Library of
Davidson College

The Politics of Inequality

Asian Studies at Hawaii, No. 22

The Politics of Inequality
Competition and Control in an Indian Village

Miriam Sharma

ASIAN STUDIES PROGRAM
UNIVERSITY OF HAWAII
THE UNIVERSITY PRESS OF HAWAII

301.59
S531p

Copyright © 1978 by The University Press of Hawaii
All rights reserved
Manufactured in the United States of America

Library of Congress Cataloging in Publication Data

Sharma, Miriam, 1941–
  The politics of inequality.

  (Asian studies at Hawaii ; no. 22)
  Bibliography: p.
  Includes index.
  1. Villages—India—Case studies. 2. Local government—India—Case studies. 3. India—Rural conditions—Case studies. 4. Caste—India—Case studies.
  I. Title. II. Series.
  DS3.A2A82 no. 22   [HV683.5]   950'.08s
  ISBN 0-8248-0569-0   [301.5'92'09542]   78-5526

All photographs are by the author

Map 1 by Iris Shinohara

To the people of Arunpur
    and
Jagdish, Arun, and Nitasha:

for the goodness they have shared with me

Contents

LIST OF ILLUSTRATIONS	x
LIST OF TABLES	xiii
PREFACE	xv
CHAPTER 1 POLITICS IN INDIAN VILLAGE SOCIETY	3
Politics in Arunpur	5
The Dialectic	8
Fieldwork and the Collection of Data	12
CHAPTER 2 THE VILLAGE OF ARUNPUR	19
Locale of Arunpur	21
Village History	24
Water, Land, and Labor in the Agricultural Cycle of Arunpur	28
Traditional Mode of Conflict Resolution: The *Panchayat*	37
The Distribution of Resources in Arunpur	40
CHAPTER 3 ARUNPUR AND THE OUTSIDE WORLD: THE EXTENSION OF GOVERNMENT ADMINISTRATION	49
Extension of Government Administration	49
New Alternatives for Conflict Resolution	53
New Resources and Relationships with Government Personnel	55
Expansion of Government Administration and the Political Arena	59

CHAPTER 4 CASTE AND KIN: THE NETWORK OF SOCIAL RELATIONS	61
Formal Relations among Castes: Dominance and *Jajmani*	62
Informal Relations among Castes: Friendship and Sex	76
Kinship in Arunpur	79
CHAPTER 5 CONFLICT IN ARUNPUR: DISPUTES THAT DO NOT ESCALATE	88
Conflict within the Family	89
Conflict among Affines	97
Conflict within the *Khandan*	103
Disputes within *Jajmani* Relations	105
Containment of Conflict	106
CHAPTER 6 THE ANATOMY OF LEADERSHIP: BIG MEN OF ARUNPUR	109
Cultural Categories of Village Leadership	109
Big Men in Arunpur before Independence (1947)	114
Big Men in Arunpur Today	118
Cultural Categories and Village Leaders	130
CHAPTER 7 THE POLITICAL ARENA IN ARUNPUR: FACTIONS	134
Origin of *Partibandi* in Arunpur	135
Factions and the Organization of Conflict	141
The Dynamics of Factions: Escalation of Conflict to the Political Arena	144
Recruitment of *Partibandi* Personnel	148
The Organization and Interactions of *Partibandi* Conflict	155
CHAPTER 8 THE POLITICAL ARENA IN ARUNPUR: CLASS CONFLICT	160
Caste Culture of the Chamars	162
The Conditions of *Mazburi:* Agricultural Labor among the Chamars	166
Disputes between *Malik* and *Mazdur*	171
Factions among the Chamars	177
Change and Class among Arunpur Chamars	181
CHAPTER 9 THE POLITICS OF WATER	185
Distribution of Water in Arunpur	186
Competition for Water Organized by Factions	188
Competition between Classes	191
Competition among Individuals	194
The Structure of Conflict	197
CHAPTER 10 ELECTORAL POLITICS IN ARUNPUR: THE 1969 MIDTERM POLL	201
Village Participation in State Politics	202

Perceptions of Voting and Political Ideologies 203
Village Factionalism and the Election 207
Class Tensions and the Chamar Vote 210
Arunpur Intercollege and the Midterm Poll 213
Election Day in Arunpur: Regional Politics and the Village Arena 214

CHAPTER 11 CONCLUSIONS 219
The Political Arena in Arunpur 219
From British Raj to Entrepreneurial Big Man 223
New Alternatives for Action 225
Competition for New Resources 226
Effect of a Changed Political Arena on Factional Conflict 227
Development of Class Conflict 229
Caste and Class in Indian Politics 232

GLOSSARY 237

BIBLIOGRAPHY 239

INDEX 251

Illustrations

MAPS
1. Map of India, showing location of Banaras District in the state of Uttar Pradesh   2
2. General locale of Arunpur   7
3. Arunpur and immediate environs   22

CHARTS
1. Genealogy 1: Descendants of Arun Singh, Main Pura   26
2. Genealogy 2: Little Pura Bhumihars   27
3. Conflict over resources: Water from the government tubewell   198

FIGURES
1. Manual boring of a tubewell.   30
2. Laborers irrigate a field from a ditch.   32
3. Cutting fodder by hand.   34
4. Carrying fertilizer of dried manure from the fields.   36
5. A Community Development worker helps a villager sign his name in the registry during a village meeting in which the possible installation of a government tubewell in Kusampur is considered.   51

ILLUSTRATIONS xi

6.	A Brahman from a nearby village performs traditional priestly functions during the naming ceremony for a newborn Bhumihar.	65
7.	A Lohar works on a plough.	70
8.	A Musahar gathers wood.	72
9.	A Kohar sits before his potter's wheel. Pandeyji is behind him.	75
10.	Villagers participate in wrestling matches and feats of strength on the festival of Tij.	77
11.	Men of all castes share the *ganjha chilam*. From left to right: a Brahman, two Dharkars, and a Bhumihar enjoy a smoke while sitting along a tubewell canal.	80
12.	Bhumihar children from Narain Singh's house.	83
13.	Giving an oil massage to newborn infants is a villagewide practice.	85
14.	Women gather in the Pradhan's house to bid a sad farewell to a daughter who is leaving for her in-laws' house, after the *gauna*.	99
15.	Present descendants of Arun Singh, the elders of the Pradhan's house, husk corn. Amar Singh is at the far right.	116
16.	The Pradhan.	121
17.	Raj Kumar Singh.	122
18.	Chandra Singh, drinking tea while campaigning for the Jan Sangh, is flanked by a Saranpur supporter on the left and Lalji Singh standing behind him.	124
19.	Jai Singh, on the left, and his staunch Arunpur supporter campaign for the Jan Sangh in the constituency.	125
20.	Brahman priests officiate at the ceremony to sanctify the land upon which Krishna Singh's house will be built. Krishna's two brothers are standing, while a third squats with his wife behind him.	128
21.	Entertainers at a feast honoring a Chamar woman who died at a very old age.	163

22.	Enjoying the antics of a performing monkey in Chamar Pura. The woman at the extreme right is of the Teli caste.	165
23.	Ploughman holds two ploughs.	168
24.	Chamar and Musahar laborers pick what remains in Chandra Singh's potato fields.	173
25.	Raj Narain, member of Parliament (now Minister of Health and Family Welfare in the central government), gives a campaign speech during an SSP rally in Dallia bazaar.	206
26.	Women wait to cast their votes at the Arunpur Intercollege polling station.	215

Tables

1.	Caste hierarchy in Arunpur	6
2.	Population of Arunpur	23
3.	Land ownership in Arunpur by caste (in *bigha*s)	35
4.	Land in Arunpur by amount owned	42–43
5.	Land by categories of ownership	44
6.	Land ownership among Bhumihars	44
7.	Caste and occupation in Arunpur	45
8.	Estimated annual cash income (in rupees)	46
9.	Education in Arunpur	47

Preface

Although I write here about politics and inequality in India, both are universal aspects of human society. As the form of political activity will differ from one culture to another, so too will the way in which inequality is manifested in behavior and sanctified (or condemned) in ideology. India has proven a fascinating place to look at the dialectics of political interaction that occur within a traditional ideology of caste—which legitimizes inequalities through a belief in the divine order of hierarchy—and within the alternative ideology of equality, to which the national government has affirmed its commitment. The example of India also permits us to examine the ways in which contradictions between these two ideologies affect political behavior in a changing environment.

In many ways, a specialized study of any selected aspects of a culture will present a distorted view, especially to those readers who may be unfamiliar with other parts of the whole. A generalized ethnographic approach would avoid this pitfall, in the main, although it rarely allows for detailed study of any single activity system. Since politics deals with conflict over the allocation and control of things valued in society, an ethnography of a political system will necessarily focus on what may appear as the more disruptive elements of the social fabric, ignoring areas involving cooperation and direct concern for one's fellows. During the course of three visits and two and a half years of living in India, I have amply witnessed and been affected by this latter part of social life. The lack of focus on cooperative activity here is no comment on the extent of its existence within Indian society and culture.

This study has come about as a result of an evolution of personal interest and research that dates from the time I was an "occasional" student at the University of London, when I concurrently met two people. One introduced me to the rich culture of India and the other to the equally rich discipline of anthropology. My husband Jagdish, and subsequently all members of my *sasural,* have imbued in me a respect and love for things Indian, while at the same time they have not blinded me to what they see as the shortcomings in their way of life. Doranne Jacobson has shared with me her commitment to anthropology, knowledge of India, and regard for the country. Additionally, Professors F. G. Bailey and Adrian Mayer, at the School of Oriental and African Studies (London), helped me gain a foundation of learning that I was able to build upon subsequently at the University of Hawaii. Teachers and fellow students here have provided a stimulating environment in which to carry on further study. Specifically, I would like to acknowledge Jack Baumer, who taught me Hindi, and Bob Harrison, Ben Kerkvliet, and Woody Watson, for their concern and patience in helping me to formulate the dissertation on which this book is based. Alice Dewey has been both mentor and friend and a constant source of encouragement through the years.

My greatest debt is to those who supported and aided me during the period of research in India. The Registrar at Banaras Hindu University was kind enough to let me live in the Women's Hostel early in my stay, and friends there facilitated my easy transition into Indian society. Professor A. K. Narain, Ushaji, and their wonderful family were "my family" in the city. Dr. C. P. Goel of Kashi Vidyapith University and members of the Kashi Vidyapith Community Development Block headquarters helped in my search for a village to study. Professor S. K. Srivastava of Banaras Hindu University recommended one of his most promising students, Sri C. B. Pandey, to be my assistant. It is to my coworker and the people of Arunpur* that I am most in debt. Pandeyji was an indispensable part of the research project, and the extent to which he must have had to adapt himself to live with us I have only realized fully in retrospect. It is difficult to express true feelings of gratitude, beyond what may appear as a perfunctory acknowledgment, to the people among whom an anthropologist lives. Perhaps I need not try—shared, reciprocal relationships in India do not demand a verbalized "thank you."

Lynette Jagbandhansingha-Wageman, South Asia Specialist at the University of Hawaii Library, stoically bore my frequent raids on her uncatalogued PL 480 books and dealt with other demanding requests for material. Jean Kennedy, another good friend, made the maps and diagrams, while Freda Hellinger typed from the original nightmare that was

---
*Pseudonyms are used for all villages and villagers named.

this manuscript. Maud Nishimoto gave me time in which to write, and Harry Lamley, formerly chairman of the publications committee for this series, encouraged me to submit the work for publication. Many have read and commented on parts of this study; the remarks of anonymous (and not so anonymous) reviewers were among the most critical and the most useful. I should also like to acknowledge financial support from the an N.D.E.A. fellowship, Fulbright Predoctoral Research and N.S.F. grants, and moral support from my mother and *pihar*.

I wish I could thank a long-suffering wife—one who aided unflinchingly in the collection of much of my data, carried out the daily concerns of organizing households and family in the field and at home, and laboriously typed all the drafts of this much revised work. I unfortunately cannot, and those who can should be truly grateful.

The Politics of Inequality

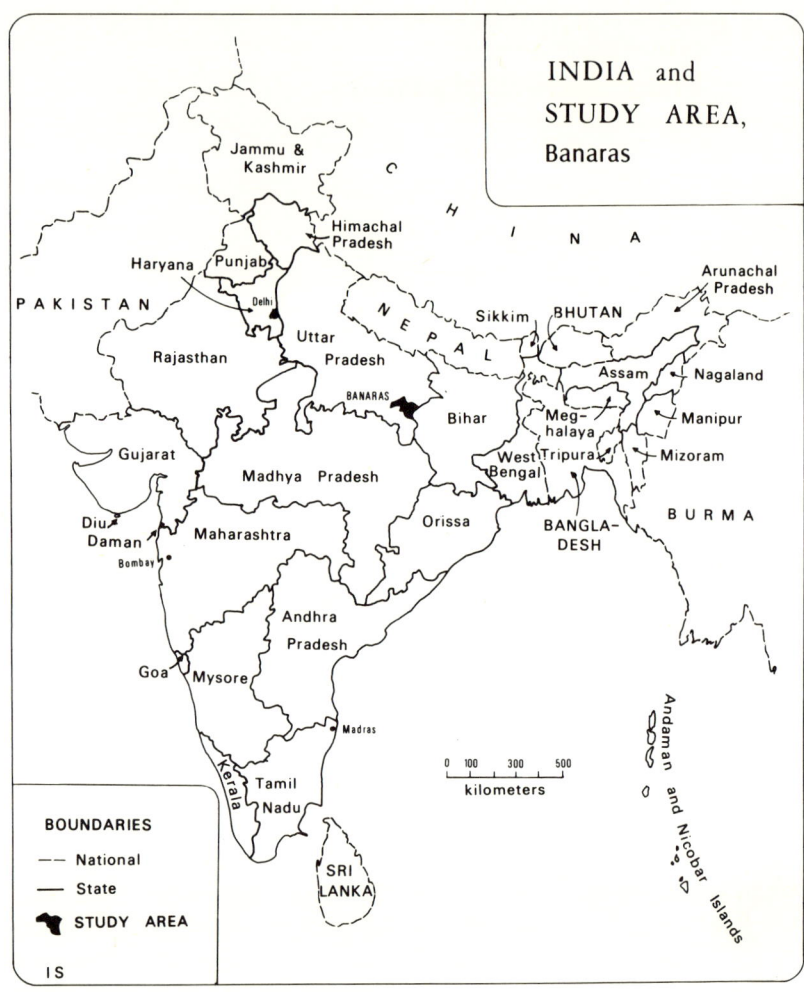

MAP 1. Map of India, showing location of Banaras District in the state of Uttar Pradesh. Based on map issued by the Registrar General and Census Commissioner of India, 1971.

CHAPTER 1
Politics in Indian Village Society

I think, and people in the village think, that if you speak against a powerful man you will get only trouble from him or anyone else against whom you speak. Take my case, I didn't want to contest the election for village head *(pradhan)* but Jai Singh stood against me. I was opposed to making the election a contest and did not file any papers for it. But others in the village went and filed my name. As most people supported me, I thought that if I accepted the post I might lessen factionalism *(partibandi)* in our village. I also knew that our village has spent some 50,000 to 60,000 rupees since 1960 or 1957 in court cases. For there was always competition that if someone did something, the other would like to outdo him so that he didn't suffer dishonor.—the Pradhan of Arunpur

The presence of powerful men, conflict, animosities, elections, disputes leading to court cases, competition, and feelings of prestige are all recognizable parts of political activity in an Indian village. The idealized Metcalfian vision of villages as "little republics" that existed in harmony and without conflict has been discarded by those who have studied any aspect of political activity in rural India.[1] Another view has appeared in its place, in which the "language" of traditional (i.e., village) politics is articulated through caste and comes increasingly into conflict with the language of modern politics spoken through the idiom of "policies and interests, programmes and plans" (Morris-Jones 1964:53; also 48ff).

When, more than a decade ago, Morris-Jones wrote his provocative essay outlining India's political idioms, he attributed great significance to the work of anthropologists in charting the unknown terrain labeled "Indian politics." "For they," he stated, "have to follow caste as a social institution wherever it may lead them, and it has led them firmly into politics" (1964:65; first appearing in 1963). The anthropological insight that the relation between society and politics in non-Western and predominantly rural societies will be different from what we are led to expect from the Western experience has considerably advanced our understanding of the Indian scene. Yet because the many different aspects of social life are so intermeshed in rural society, it is difficult even for anthropologists to identify analytically what is political. A primary concern with the social organization of Indian society has led them to approach politics mainly through a study of the caste system and to explore political activity to the extent that it reveals something of that institution. This focus has produced a considerable body of research dealing with factionalism. A small but growing number of studies also look at conflict from the perspective of intercaste or specifically class relations.[2]

Given the importance of a political idiom that has its roots in communities comprising some eighty percent of the total population, it is surprising that no comprehensive political ethnography of any village exists. Anthropologists have not yet done for politics what has been so aptly done for caste, that is, follow it where it may lead. This study, in presenting such an ethnography, attempts to fill the gap. It concentrates solely on political activity as an essential part of all Indian behavior (as it is of all human behavior) and follows that activity into whatever areas of village life it permeates. Political activity relates to decisions about the allocation of scarce and valued resources and control over men (Easton 1959:226). The essence of politics is conflict—conflict over the attempt to gain control of these resources, to influence behavior in a certain direction, and to acquire or exercise power (Mark and Snyder 1957:218). When conflict is so broadly defined, much of human behavior may be regarded as political.

This study focuses on political activity in that wider sphere which affects most community members and then delimits the boundaries of what may be considered the political system of a villagewide "arena," the social and cultural environment within which such activity takes place. It points out the ways in which the boundaries of the villagewide arena become fluid and extend outward. An arena contains several fields of action composed of the actors who are directly involved in the processes being studied (Bailey 1963b:224–226; Swartz 1968:6ff). Such fields represent different cleavages that cut across village society and organize the arena.

Arenas are also organized by rules which define the acceptable ways of getting things done and impose some kind of limits on possible action. They prescribe who makes decisions, how decisions are made, and the way in which conflict over such decisions is resolved. The rules also disclose the objects of value in a society (its resources) for which people compete. Knowing these rules permits identification of participants and their respective sides and this, in turn, reveals the boundaries of the political arena. As the case material will illustrate, however, there is an area of discretion and choice where actors can manipulate the means to achieve their ends within these limits. While the rules organize the activity of "politicians" and political groups, the cleavages orient the latter to one another and define the extent of political activity (Bailey 1960:11, 13, 251; 1963b:223-224; Gamson 1961:374; Mark and Snyder 1957:217; Nicholas 1968a:246).

The field data upon which the research is based are presented as a series of case histories that deal with three major questions integral to a political ethnography. First, is it analytically possible to distinguish between the political activity that pervades all human behavior and that which may be confined to the designated arena under observation, in this case the villagewide political system? Second, can the designated political arena be circumscribed, and what are the points at which it becomes involved in networks of relationships that extend beyond the arena boundaries? Third, what are the rules for this particular arena relating to who makes decisions about resource allocation, how these decisions are made, and how conflict is resolved?

POLITICS IN ARUNPUR

It is known that conflict within a caste and among castes occurs in rural society. To find out how this political activity is organized and whether other cleavages may be present, I carried out fieldwork in Arunpur, a village in the northern state of Uttar Pradesh. Arunpur is eight miles from the urban center of Banaras, within a district of the same name (Map 2). Its population of 1,047 people, divided into sixteen castes, is big enough to reveal the many different levels at which politics works in village life. The numerically large and traditionally dominant landowning caste of Bhumihars (see Table 1) is divided into two main factions. These are coalitions of powerful Bhumihars known as the village "big men." Faction leaders seek to gain the support of other villagers by using a diversity of ties to attract them to their side. The village also has a large group of Untouchable Chamars, traditionally leatherworkers, who provide the Bhumihars with cheap agricultural labor.[3] They are mostly illiterate and poverty stricken, but rising consciousness of a unity of interests has brought them into conflict with their masters on several occasions. Between these two extremes of the caste hierarchy lie a number of other castes, of which the agricultural Kurmis are politically and economically the most important.

Factionalism within a dominant caste or group of closely allied castes, which runs vertically through the village, is the traditional and still predominant form of political activity in rural India (Nicholas 1968a:278). Arunpur proved no exception to this rule. Most competition and the effective allocation of resources are determined by decisions of the two coalitions of powerful Bhumihar big men, each with their respective bands of followers and general supporters. Given the small, face-to-face nature of a village community and the high degree of interdependence among its members, few villagers could remain aloof or unaffected by factional politics.

In contrast to factionalism, which involves most of the inhabitants, it was found that Arunpur also contains a horizontal cleavage between the

Table 1. Caste Hierarchy in Arunpur

	Caste	Traditional Occupation	*Varna*[a]
1	Brahman	Priest	Brahman
	Bhumihar Brahman	Cultivating "priest"	,,
2[b]	Agrawal	Merchant	Vaishya
3 (A)	Kurmi (Kunbi)	Cultivator	Shudra
3 (B)[c]	Kahar	Waterbearer, fisherman	,,
	Lohar	Blacksmith	,,
	Kevat	Fisherman, cultivator	,,
	Parihar	?	,,
	Nai	Barber	,,
	Kohar (Kumhar)	Potter	,,
	Kalwar	Distiller	,,
	Noniya	Saltpeter worker and earthworker	,,
	Teli	Oil presser	,,
4[d]	Pasi	Pig raiser, toddy tapper	Untouchable
	Chamar	Leatherworker	,,
	Musahar	Wood collector	,,
	Dharkar	Basket weaver	,,

[a] Arunpur has no caste considered to be in the *kshatriya varna*.
[b] Only the ex-zamindar belonged to this caste. He is not considered a village resident.
[c] There was great variability in the way that villagers ranked castes according to cards listing names of castes individually. This order represents the ranking most often mentioned. Villagers distinguish between two major categories of caste: high caste *(unchjat)* and low caste *(nichjat)*. Those in categories 3 and 4 are considered low caste. The Indian government regards castes in category 3, along with the "Scheduled Castes" of category 4, as belonging to the "Backward Classes" and therefore eligible for certain preferential treatment (Béteille 1969b:105ff). Some social scientists regard category 3 as representing the "middle" castes.
[d] The category of Untouchable is usually considered outside the fourfold *varna* classification.

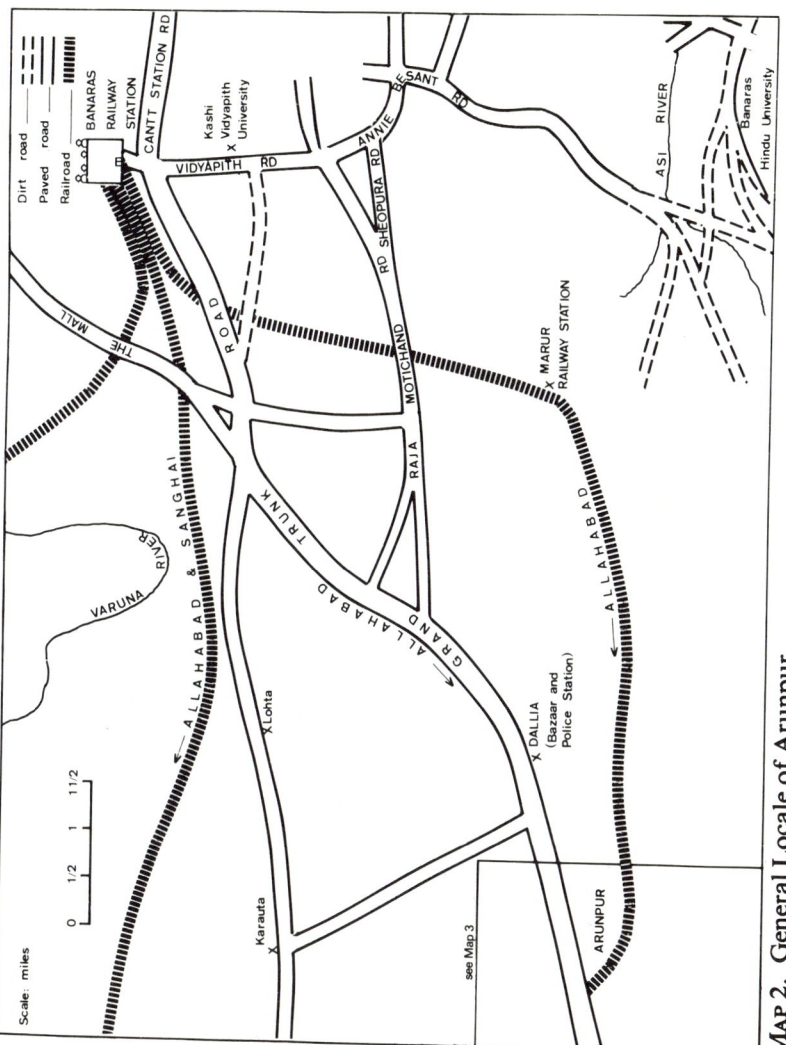

MAP 2. General Locale of Arunpur.

landed, upper-caste Bhumihars and their landless, Chamar agricultural laborers. The nature of this cleavage makes it more amenable to analysis in terms of class. This cleavage has become exacerbated because the Chamars have not effectively participated in the economic and political mobility which has characterized much of Indian society as a whole and which is exemplified by the achievements of the Kurmi caste locally.

Factionalism, representing a primary cleavage within the dominant caste that has spread vertically to encompass other villagers, is intimately related to the horizontal cleavage which occurs between castes acting as corporate classes. Two major conditions affect the relationship between factions and class conflict in the village arena. First, the existence of factions within the Chamar caste that are connected to those among the Bhumihars has a limiting effect on the solidarity of the Untouchables in relation to their superordinates. Second, the frequency of class conflict has a decided effect upon the nature of factionalism within the dominant caste because it forces the two factions to close ranks before a common opponent.

Competition for water from the government tubewell is a special factor that enters the arena of villagewide conflict. The peculiar feature of this resource, when compared with other government aid or land, for example, is that it is always available and yet perennially scarce. Water is supplied almost daily from the tubewell, but the supply can never adequately fulfill the demand (especially in the peak seasons of irrigating potatoes and rice). This means that there is constant rivalry for this commodity. As such, the conflict for water involves not only the vertical and horizontal cleavages mentioned earlier, but also spreads out to involve villagers along other lines of dissension—between the two Bhumihar *puras* (settlements), among factionally aligned and neutral villagers, and among men who are considered as belonging to the same faction. Much of the competition for water takes place among individuals who happen to require this commodity at the same time and is not encompassed by the two main types of conflict.

THE DIALECTIC

Defining the presence of both factional conflict within a dominant caste and class conflict between castes does not fit in easily with prevailing views about the nature of Indian village politics. A major theoretical assumption of many anthropological studies has been that political activity must be subsumed under, encompassed by, and articulated through the major social institution of caste. Caste is the arena within which all political activity takes place, and caste society is regarded as antithetical to (and not allowing for) the existence of classes. Such studies assume that for classes to appear, castes must disappear. A caste society must somehow be transformed into a class society. This interpretation has come about through a particular view of caste as an ideological system and a particular view of the roles of dominance and factions in the system.

Most studies on village politics argue that caste society does not allow for conflict between castes. Castes are regarded as mutually interdependent groups which cooperate and do not compete in the ideal view of the system (Bailey 1963a:121; Leach 1960:7; cf. Srinivas 1962; Béteille 1969a). It is recognized, however, that in reality the system is held together not so much by ties of reciprocity as by the concentration of force and coercive sanctions in the hands of a dominant caste (Bailey 1960:258; 1963a:110; Rudolph 1961:386).

Srinivas has emphasized the need to distinguish between ritual status based on ideology and the distribution of wealth and power in Indian villages with his concept of the "dominant caste." A dominant caste is one that predominates numerically over other castes and also wields predominant economic and political power. "A larger and powerful caste group can also be more easily dominant if its position in the local hierarchy is not too low" (Srinivas 1955:18). The criterion of Western education was added later, as it "is the means by which such dominance is acquired" (Srinivas 1959:1). Dominance implies the replication of the royal *kshatriya* function on a much smaller (i.e., village) basis. Its main characteristics can be summarized as: (1) relatively eminent right over land, (2) the resulting power to grant land and employ members of other castes, (3) the power to dispense justice, (4) the general monopoly of authority, and (5) the tendency to claim royal caste status (Dumont 1972:207).[4] The concept is particularly suited to the political structure of the Banaras region, where, since the eighteenth and nineteenth centuries, the basic jural unit was the "little kingdom," with the dominant caste controlling all beneath it (Cohn 1959:81).

Although few anthropologists would deny that even in the traditional situation competition and conflict have always been present, they accommodate such activity within the rules of the system by confining political competition to the dominant caste (e.g., Bailey 1960:169; Dumont 1972:348; Leach 1960; Yalman 1960)[5] and by noting the congruence between caste, class, and power (Bailey 1963a; Béteille 1965; 1969b:57ff). Competition confined within the dominant caste produces cleavages that are characteristic of factions. They represent a vertical breach in the village, and members of all castes may be found in one camp or another. "Cooperative relationships run up and down between families in the dominant caste and families in the service castes" (Bailey 1963a:118; also Elliott 1970:134). There is no single principle by which faction personnel are recruited, and leaders make use of many different ties to gain supporters. Factional conflict takes place between structurally equivalent bodies with no specified criteria for inclusion or exclusion, while conflict between classes (discussed later) takes place between social strata characterized by superordinate-subordinate relations (Boissevain 1968:551).

Dominance, then, implies that competition along factional lines within a single caste is extended to other castes only because of the need to gain supporters. This reinforces the definition of castes as "non-antagonistic" strata in a social system (Béteille 1969a), and much of the literature on rural politics in India is devoted to this phenomenon.

Opposed to the interdependence of castes is the conflict associated with classes. While there is no unanimity on exactly what constitutes a class (cf. Dahrendorf 1959:237-238; Lenski 1966:74-75; Lenin 1971:231; Marx 1963:124; Weber 1966:21ff; see also discussions in Alavi 1973:25ff; Béteille 1974b:73-93; Lipset 1968), it is regarded essentially as an aggregate of persons who occupy the same position in relation to the means and organization of production. They share a specific causal component of life chances and common economic conditions (Bendix and Lipset 1966:7; Weber 1966:21). Like factions, classes never exist on their own but are encountered in the plural. Beyond this, however, it must be seen that ultimately, "classes are political groups united by a common interest. The struggle between two classes is a political struggle" (Dahrendorf 1959:16). Differential position in an authority structure and property form the bases of classes (Dahrendorf:13ff). In contrast to castes, then, classes are marked by a conflict of interests and horizontal lines of cleavage in terms of superordinates and subordinates. A caste society has been characterized as a basically stable and unchanging society wherein inequalities are legitimized through an ideology of hierarchy. A class society, on the other hand, is marked by instability and change due to divergence between actual interests and prevailing ideology (Béteille 1972; 1974a:110ff; 194ff).

Though strikingly parallel to the modernity-tradition model that has sparked a long debate, it is equally striking that, with the major exception of Béteille's writings, this dichotomy has not been theoretically examined. Similarly, while considerable attention has been paid to the presence of caste outside of India, barely any serious thought has been given to the suitability of the term "class" within Indian society.[6] Factionalism has been so defined that it is recognized as an integral part of every society, group, and organization, but the utility of a similar approach to a definition of class has not been treated.

There is, however, an alternative approach to this "either-or" division into caste and class societies with their a priori categorization of the nature of political activity. Anthropologists have long acknowledged that all people do not structure their world in the same way and that the categories of one culture may not necessarily be applicable to another. It is not that groups similar to our own may not be present in Indian society, "but rather that they are not defined in the same way" (Nicholas 1973:153). This seems to be particularly true for the notion of class and the role of class conflict in Indian politics. Thus, a starting point lies with an examination of the cultural categories for relationships indicative not of caste but of what we mean by class. Thorner proposed looking at the agrarian system of rural India in terms used by the people themselves. He specified *malik* (master), *kisan* (peasant) and *mazdur* (laborer) as representing important divisions within the agricultural population (1956:4–6). Eight years later, Pocock referred to the existence of indigenous terms relating to different kinds of relationships between landowner and laborer to support his argument that *jajmani* (the ritualized exchange of economic services) may not represent a single system of relations (1962:88; also Harper 1968; see later, pp. 71ff).

Béteille has advocated the need to study the dialectic between ideas and interests in Indian society in terms of those relationships centering around the ownership of land for which native categories exist (1974a:43, 117ff,126).[7] He remarks pointedly that although Marx conceived of class and class conflicts in terms of property relations, it is strange that the concept has not been applied in those very societies in which ownership of land is preeminent (1974a:53). Two other original essays employ the concept of class to analyze the *bhadralok-chhotolok* ("gentlemen"-"lowly people") dichotomy in the social and political development of nineteenth-century and present-day Bengal (Mukherjee 1970; Sinha and Bhattacharya 1969).

The argument of this work is, therefore, that the scholarly study of village politics has been inhibited by the scholarly study of caste. The ideology of caste is remarkable in the extent to which it has successfully enforced and immobilized an existing system of class relations and granted a legitimizing status to all types of inequalities in society. It has likewise been remarkable in the degree to which it has masked the extremely differing socioeconomic interests of groups and made them less amenable to study. "The mask is not always consciously worn but it is for that reason no less there" (Béteille 1974b:104). This study will investigate the ways in which participants themselves structure their perceptions about political activity and examine the extent to which certain relationships may be indicative of class.

The study of class relations is located primarily within the structure of landownership in India, and the political activity of classes does not necessarily depend upon the presence of organized conflict on a national scale or on a unified class consciousness. Such strict prerequisites entail the danger of possibly defining classes "out of existence" (Béteille 1974a:52-53).[8] Alavi has reasoned convincingly that "the complex mediations of the processes by which class solidarity is established and manifested, escapes the attention of those Marxists who focus exclusively on dramatic demonstrations of class solidarity of peasants in revolutionary action" (1973:59), and this may prove to be the most crucial aspect of the study of class (also Béteille 1974a:141; Terray 1975:92).

The concentration on a case in which a local group is in the process of class formation reveals the way in which class is becoming a more important variable in Indian political conflict. Because of the presence of competing ideologies, along with other changes in society, the legitimacy of caste (and its relations of dominance and subordination) as an accepted code for all behavior has been undermined. The strength that it still has in ordering actual relations, however, has not been undermined. Villagers increasingly have become aware of the existence of two different systems of social relations, one pertaining to the village and the other to that which derives its strength and legitimacy from the world outside (see below, pp. 61ff). Only when the many ways in which people divide up their social universe are understood may the dialectic between ideas and interests be seen.

FIELDWORK AND THE COLLECTION OF DATA

It is a truism that the findings of a study can be no better than the data upon which it is based. Yet all too often, this principle is forgotten and information about the actual collection of research material is relegated to a secondary position. It is possible that someone else looking at the political activity of Arunpur may come to different conclusions than those presented here. I feel, however, that a clear statement of the way in which fieldwork was conducted and the problems that were faced would go far to explain such possible differences.

There are four important points to be considered in the evaluation of the data. These are: (1) the role which I assumed as a fieldworker, (2) the methods used to collect data, (3) the nature of information obtained when the major mode of organizing political action is factionalism, and (4) the involvement of me and my associates in village politics.

The very first appearance of an anthropologist at the research site often provides the strongest, if not most lasting, impression. I entered Arunpur in a jeep one day, accompanied by a driver, a professor from a Banaras college, a minor official from the local Community Development office, one of the most important local political figures from a neighboring village, and the *pradhan* (elected village head) of Arunpur. I was wearing a sari and a short, sleeveless blouse. Much, much later, villagers confided that it was rumored that a film actress had come to shoot some scenes in Arunpur (because I was of "fair" complexion, as are the film stars). Some also thought that I was a dancing girl cum prostitute *(randi)* because I first came at the height of the marriage season in May. Who else but a *randi* would wear a sleeveless blouse in the village (and I never wore one again)!

The most crucial liabilities, over which I had no control and which determined much of my subsequent role, were that I was a woman, a Westerner, and married to a Brahman. Sitting and talking with men in a highly sex-segregated society, where wealthy and high-caste women (whose status I was later accorded) are in "seclusion" (purdah), was regarded as an unacceptable form of behavior by some villagers throughout my stay. I also had to dispel many of the preconceived notions of what a *mem sahib* was like, gleaned mostly from Western films, by scrupulous attention to modesty and decorum; this included wearing a sari as well as controlling all other aspects of my physical and verbal behavior.

With a few men, in addition, I also had to take the role of a passive member of the group and let my assistant do most of the talking, while I spoke only when I had a specific question. To some extent (so I like to believe), my personality as it was perceived by those among whom I lived went far to overcome these liabilities. The addition of my husband's mother to our household, some six weeks after our arrival in the village, gave me an added respectability and put an end to gossip about my actual relationship to my husband and assistant.

Once I had established some sort of place for myself as an accepted, albeit outside and temporary, visitor in the village, much depended upon the methods we used to collect material. The standard anthropological technique of participant-observation was most often employed. This meant sitting with, watching, and listening to others and participating in informal talks and interviews as a part of our daily routine.

Most of the information on politics I gained by talking with village men, especially those who were leaders of the two factions, their kinsmen, and other people who actively supported one side or the other. The Chamars were most willing to tell us of their miserable conditions in the hope that we might be able to do something for them. More intimate details of their relations to the Bhumihars, however, came primarily from younger men and from those known to belong to the anti-Bhumihar faction of their *pura*. In addition, we spoke to many other men of neighboring villages and often visited these places. We also had extensive contact with minor government officials that included the Village Level Worker in the Community Development Program, the Seed-Store Inspector and, to some extent, the Block Development Officer and his entourage.

We gained little knowledge of village politics from the women, for that was not their major concern. Yet I found that as the work progressed, more and more of my time was being spent in their company, while my assistant stayed with the men. There are two reasons for this. First, women became less shy and more insistent that I come into their homes as I became a familiar part of the village scene. Second, the more I came to understand their culture, the more acutely I began to feel that my behavior in sitting and talking with men was anomalous. I had to come to terms with this feeling for the duration of my stay so that fieldwork could be continued. The tendency (if not the necessity) to slip into socially accepted sexual roles is most seductive in a highly sex-segregated society like India.

A detailed census of all households was taken in the early weeks of fieldwork. This was later supplemented by genealogies of important Bhumihar and Kurmi families. A socioeconomic interview schedule was also prepared for all heads of households, and it contained a number of questions relating to opinions on political affairs. There were also lengthy, more standardized interviews with a number of men conversant in village affairs, from Arunpur and neighboring villages, regarding the different *panchayat*s (local councils) and the changes that Local Self-Government has made. It was possible to collect on-the-spot information about a number of disputes which occurred while we were in the field.

The case history method was used extensively for organizing the data. The material fell conveniently into rather discrete, albeit interrelated, dispute events because political activity relates to conflicts over specific decisions. All the scattered references pertaining to a specific encounter were put together and the event was coherently described in the form of a case history. I also attempted to give a processual view of each dispute, as far as knowledge regarding it permitted, so that the course of the event through time would be understood. Many of the events described refer to conflicts which took place in the past and about which the villagers could speak with relatively greater freedom. Yet the picture remains necessarily incomplete and sketchy, while also subject to the biases outlined below. The texts of the cases also incorporate those interpretations or items of information that are greatly disparate and are significant to understanding the event under consideration.

Besides the particular drawbacks of being a Western *mem sahib* that hampered my own work, any fieldworker who seeks to collect information about politics in an arena organized mainly by factions is put in a difficult situation. I realized beforehand the importance of remaining both neutral and discreet if the information we desired was to be obtained, and I sought to enlist the understanding of my assistant and my husband in this matter. Although the latter did not actively take part in fieldwork and was not often in the village (our house being somewhat apart), many men would come to visit him and he had several good friends among them.

It soon became clear that the political situation was a delicate one. Factionalism requires fierce loyalty (even if only temporary) to one's leader; hence, any divulgence of information is also treated as a personal matter. The only people with whom one speaks of such things candidly are the members of the same faction. Since we attempted to remain neutral, we were suspected by both of being loyal to the opposing side. This was highlighted by the villagers' much more open talk of their involvement in the midterm local election that took place during our stay and was not greatly influenced by factional considerations.

Much of the information gathered about factional politics was from the extreme gossip, frequently quite malicious, that one side told about the other. It is, of course, difficult to assess the reliability of such data, and I often questioned whether I was learning anything at all of the true situation in the village. A few features, however, saved me from abandoning hope altogether. There was usually some basic agreement between the version each faction gave of a certain situation. The major difference was their moral assessment of who was in the wrong. In addition, on rare occasions one faction would substantiate a particular interpretation given by the other side. Finally, the information given by people who were either known to be neutral or from outside the village, and hence uninvolved, was taken to be fairly reliable.

Knowledge about the Chamars' situation came from two major sources. The Bhumihars who employed them as laborers told us about the conditions of their work. This was double-checked by eliciting the same information from the Chamars. The events which took place during our stay in the village were also corroborated by our own observations and discussions with others. But by far the major bulk of the information regarding their plight was obtained from the Chamars themselves in a series of "secret" meetings arranged for that purpose. Chapter 8 discusses this further.

We had to be known as neutral and trustworthy people before anyone would talk to us of these controversial affairs; we could not divulge any confidences. I was strongly committed to this approach and was eventually regarded as being either neutral or insignificant. My husband and assistant, however, each became closely associated with opposing sides and I am not sure of the success we had later in attempting to counterbalance this situation.

The role of my assistant was more crucial, for he was intimately involved in the fieldwork situation and I had to depend on him for the material he gathered independently as well as for aid in translations and interpretations of events. I soon became aware of the discrepancies of some of his translations and even general interpretations, since I had a fair command of Hindi. His own attachments, personality, and feelings also affected the information he passed on to me, although he was conversant with the requirement of objectivity in research. He became closer to the faction which opposed the Pradhan, perhaps partly because of the competition he felt from the latter's highly educated kinsmen. Most of the opposing faction's leaders and key members are educated only up to the primary or intermediate levels. My highly educated (M.A. in sociology) assistant felt that they gave more respect to his learning. In addition, they seemed to have a greater appreciation for his status as a non-Bhumihar Brahman.

A similar course of involvement followed with the Chamars. I tried to overcome the usual high-caste bias that so easily slips into fieldwork, especially since all groups in the village were affected by political activity. My assistant, a *pakka* ("pure") Brahman and staunch believer in the ideology of the right-wing Jan Sangh political party, had great difficulty in interviewing the Chamars at first. However, after we agreed that it was necessary to sit and speak with them because part of my fieldwork depended upon doing this, he soon switched into the role of a leader.

From that time until he left Arunpur, his role became that of a young, educated Brahman concerned with the welfare of poor Untouchables. Although I feared possible reprisals from upper-caste village people, especially the Bhumihars upon whom our successful stay in the village ultimately depended, he continued his association with the Chamars. This created a potentially explosive situation (see Chapter 8). It was only after his departure, when some high-caste villagers commented about their feelings toward him and his interference, that I could assess how much he had become involved. It may be that the situation of conflict between the Bhumihars and Chamars was latent, but our arrival on the scene and my assistant certainly added to it in such a way that the cleavage and alignment of personnel were clearly revealed. It is also possible that our very presence produced some conflict that might otherwise not have occurred.

NOTES

1. That the vision is still not without a certain allure may be seem from such works as Ishwaran (1966) and Beals and Siegel (1966: especially p. 158). Cohn stresses that it is one of the main sources for the "tendency in the study of Indian factionalism, and for that matter of all forms of conflict, to view these situations as abnormal or bad" (1965:96).

2. On factions, see, for example, Beals and Siegel (1966); Siegel and Beals (1960a; 1960b); Lewis (1958); Singh (1961); Nicholas (1965; 1966; 1968a; 1968b); Firth (1957); Yadava (1968). On intercaste or class conflict, see, for example, Bailey (1957; 1960); Béteille (1965); Caplan (1972); Gough (1960; 1970; 1973); Nicholas (1968a); Shepperdson (1969); Sivertsen (1963); Srinivas (1962). The interests of political scientists lay more in the direction of analyzing the formal politics of *panchayati raj* (Local Self-Government) institutions and elections.

3. The percentage of Chamars in Arunpur, 24 percent, is somewhat larger than their numerical strength in the state and district—about 18 percent—while the total for all Scheduled Castes and Tribes (the latter quite small) is 21 percent for these levels. Chamars thus constitute the overwhelming majority of this category. Further, the *tehsil* subdivision of which the village is a part contains 40 percent of the district's total number of Scheduled Castes (Government of India 1965).

4. Srinivas has been criticized on several points relating to his concept, specifically on the necessity for a caste to be numerically dominant in order to dominate in general (see, e.g., Dumont 1972:206; Mayer 1958:425). The dominant caste need not always be a majority (either the largest single caste or larger than the rest put together). Nor is the same dominant caste present in all villages in a given locale. The Bhumihars are clearly dominant in Arunpur, but in a neighboring village, where there are no Bhumihars and practically the entire population is of the Kurmi caste, a different situation prevails. There are two dominant castes within the wider Banaras region, the Bhumihars and the Rajput Thakurs. The identification of a dominant caste is thus a function of the level that is being studied; the village, multivillage, or regional areas (Mayer 1958; Béteille 1969a:21).

    Nicholas discusses the presence of more than one dominant caste in a village (1968a:273), while Gardner analyzes differing referents for the term (1968). Miller has a good summary of these and other positions (1975:105ff). Such criticisms not withstanding, the concept remains singularly useful for the study of Indian village politics. Furthermore, no theoretical discussion of caste and politics exists which does not employ this concept in some way.

5. For detailed criticisms of Leach's position, see Bailey (1960:258; 1963a:110, 117-118), and Béteille (1969a:21).

6. Some anthropologists have examined class in other precapitalist societies. See Terray (1975) and his bibliography.

7. Just how strong the pull of ideas is, even for those interested in examining class relations in India, can be seen from Béteille's own writings. At one point he questions the "relevance of native categories such as caste as compared with general analytical concepts like class; or to put it a different way, the use of mechanical as opposed to statistical models" (1974a:35). In a later essay, however, he does mention certain native categories which may be regarded "provisionally" as being of the class type (1974a:126). Mencher, whose major interest is the study of

class relations in South India, muddles an otherwise cogent discussion of a view of the caste system from the bottom. Although she refers to numerous revolts and conflicts between landlords and lower castes, she maintains that the caste system prevented "the formation of social classes with any commonality of interest or unity of purpose" (1974a:469). It is difficult to understand what were the bases for organizing such conflict, then, in lieu of common interests and goals for different groups, even though the conflict may have been localized and short-lived.

8. Marx's observations on the French peasantry led him to conclude:

> In this way the great mass of the French nation is formed by simple additions of homologous magnitude, much as potatoes in a sack form a sack of potatoes. In so far as millions of families live under economic conditions of existence that separate their mode of life, their interests and their culture from those of the other classes, and put them in a hostile opposition to the latter, they form a class. In so far as there is merely a local interconnection among these small-holding peasants, and the identity of their interests begets no community, no national bond and no political organization among them, they do not form a class. (1963:124)

CHAPTER 2
The Village of Arunpur

Anthropologists make a conscious decision when they choose a particular village and are also influenced by factors beyond their control. In my own case, I tried to locate a village which met certain criteria that seemed relevant to the topic chosen for study. I had decided beforehand to work near the ancient and holy city of Banaras. This particular area was chosen for personal reasons, not the least of which was the presence of friends and facilities which could provide invaluable help. I learned of the great difference between the standard Hindi I had studied and the dialect spoken here—Bhojpuri—only after reaching Banaras. Many village men were bilingual in both Hindi and Bhojpuri, but I always experienced difficulty communicating with and understanding most of the women, who spoke only the dialect.

The Bhojpuri area, from eastern Uttar Pradesh through western Bihar, forms a cultural region where the people are united by a dialect and the existence of certain caste groups and customs that are common to all (see Schwartzberg 1968). The region is one of the most densely populated in India and is considered economically and socially backward. This position is epitomized by the city of Banaras, which seems to cater more for the needs of the soul than the body, and strongly influences life in the surrounding countryside. At the same time, the trend in modern India is toward an increasing communication and mobility between urban and rural centers, via the transit and transistor revolution.[1] I felt that the kinds of changes that are taking place in the political arenas of communities near an urban center are those that will most likely come to affect the more than half a million villages of India.

Besides location near an urban center, I had several other criteria for choice of a site. There should be a population of at least seven hundred and fifty persons, to ensure the existence of a sufficiently large and active political arena to be reasonably studied in a year; both traditional and statutory *panchayat*s (councils); contact with government development programs that provide new resources requiring distribution; and a primary reliance on agriculture for subsistence (since this is true of practically all Indian villages).

Three more criteria were added after I began to look for a village. First, one of the two major landowning and traditionally administrative castes in the area should be represented. These are either Rajputs or Bhumihars and they are usually mutually exclusive in a given village. The Bhumihars predominate in the region around Banaras by virtue of the fact that the maharajas of this ex-princely state had belonged to this caste. Second, the village should also have at least a dozen or more different castes so that intercaste as well as intracaste conflict might be observed. Finally, the "people" (usually meaning the elected head of the village or any other influential men through whom initial contact was made) would have to welcome my intrusion and be able to suggest some accommodation for me.

The criterion of religion was conspicuously absent, for I was unaware at the time of its importance in the Banaras region. India is predominantly Hindu, but in certain areas other religious groups are present in significant numbers: Christians, Jains, Zoroastrians (Parsis), "neo-Buddhists" (among Untouchables), tribal religious groups, and, of course, Muslims. The 1961 Government of India Census lists Muslims as constituting 10 percent of the people in Banaras District. Many villages around Arunpur had varying proportions of Muslim inhabitants. The study of religious conflict, in addition to and intertwining with that of caste and class conflict in the political arena, would have greatly enhanced the content of this work.

The notes of my diary reveal that the search for a village was complicated by other unforeseen problems, primarily those of heat, exhaustion, frustration, and lack of transportation. A crucial factor affecting my ultimate choice seems to have been the necessity to depend upon others at all stages of locating a village. I had to consider their views, from the initial process of becoming familiar with the general area to the final ones of deciding which villages could be visited and which would be most suitable.

Having now described my odyssey, let me now turn to the place where the journey ended.

THE VILLAGE OF ARUNPUR

LOCALE OF ARUNPUR

My search ended some eight miles west of Banaras, along the ancient Grand Trunk Road. A dirt path leads from there for half a mile, crosses the railroad tracks, and ends in the main settlement *(pura)* of Arunpur (see Map 3). The railroad station, small market of Dallia, boys' and girls' primary schools, and the Intercollege are all on the main road and are easily accessible from the village. Tea stalls and betel stands are located just across from the Intercollege, as is the huge enclosed mansion of the ex-zamindar (landlord) of Arunpur. He is considered the main benefactor, since he donated most of the land for the school. The Intercollege and ex-zamindar's house have electricity, and the latter has the only telephone in the area. The only electricity Arunpur has is generated by a single private pumping set. Other substantial stone buildings are interspersed with temporary and mobile stalls all along the Grand Trunk Road which provide many goods and services (haircut and shave, cycle repair, school supplies, betel, cigarettes and *ganjha—cannabis sativa*).

Arunpur is surrounded by eight villages and has relations with all on the basis of kinship, marriage ties, services rendered and received, friendship, disputes, and through participation in the "big men" *panchayat*. An appreciation of the location of the village would not be complete without reference to its proximity to Banaras. This makes it what Somjee has termed a "peri-urban" community (1964). Village men work in the city, daily cycling the eight miles back and forth with ease, and students attend its university and other institutions of learning. People go to Banaras on business, to use the courts, shop, meet with relatives and friends, see films or enjoy other forms of amusement, and take a dip in the holy Ganges. They go by cycle, rickshaw, bus, car, train, bullock cart, or on foot.

Villagers know about the activities of the city and are able to expand their world by reading the local Hindi daily paper *(Aj)* or any one of the national papers and magazines. Like the area around Baroda studied by Dr. Somjee's students (1964:2), people here are threatened with the proposed expansion of the Banaras municipal limits and feel that their land may eventually be taken away *(Aj 8/25/68:7-9)*. Though Arunpur looks like any other village in the region, it is exposed to much greater information and influence from outside communications. This increased information has widened the political arena of the village and presented new possible alternatives for action. Despite this, there are many areas of life which seem to be hardly affected by these changes. This specifically relates to the family, kinship, and the position of women (see Chapter 4).

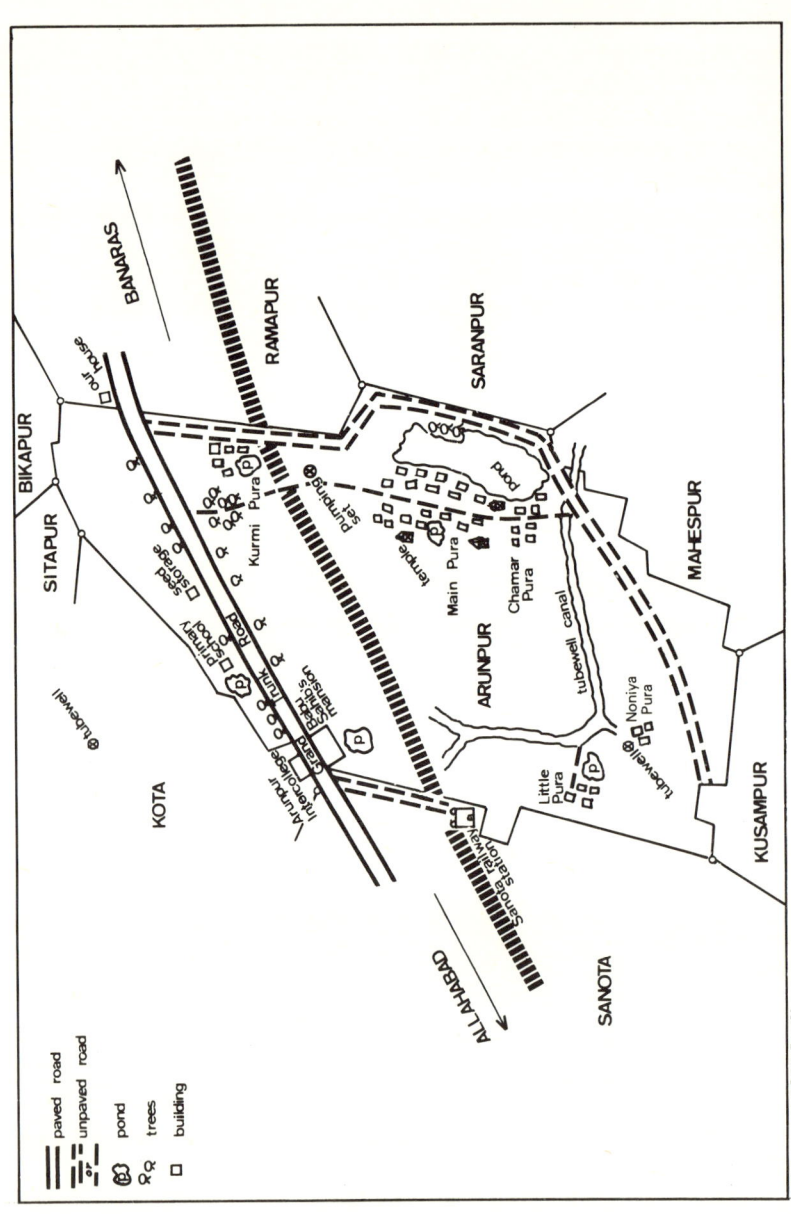

MAP 3. Arunpur and immediate environs. The open squares do not represent the actual number of buildings.

Table 2. Population of Arunpur[a]

Caste	Main Pura Population	Main Pura Households	Little Pura Population	Little Pura Households	Chamar Pura Population	Chamar Pura Households	Noniya Pura Population	Noniya Pura Households	Kurmi Pura Population	Kurmi Pura Households	Totals Population	Totals Percent of Total Population	Totals Households	Average Household Size
Brahman	48	10									48	4.6	10	4.8
Bhumihar	218	19	64	6							282	27.0	25	11.2
Kurmi	87	10	35	6					74	9	196	18.7	25	7.8
Kahar	12	2							25	3	37	3.5	5	7.4
Lohar	33	5									33	3.2	5	6.6
Kevat							3	1			3	.03	1	4.0[b]
Parihar	13	3									13	1.2	3	4.3
Nai	17	3									17	1.6	3	5.6
Kohar							24	3			24	2.3	3	8.0
Kalwar	29	2									29	2.8	2	14.5
Noniya							20	3			20	2.0	3	6.6
Teli	48	6									48	4.6	6	8.0
Pasi							1				1	.01		–[b]
Chamar					255	44					255	24.3	44	5.8
Musahar							29	4			29	2.8	4	7.3
Dharkar							12	2			12	1.0	2	6.0
Subtotals	505	60	99	12	255	44	89	13	99	12	1047	99.64	141	7.4

[a] This does not include the ex-zamindar's household or several other houses along the main road which are not part of the community.
[b] The single Kevat in Arunpur lives with a Pasi woman. They have two children.

My impressions and findings on the feeling of unity that the villagers have with one another, as well as their pride in belonging to the same village, are also similar to what Somjee has found. Such a unity insofar as it ever existed, seems to be dissipating. Part of this is due to the fact that the city offers an alternative sphere of action for those men who would have as little to do with their fellow villagers as possible (Somjee 1964:4). For example, the small group of highly educated young men in the village who teach in the Intercollege have practically no social relations outside of each other's company or that of fellow teachers', and their own lineage members *(pattidars)*. The bond of friendship between them is often also reinforced by kin ties. These young men, as well as most other villagers, have little regard for an appeal to "our" village or the prestige of the village in terminating a quarrel, reaching a unanimous decision, or attempting to overcome indifference toward a public cause. This is one of the reasons given for the increased factional fighting within the village as well as the high frequency of court cases.

Yet the decline in the feeling of village unity cannot be solely attributed to the propinquity of Banaras. There is, rather, a continual dialectical process whereby certain factors in the village (e.g., presence of factions, other disputing groups, educated men, and the settlement pattern itself) constantly interact with the alternatives offered by the city and the changes that are occurring in the society at large. It is also conceivable that the unity found in the villages of western Uttar Pradesh may not have existed here in the eastern region because villages in this region are composed of a number of settlements *(puras)*. The main settlement is separated from smaller ones ("hamlets") by fields lying between them. In Arunpur there are five such *puras* and each of them was populated at a different time. Three contain only low castes and the other two have nearly always been in opposition to one another (Table 2). Historical antecedents seem to have combined with certain contemporary communal forces to produce a feeling of community unity more at the level of the individual *pura* than of the village as a whole.

VILLAGE HISTORY

The fact that the two settlements of Bhumihars (Main Pura and Little Pura) were founded separately and by different ancestors has affected village politics. It is said that Arun Singh, a relative of the then Maharaja of Banaras, came to the village some one hundred eighty years ago and settled in what is now known as Main Pura. The village is named after him, and the largest and most influential families in this *pura* today are his descendants (Chart 1). Other Bhumihars and castes came later. The first Bhumihar came to Little Pura about a hundred years ago to work in an Englishman's indigo fields. The crop was planted throughout the present village and surrounding area at that time. This Bhumihar was Chait Singh (Chart 2), who supervised some hundred indigo laborers as the foreman. When the Englishman left, his lands went to the villagers who had worked for him. Chait Singh received a large amount of land in what was subsequently called Little Pura. Apart from a few households that were established before the founder Arun Singh came to the village, most of the low castes came after, and primarily to work for, these two Bhumihar groups. Some low-caste people lived in separate *pura*s and this was mandatory for the Chamars.

There has been a history of antagonism between the descendants of Arun Singh and those of Chait Singh since the founding of Main Pura and Little Pura. Arun Singh's descendants claim that their ancestors were the original zamindars of the village until they neglected to take proper interest in the land and part of the government revenue was left unpaid. The Maharaja then put the post on "auction," for he was anxious to have a landlord who would successfully obtain the government's share. It fell to the grandfather of the last zamindar, Babu Sahib, who was of the Agrawal merchant caste. The latter took control of the village with the help of guns and the police. The result was an uneasy relationship of simmering hostility between the old zamindars and the new. Babu Sahib's grandfather, however, was quite clever and invited the displaced landlords to his marriages and other functions, thereby gaining their respect and gratitude. Arun Singh's descendants, in turn, responded by compromising with the new situation.

To be certain that he received all the revenue due him, Babu Sahib's grandfather did not employ these ex-zamindars as messengers who informed the farmers to pay their taxes to the collector. Instead, this task fell to the Bhumihars of Little Pura. They were now used by the new zamindar to buttress his authority and this fostered further rivalry and hostility between the two Bhumihar settlements. The policy worked well. Much of the village power struggle today may be seen as a legacy from this past.

Because of their connection with Babu Sahib's grandfather, the Little Pura Bhumihars came closer to the seat of power in the village. The new zamindar's first tax collector was Chand Singh (Chart 2). This position subsequently passed on to his son, Cheddinath, who is reputed to have been a physically imposing as well as notorious personage. The link between the Little Pura Bhumihars and the power structure became even stronger when Cheddinath was also appointed village headman *(mukhiya)* by the British. It was he who called the village *panchayat,* presided over it, and settled all disputes within his jurisdiction. He was also the

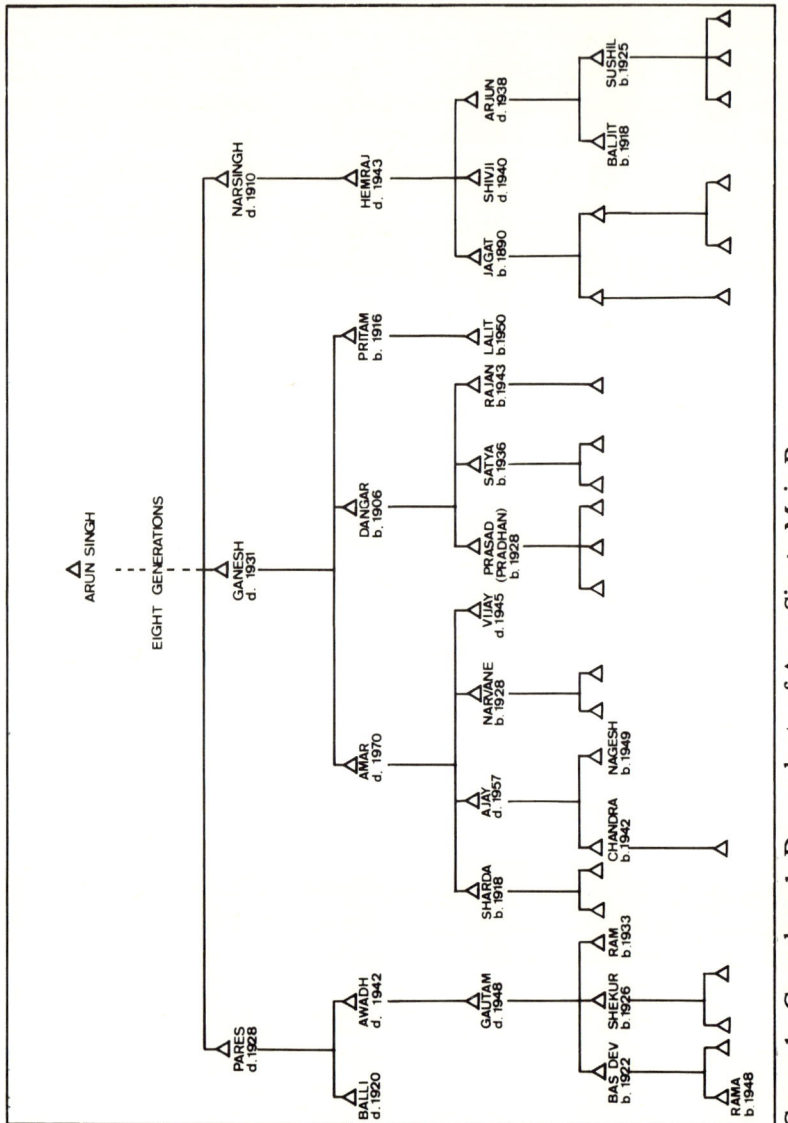

CHART 1. Genealogy 1: Descendants of Arun Singh, Main Pura.

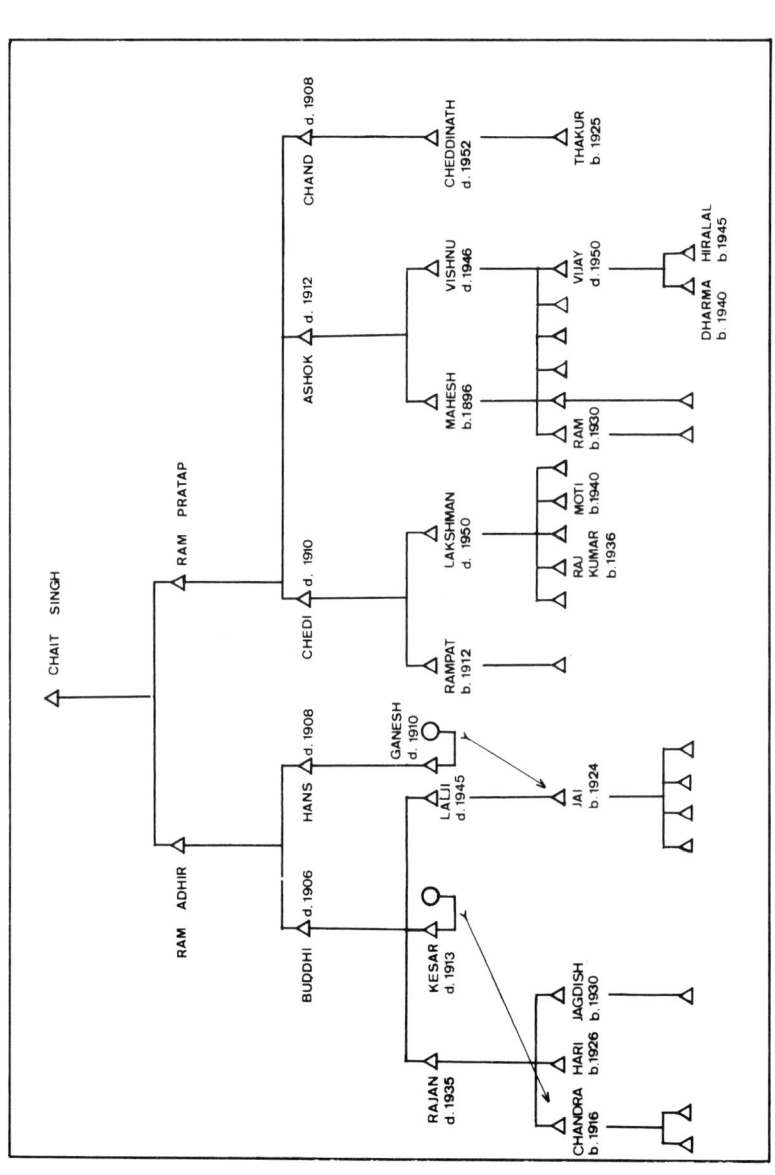

CHART 2. Genealogy 2: Little Pura Bhumihars.

chief member *(sarpanch)* of the British local *(amin) panchayat,* which included Arunpur and the eight surrounding villages.

The Independence Movement that started at the beginning of this century set the stage for the next major period of conflict between the descendants of Arun Singh and Chait Singh. During World War II, Arunpur and the neighboring area were included in a large British military depot. Members of Amar Singh's household in Main Pura (Chart 1) had by this time become active in Gandhi's Non-Cooperation Movement of 1942, and several men were sent to prison. I was told of the hardships they suffered during this period and how Amar's house was searched by government police nine times.

The Little Pura Bhumihars sided with the rulers, since their leader was the British-appointed headman, and appeared as government witnesses against the village freedom fighters. After Independence, however, they supported the Congress Party, while the Main Pura families of Amar Singh, his kinsmen, and followers voted for the Socialists. Although the father of the present ex-zamindar had been allied with the British and aided their troops, Babu Sahib himself now leads a quiet life since the abolition of zamindari. He is involved in his own family affairs and farming enterprise and stays aloof from the politics of Arunpur or any other village. His only connection with village affairs is through his position as manager of the Arunpur Intercollege. When Ajay Singh (Chart 1), the most active and famed freedom fighter in the village, started to work for the foundation of the college, Babu Sahib supported the effort and donated much of the land on which it was constructed.[2]

This historical background uncovers the roots of one major form of political conflict in Arunpur, the existence of factions among the Bhumihars. Factionalism and other political conflict in the village arena are primarily concerned with competition for the distribution of the scarce resources of land, water, and labor. Their place within agriculture, the most important economic activity, must be explained before we can understand the disputes over these resources.

WATER, LAND, AND LABOR IN THE AGRICULTURAL CYCLE OF ARUNPUR

A peasant's work is arduous when he must eke out an existence from the soil armed only with one or two bullocks, a wooden plough, and a few "machines" that are run by his own sweat. An elderly man told of his labors:

> I get up at 4, feed the animals, and then take them to the field and plough until 10 a.m. Then I bring the bullocks back to the house and return to the fields to cut two headloads of fodder which I take home in two trips. I cut these by hand and finish at noon. Then I feed the animals, eat, and it is 1:30.

I take the bullocks to the fields again and plough until 5 or 6. I return home and go to the market and come back by 8. Then I feed the animals and eat. Then it becomes 10 at night. Because of all this work I sleep like a dead man.

A description of the agricultural cycle may begin with the arrival of the monsoon rains by late June, which serve to break the intense summer heat. At this time, the rain crops *(kharif)* are sown, of which rice (both early and late varieties) is the most important. In addition, there is maize, sorghum, millet, and jute—much of the three latter crops are used for fodder. The rains often fail and a great deal of the crops dry up. Agriculturalists depend upon either the government tubewell, a private pumping set, or other more primitive methods of irrigation at such times. While these rain crops are harvested during September and October, the most strenuous agricultural work is simultaneously begun with the preparation of the fields for the winter crops *(rabi)*. The winter harvest provides most of the staples for a north Indian village.

During October and November, the newly ploughed fields are sown with wheat, pulses, potatoes, peas, mustard, and sesame. After sowing, the major work is providing irrigation for the potatoes during the dry winter months, cutting, crushing, and preparing molasses from the now matured sugar cane, and cutting and husking the rice. By February, these tasks are complete and it is time to harvest the peas and potatoes, cut the wheat, and pick and crush the mustard and sesame. At the same time, beginning in March, the difficult job of ploughing starts once again, this time to prepare the fields for planting sugar cane. Great effort is required to follow through a zigzagged ploughing scheme which may overturn the earth as many as ten times. Although potato is the major cash crop in the village (because of the general lack of sugar-crushing mills in the area), many of the larger landowners are able to market some of their surplus molasses.

By May, when the temperature reaches its peak and the infamous dust storm *(loo)* makes its appearance, work is complete. People spend most of the day indoors and the only preparations made are those of arranging for or participating in a marriage. Few people will bother to plant the hot weather crops *(zaid),* which yield only vegetables and some melons.

It is well known that the main impediment to increased agricultural production throughout the entire northeastern section of India—stretching from the eastern districts of Uttar Pradesh through Bihar and vast regions of Bengal—is the lack of irrigation. The lands between the Ganges and the Jamuna in the west enjoy an extensive canal network through which water flows naturally. In the east, however, the river beds are often below the level of the fields and an expensive pumping method is required to bring the water up to field level. "Canal irrigation here is fifty years behind the western areas" (Etienne 1968:155).

In Arunpur there is only one tubewell, located just outside of Little Pura, which was installed by the government in 1953. During the dry winter months, when irrigation is required for potatoes and when the monsoon may come late or even fail, there is tremendous demand for tubewell water. Thus, it is not surprising that the major number of disputes in Arunpur occur over the distribution of this extremely scarce resource. The only privately owned pumping set in the village began operating during my stay and irrigates the twenty-*bigha* (one *bigha* = .67 acre) field belonging to the family of Amar Singh (Chart 1). They also plan to sell water to others at the rate of four rupees (one rupee = U.S. $.13) an hour and believe that their agricultural output will double or treble in just a single year after introducing this innovation.

While a tubewell provides more water than a pumping set, it is much more expensive to install and requires an outlay of some 20,000 to 30,000 rupees. The pipe in the well is bored deep into the ground and a fifteen to twenty-horsepower engine is then employed to bring the water up to the level of the fields. A pumping set, on the other hand, can be installed on an already existent well and is run by a maximum five-horsepower elec-

FIGURE 1. Manual boring of a tubewell.

THE VILLAGE OF ARUNPUR 31

tric (or diesel) generator. It costs only about 12,000 rupees but may possibly run dry. Six farmers were in the process of filing applications at the Community Development Block office and at the electric company for new pumping sets and electricity connections by the time I left Arunpur. There is competition among them over who shall get a set (for there are regulations about their spacing) and who shall have it installed first. Applying and successfully receiving approval for the installation of a pumping set is a tedious business which requires familiarity with the workings of the official world as well as the acumen to calculate maneuvers and alter strategies to achieve this goal.

By far the most usual method of irrigation, however, is the old system which entails the use of a large leather bag *(mot)* drawn from the well by a pair of bullocks who walk up and down the well ramp. This is hard work for the animals as well as for the man who drives them, and the man, woman, or child who must pull the bag over the top of the well so that the water can flow along one of the small channels to the fields. Much water falls back into the well, and it is necessary to stop for rest more often than with a Persian wheel, the device common in the western part of the state. It is estimated that two bullocks, pulling one bag each, can irrigate a little less than one *bigha* in a day, while a Persian wheel irrigates two *bighas* per day (Etienne 1968:153).

Another method for moving water from either a pond or a depression where it has accumulated to a higher area is the use of a tubelike construction operated by two persons who constantly move it up and down. I have even seen water arduously transferred by means of metal pans.

The competition for water is based upon the possession of land, which is itself another major cause of disputes in Arunpur. This competition usually takes two forms: (1) conflict over the possession of land and (2) conflict between the landed farmers and their landless laborers, who receive a small plot of land as part of their wages. A preliminary to this discussion, however, is some knowledge about the nature of land tenure.

In 1950, the Uttar Pradesh Legislative Assembly passed the U.P. Zamindari and Land Reform Act, which reduced a plethora of land tenure statuses to two main types—*bhumidar* and *sirdar*. The law went into effect in 1952 and affected Arunpur as it did all other villages in the state. The ex-zamindar was allowed to retain ownership of the land he had cultivated directly with the help of agricultural laborers *(khudkasht)*. As compensation for the loss of other lands, he received ready cash and government debentures or bonds which were equal to eight times the annual revenue collected. The landlord then became a *bhumidar* (absolute owner with the right to sell) on his own land and paid only half the annual tax previously levied on that property.

FIGURE 2. Laborers irrigate a field from a ditch.

Those who had been the occupancy-tenants of the zamindar, for the most part people who now have land in Arunpur, became *sirdars* and paid the state a tax which was equivalent to the rent previously charged by the zamindar. These ex-tenants retained all their former rights enjoyed under zamindari, including use of the land and its transference to their heirs. The only restriction was the prohibition on subletting. In addition, as in the past, *sirdars* were not allowed to sell their land until they became *bhumidars*. A very important provision of the act authorized, and even encouraged, this change of status by reducing the *sirdar* tax by half if a farmer agreed to give ten times the annual revenue initially and thereby become a *bhumidar* (Etienne 1968:59). The village record-keeper *(lekhpal)* informed me that most of the people in Arunpur hold land as *sirdar* despite the fact that he often tried to convince them of the tax saving under *bhumidar* ownership. The farmers, in turn, find it too difficult to raise the tenfold amount initially required and hence do not change their status until they are ready to sell their land.

It is easy to say that practically nothing has been gained by zamindari abolition, since former tenants merely became *sirdars* and pay to the state what was previously paid to the zamindar. The landless remained so (see Table 3; also Cohn 1955:55). Some land, however, did come on the market and the zamindar's rights as lord of the village were abolished. But not all villagers are pleased with the passing of zamindari. A Kurmi farmer told me:

> If anything, things got worse. Babu Sahib [the last zamindar] was good; if we had no money he understood and would suspend tax collection for two or three years until we could pay. Now, if we don't give the tax to the revenue collector immediately, they take away our bullocks and belongings.

He further said that, in a way, the Kurmis received less land by abolition. All the land they own today was held prior to 1952; after that, when land came on the market they could not buy it, for this precious resource was "grabbed up by the Bhumihars. It is they who gained the most."

The plight of those without land remains the same. Some Chamars used to lease land (altogether, about eighty *bighas*), and during the days of zamindari they paid their taxes to Cheddinath Singh, the village headman and tax collector for the zamindar. Instead of passing the money on to the zamindar, however, Cheddinath "ate it up." The zamindar never knew that the rent had been paid and placed the Chamar's land on auction. Many Bhumihars, Kurmis, and some others purchased the property. The Chamars filed a case in the court, but "nothing happened." Hence today they are practically all landless and rely on their labor and the land received as wages to keep body and soul together. They also told

FIGURE 3. Cutting fodder by hand.

Table 3. Land Ownership in Arunpur by Caste (in *Bigha*s) [a]

| Caste | Settlement | | | | | Totals | | |
	Main Pura	Little Pura	Chamar Pura	Noniya Pura	Kurmi Pura	Land Owned	Percent of Total Land Owned	Per Capita Ownership
Brahman	28[b]					28	6	.60
Bhumihar	210	106				316	63	1.10
Kurmi	51	26			31	108	21	.55
Kahar	3			9		12	2	.30[c]
Lohar	2					2	.5	.06
Kevat				0		0	0	0
Parihar	0					0	0	0
Nai	10					10	2	.58
Kohar			5			5	1	.20
Kalwar	0					0	0	0
Noniya				2		2	.5	.10
Teli	15					15	3	.30
Pasi				0		0	0	0
Chamar			6			6	1	.02
Musahar				0		0	0	0
Dharkar				0		0	0	0
Subtotals	319	132	6	7	40	504[d]	100	0.48

[a] 1 *bigha* = 0.67 acre.

[b] Figures incomplete for two households.

[c] The amount of land the Kahars own is not exact because of their involvement in a dispute with the village over a pond.

[d] The total area is larger than the amount included in the village boundaries (i.e., 291 acres or 434 *bigha*s), since some villagers owned land outside Arunpur.

of still having to perform forced labor without pay (*begar,* the traditional due of the zamindar) for their Bhumihar masters. Some of the latter confirmed this fact.

As a result of losing their land and relinquishing their traditional occupations, Chamars are now almost totally reduced to being landless laborers who plough and work the land of the upper castes. The Bhumihars in Arunpur, as elsewhere in the region, feel that it is beneath their dignity and prestige to touch the plough. One of them said:

> It is our custom not to plough just as it is a custom that the big man must give some land to the poor man; if not in the form of a donation, then in the form of wages. If we big men do not keep laborers and give them land, then the people of the area will taunt us—"You say that you are big but you can't even give a *bigha* of land to a poor man."

FIGURE 4. Carrying fertilizer of dried manure from the fields.

The situation is much the same as Etienne describes for the village of Nahiyan, twenty-eight miles north of Banaras, where farmers grant part of their land to laborers on a sharecropping basis as a part of their wage. To prevent any legal tangles whereby the tiller may eventually claim the land he works as his own, the plot is frequently changed each year.

This system of rotating the sublet land *(mafi)* is so flexible that it escapes the law and laborers are reluctant to make complaints for fear of losing their jobs and land (Etienne 1968:157). Although there is no shortage of labor in Arunpur, so that one pair of hands could easily replace another, such replacements are difficult, if not impossible. The credit that a laborer obtains from the landowner tends to bind them together permanently, and the debts of the father are inherited by his sons. When such debts accumulate at an annual interest of 20 to 36 percent, repayment at the present "wage" becomes impossible.

Traditional Mode of Conflict Resolution: The Panchayat

Land, water, and labor are the resources most often fought over in Arunpur. The more frequent conflicts over the distribution of water are usually settled by the parties concerned, and the decision reached is based on the implicit or explicit threat of force. The same is generally true of conflict between landowners and laborers. Conflicts over land, however, are more technical and serious and are referred to some external dispute-settling body. Other types of conflicts also occur, and to deal with them the villagers have access to several different modes of conflict resolution. The traditional form of conflict resolution, the *panchayat,* is described here while new alternatives are discussed in the next chapter.

When two parties are in dispute and unable to settle the matter between themselves, they will approach a third party who acts as an arbitrator in deciding the matter. The third party must initally be acceptable to both disputants and they then agree to adhere to his (or its) decision. Thus, if the arbitrator acts in a truly nonpartisan manner, he (it) will be acting nonpolitically and without any stake or interest in the dispute at hand, save that justice be done. Once a decision is reached and accepted by both parties, the matter should end there.

The major form of conflict resolution in village India where one could expect to receive such a just decision was, and to a large extent still is, the *panchayat. Panchayat,* translated as "council," literally means "five sitting in a circle" or "a meeting of five," whose purpose is to sit in judgment on the matter at hand. The men selected to reach a decision in the *panchayat,* usually four to ten people, are known as *panchas*. There are two major forms of *panchayat.* Each one demands that its members be men esteemed for their impartiality and good judgment; each conducts its actual proceedings and reaches its decision in a similar manner. But they are composed of different men and deal with separate spheres of conflict. Cohn has rightly pointed out that the *panchayat* is not so much a council, with the accompanying emphasis on membership and precedence, as a set of processes relating to arbitration and adjudication (1965:90).

The caste *(biradari) panchayat* is a formal entity among the lower castes and deals with disputes that primarily involve marriage, divorce, familial relations of caste members, and contraventions of caste rules. It is regarded as dealing with personal matters, and the *panchayat* members chosen to give judgment are solely from the caste concerned. Others from different castes, however, may also attend the meeting. The head of a caste *panchayat* is the *chaudhuri,* whom the aggrieved party originally requests to call and organize a meeting of a *panchayat*. The head may represent a circle of ten to twenty villages, fifty villages, or even more. Depending upon the nature and seriousness of the matter, the appropriate caste leader will be called upon. No such formal institution exists among the Brahmans and Bhumihars. Here people simply decide among themselves who has broken a caste rule and, as in the case of an "outcaste" Arunpur Bhumihar, take the necessary steps to cut off those concerned from social relations. Upper-caste men can come together in a *panchayat,* which takes the form of a general meeting, when they wish to discuss a matter of interest to the entire caste or which affects the caste as a whole.

If a dispute is between members of two different castes or members of the same caste and involves a quarrel, fight, or conflict over property, water, wages, money, and anything of interest of concern to the general public *(sarvajanik),* it is referred to a *panchayat* of big men *(bare admi)*. Ideally, this *panchayat* is not composed along caste lines and consists of a number of respected and influential men who can be counted upon to give the dispute a good hearing and reach an impartial decision. In actuality, however, high-caste men will often be judged sole by their caste peers. If one or both of the parties is from a lower caste, then one or two men from that caste may be invited to sit in the *panchayat*. Yet even the Bhumihars admitted that in such a case these lower-caste *panchas* would feel intimidated by their superiors. Considerations of wealth and power often figure in the selection of *panchayat* members, although honesty and impartiality are regarded as the prime virtues. It is said that it is important to have influential and powerful men give the decision so that the disputants will be afraid to disregard the judgment.

The different spheres of influence relegated to the two forms of *pan-*

chayat are not, however, always that clearly demarcated. The personal circumstances and predilections of the aggrieved party may account for the type of *panchayat* called. For example, a purely (low) caste matter can be referred to a big man *panchayat* (as in Cases 4 and 9 in Chapter 5) or even to an on-the-spot *panchayat* (Case 17 in Chapter 7). The disputants may want to avoid the cost and formality of calling a caste *panchayat*. A high-caste man may also be invited to sit and give counsel on a caste *panchayat*, although no one of low caste is ever invited to any meeting where high-caste affairs are discussed. Cohn has found, for a village in a nearby district, that "frequently it would seem that members of the dominant caste interfere with the workings of lower-caste councils to support clients or to achieve political or economic ends of their own" (1965:103). Two men who are in disagreement may also approach a group of other villagers who are socially sitting together and choose several among them to settle their dispute.

The conduct of both types of *panchayat*s is similar. It is the party who feels wronged, usually the weaker one, who makes the appeal for a *panchayat*. Both disputants must be present at the actual meeting and agree to abide by whatever decision is reached before the *panchayat* proceeds further. The disputants, or those in attendance, then talk among themselves and decide who among the influential and powerful men present are to be selected as *panchayat* members and will give judgment on the case. These four to ten members must be agreeable to both parties, and one of them becomes the leader *(sarpanch)* who conducts the meeting and leads in the decision making.

The one who has called the *panchayat* is asked to speak first and explain the dispute. The other party is then called upon to state whether the charges are true or false and to present his version. Witnesses come forth and other evidence (i.e., written deeds, notes, and so on) is also given.

When the *panchayat* members have thoroughly examined the case, they retire to discuss what decision they will give. It is said that people in a *panchayat* cannot be fooled by false evidence because they are all local men who have an intimate knowledge of the lives of their fellow villagers. If the leader is wise and persuasive, he may succeed in getting all to agree to a common decision. If not, then the decision proposed by the majority *(bahumat)* of the members is accepted and presented to the meeting as the decision with the consensus of all *(sarva samiti se)*. Decisions reached by the *panchayat* used to be solely oral. In important disputes today, in cases where the people involved are skeptical about whether or not the decision will be implemented, or if they wish to use it as evidence in a law court, the decision will be written down, signed, witnessed, and officially registered.

The judgment and punishment imposed in the big men *panchayat* are usually in the form of a declaration that the party who is found to be correct should receive what he demands and the offender be fined. There is no actual way effectively to force the decision of this *panchayat* upon the two parties concerned, save making them afraid of going against the verdict of big and powerful men and antagonizing society as a whole by their disobedience. The caste *panchayat,* from which there is usually no other court of appeal, is much more effective in achieving compliance with its decisions because it can threaten total social ostracism. The punishment imposed on the offending party is most usually a fine in the form of a feast. Money, repair of a temple, or clearance of some path or crosswalk, and so on, might also be requested. The person who does not obey this *panchayat*'s decision can then become an "outcaste" (which may be an initial punishment as well), when people will cease to sit, to eat, and to have marriage ties with him.

Today, however, villagers often say that the *panchayat* as a mode of conflict resolution is losing its hold on society. People no longer fear what others think, nor are they hesitant to ignore the decision reached. Every man thinks himself big and thus comes to the *panchayat* not for justice but for a favorable verdict. If they fail to obtain this from the traditional bodies, they are able to appeal elsewhere, outside of the village locale. Most often, men will go to officials in one of the government institutions.

The Distribution of Resources in Arunpur

From an examination of the tables presented in this chapter, it can be seen that land and other forms of wealth are highly concentrated in the hands of Bhumihars and that the gulf between them and the Untouchables is extreme. Of the 504 *bigha*s owned by Arunpur residents, 316 belong to the former, who number 282, while 6 *bigha*s belong to the latter, numbering 297. In other words, 27 percent of the population owns 63 percent of the land, while 28 percent, who rely almost solely on employment in agriculture, own less than 2 percent of the land. This difference is seen more sharply when the average land per capita is computed. For Bhumihars, it is 1.1 *bigha*s and decreases rapidly until among the Untouchable castes the Chamars have only .02 *bigha*s per capita and Dharkars, Musahars, and the single Pasi have nothing.

Tables 4 and 5 present basic information regarding land ownership from different perspectives than that primarily of caste. Table 4 details the land that different caste groups own according to categories of holdings (figures rounded out from data just given). A quick glance reveals that while 33 percent of the total population are completely landless, the Untouchables form 68 percent of that number. At the other end, we find that 4 percent of the village population holds 15 percent of its land resources. The table reflects the high concentration of land in the hands of a few, again mainly Bhumihars. The degree of concentration is shown more starkly in Table 5, which collapses some of the categories of landholding from the previous table. If the landless and the small landowners (up to ten *bighas*) are put together, we find that 17 percent of the population controls 51 percent of the land in holdings of eleven *bigha*s or more. Finally, Table 6 shows land ownership among the Bhumihars, the caste which has the most dispersion of holdings. Here again, there is a trend toward concentration even within a single caste, although it is not as great as the disparities between castes or categories of holdings (Tables 3 and 4).

Table 7, reflecting occupational dispersion in Arunpur, explains a number of things about the distribution of cash income (Table 8). The comparatively high annual monetary income of the Bhumihars (estimated at 563 rupees per capita) is primarily due to their outside professional employment, small but lucrative involvement in business, and sale of surplus agricultural produce. Although almost every Bhumihar landowner grows some cash crops (mainly potatoes or sugar cane) for the market, only a small number of some half a dozen households have significant farm surpluses and may be seen as engaging in capitalist farming activities. Economic differentiation within this caste is increasing as larger farmers take greater advantage of new opportunities for material gain.

The Kurmis, self-sufficient and independent producers holding small amounts of land for the most part, receive their cash income almost equally divided between sales of produce and outside employment. The Brahmans own more land per capita than the Kurmis but are much less entrepreneurial and have a smaller surplus to market. The high cash income of the Kalwars is accounted for by the fact that, despite their lack of land, they are well educated (with 100 percent literacy) and successfully employed in teaching or business.

Members of both the Kahar and Nai castes own some land. The former's income is mainly from the sale of produce (the *singhara* water vegetable and fish) cultivated in village ponds they either own or lease. Nai income is a combination of monies received from employment in both their traditonal occupation and in agriculture. Other castes, which own little or no land (Lohar through Teli), receive their cash from nonagricultural employment (see also Chapter 4).

The majority of Chamars work as agricultural laborers and receive payment in kind for the most part. The same is true of the Untouchable Musahars. Chapter 8 further details the wage structure for such labor.

Table 4. Land in Arunpur by Amount Owned

Amount of Land Owned (in *bighas*)		Brahman	Bhumihar	Kurmi	Kahar	Lohar	Kevat	Parihar	Nai	Kohar	Kalwar	Noniya	Teli	Pasi	Chamar	Musahar	Dharkar	Total	Percent Total Population	Percent Total Land Owned	Average Household Size
None	No. hsehlds.						1	3	1	2	2	2	3	–	36	4	2	59			6
	Total pop.						3	13	7	13	29	15	13	1	196	29	12	350	33	0	
Less than 1 *bigha*	No. hsehlds.	2		2		4									8			16			6.7
	Total pop.	9		9		30									59			107	10		
	Amt. land	2		1		1									6			10		2	
1–5 *bighas*	No. hsehlds.	8	11	14	5	1			1	1		1	3					45			6.4
	Total pop.	39	75	80	37	3			5	11		5	35					290	28		
	Amt. land	26	39	46	12	1			2	5		2	15					148		29	
6–10 *bighas*	No. hsehlds.		5	5					1									11			11.4
	Total pop.		59	62					5									126	12		
	Amt. land		39	43					8									90		18	

11–15 bighas	No. hsehlds.	4			
	Total pop.	46	4		
	Amt. land	55		11	11.5
16–20 bighas	No. hsehlds.	1			
	Total pop.	26	3		26
	Amt. land	18		4	
21–25 bighas	No. hsehlds.	3			
	Total pop.	47	5		15.6
	Amt. land	71		14	
26–35 bighas	No. hsehlds.	1			
	Total pop.	11	1		11
	Amt. land	35		7	
75–80 bighas	No. hsehlds.	1			
	Total pop.	44	4		44
	Amt. land	77		15	

Table 5. Land by Categories of Ownership

Amount of Land Owned	Total Population	Percent of Total Population	Percent of Total Land Owned
Landless	350	33	–
Up to 10 *bighas*	523	50	49
11 *bighas* and above	174	17	51
Totals	1047	100	100

Table 6. Land Ownership among Bhumihars

Bighas of Land Owned	Number of Bhumihars	Percent of Total Bhumihar Population	Percent of Total Land Owned by Bhumihars
1–5	75	27	12
6–10	59	21	12
11–15	46	16	18
16–20	–	–	–
21–25	47	16	23
26–35	11	4	11
75–80	44	16	24
Totals	282	100	100

The 563-rupees-per-capita annual cash income of Bhumihars may be juxtaposed against the 94 rupees per capita of the Chamars, keeping in mind that this latter figure represents a larger proportion of total Chamar income than monies received does for the Bhumihars who produce a surplus.

The information collected on debt is admittedly even more unreliable than the figures on cash income because people are generally reluctant to speak about this matter. Yet allowing for an even greater hesitancy on the part of Bhumihars to disclose such information, which may reflect upon their prestige, there is surely something significant in the amounts reported of 4,500 rupees for Bhumihars as against 16,000 rupees for the Chamars. The large disparity in the fortunes of the very high and the very low is also reflected in the average family size: 11.2 for Bhumihars and 5.8 for Chamars. Only the wealthy can afford to maintain large joint households. The castes lying in the range between these two extremes of the hierarchy have slowly begun to experience some economic mobility through newly expanding opportunities. This is most true of the Kurmis.

The prime means to an improved agriculture and irrigation also re-

Table 7. Caste and Occupation in Arunpur

Occupation	Brahman	Bhumihar	Kurmi	Kahar	Lohar	Kevat	Parihar	Nai	Kohar	Kalwar	Noniya	Teli	Pasi	Chamar	Musahar	Dharkar	Totals	Percent
Traditional occupation	4	34[a]	20[b]	7	7	0	0	0	6[a]	1	0	7	—	0	0	3	89	30
Farmer	10	7	1					2	3		1	5[b]	—	1			21	7
Businessman			1							2		4	—				15	5
Teacher		5			1					4			—				9	3
Government employee	1	12	1		1								—	2			17	6
Truck driver	1	2	1			2							—				4	1.3
Peon		3	4						1				—				8	3
Clerk		1										3	—				4	1
Housebuilder			1				2		2		2		—				7	2
Factory worker		1	4		3		1				2		—	3			14	4.7
Carpenter											1		—				1	.34
Electrician											1		—				1	.34
Weaver													—	11			14	4.7
Cigarette maker			3	2							1		—				4	1.3
Daily laborer			1	1	2	2	1					1	—	27[c]	11		43	15
Ploughman													—	28			28	10
Rickshaw driver													—	11[d]			11	4
Cycle repairer													—	1			1	.34
Well digger			1										—	2			3	1
Totals	16	65	36	10	11	2	5	8	7	6	8	20	—	86	11	3	294	100
Percent engaged in traditional occupation	25	51	57	70	67	0	0	100	14	0	0	35	—	0	0	100	31	

[a] Figure includes two men engaged in other nontraditional occupations as well.
[b] Figure includes one man engaged in another nontraditional occupation.
[c] Figure includes seven men engaged in this work on a seasonal basis, i.e., when they are not engaged as ploughmen six months of the year.
[d] Figure includes two men engaged in this work on a seasonal basis.

Table 8. Estimated Annual Cash Income (in Rupees)

Caste	Wages	Business Income	Sale of Produce	Totals	Per Capita Income
Brahman	3,320		5,440	8,670	183
Bhumihar	63,480	30,000	65,400	158,880	563
Kurmi	19,380	3,420	25,550	48,350	247
Kahar	1,080		13,000	14,080	380
Lohar	10,980			10,980	333
Kevat	1,200			1,200	300[a]
Parihar	3,000			3,000	231
Nai	1,440		600	2,040	120
Kohar	2,240		250	2,490	104
Kalwar	13,500	[b]		13,500	466
Noniya	5,400			5,400	270
Teli	6,000	1,500	5,200	12,700	265
Pasi	–	–	–	–	[a]
Chamar	24,000			24,000	94
Musahar	120			120	4
Dharkar	1,320			1,320	110
Subtotals	156,460	34,920	115,440	306,820	293

[a] The single Pasi in Arunpur is included in the figures for the Kevat caste.
[b] I could not obtain these figures.

mains in the hands of the upper castes. There are twenty wells in the village; seven belong to Bhumihars, five to Kurmis, three to Brahmans, two to Chamars, and the remaining three to those of the Nai, Kohar, and Noniya castes. The single pumping set in operation when I left the village belongs to a Bhumihar. Six others have also applied for pumping set permits, of which four are Bhumihars and two are Kurmis.

The size and type of house (mud or brick), general standard of living, and education (especially after high school) that villagers can afford (see Table 9) corresponds to the general pattern of land ownership and wealth, as does even the number of "luxury" items such as bicycles and radios (see note 1). There is also a relationship between the degree of education and occupational mobility. The most highly educated castes have the most diversified occupational structure.

The dominant group of Bhumihars has successfully retained control over the distribution of resources in the village and has extended that control to include new resources and alternative forms of conflict resolution. This brings the village as a single unit into a wider perspective by indicating the relationships it has with outsiders—specifically, the government administration.

Table 9. Education in Arunpur[a]

Caste	Primary Level or Literate (Grades 1–5)				Middle Level (Grades 6–8)				High School (Grades 9–10)		Inter-college (Grades 11–12)		B.A./ B.Sc.		M.A./ M.Sc.		Percentages of Literates					
	M		F		M		F		M		M		M		M		M		F		M+F	
	%	No.	%	No.	%	No.	%	No.	%	No.	%	No.	%	No.	%	No.	%	No.	%	No.	%	No.
Brahman	45	10	7	1	9	2	13	2	5	1							60	13	20	3	43	16
Bhumihar	40	47	27	30	20	25	6	7	11	13	14	17	5	6	4	5	94	113	33	37	65	150
Kurmi	30	25	5	3	12	10			11	9	1	1	1	1			55	46	5	3	35	49
Kahar	47	8	25	3	6	1	8	1									53	9	33	4	45	13
Lohar	65	11			17	2											66	10	0		31	10
Kevat					100	1											100	1			100	1
Parihar	14	1			14	1			14	1							42	3	0		27	3
Nai	30	3			20	2							10	1			60	6	0		40	6
Kohar	25	3			17	2			8	1							50	6	0		33	6
Kalwar	20	2	60	6	20	2			20	2	20	2	8	1	20	2	100	10	60	6	80	16
Noniya	17	2			25	3	17	1	33	4	8	1					91	11	17	1	66	12
Teli	53	8							13	2							66	10	0		31	10
Pasi																	0		0		0	
Chamar	6	8			5	4	1	1	2	3	.08	1	.08	1			14	18	1	1	9	19
Musahar																	0		0		0	
Dharkar																	0		0		0	
Subtotals	27	128	12	43	11	54	3	12	8	39	5	22	2	10	2	7	55	260	15	55	38	315

[a] This table includes everyone seven years and older in Arunpur.

NOTES

1. There are 106 bicycles in Arunpur distributed in the following manner: Brahman—4, Bhumihar—32, Kurmi—29, Teli, Kohar, Kalwar, Kevat, Nai, Lohar—34, and Chamar—7. One Bhumihar owns a motorcycle and one Chamar a rickshaw. Of the eleven transistor radios in the village, eight are owned by Bhumihars and three by Kurmis.

2. I met the ex-zamindar of Arunpur, Babu Sahib, when I first visited the village and was attempting to make some arrangements for a temporary stay and preliminary investigation there. Babu Sahib graciously met with me and agreed to let me stay at his house after his daughter's marriage. As per his request, I telephoned him a week later and after four unsuccessful attempts to reach him, I gave up. Perhaps he had changed his mind about offering me hospitality but had found it too embarrassing to say so.

    Once I came to live in Arunpur, I met him several times; most specifically when we tried to employ his help in rebuilding the Primary School well and putting a roof on the Girls' section. He was always pleasant and full of praise for our efforts, but exceedingly reluctant to do anything. On the occasions that I inquired about his family history, connection with the village and history of the village, he was noncommittal and kept saying that he knew nothing. A person cannot be pressed in that frame of mind. With great difficulty I obtained the genealogy of his immediate family, but as he preferred not to be bothered, I respected his wishes.

CHAPTER 3
Arunpur and the Outside World: The Extension of Government Administration

One of the important changes that has taken place in post-Independence Arunpur has been the increasing frequency of its contacts with the world outside, because of the proliferation of governmental interests. This is most evident from the extension of government administration to the village level. Previously, the British Raj had its local representatives in the form of the zamindar and the headman; interaction with outside government personnel was comparatively infrequent. Today, however, government reaches and affects every village by elections (and tax collections), and most villages through the Local Self-Government *(panchayati raj)*, Community Development, and education programs.

EXTENSION OF GOVERNMENT ADMINISTRATION

*Panchayat*s have had a long history in India, although the successive attempts to revive the institution by various rulers have more often led to a continuity in name rather than form. Under the British, the local *(amin) panchayat* was empowered to try petty crimes and raise money by taxation. The *panchayat* jurisdiction extended to a circle including the headquarter village and neighboring villages. Village headmen were ex-officio members of the *panchayat*. The Constitution of Independent India also empowered state governments to frame laws and rules pertaining to village *panchayat*s and to endow them with such powers and authority as might be necessary to enable them to function as agents of self-government in the village. The Uttar Pradesh *Panchayati Raj* Act of 1947 and its subsequent amendments of 1955 and 1961 provided for the establishment of village assemblies *(gram sabha)* consisting of all residents over twenty-one, village *panchayats (gram panchayat),* and justice *panchayat*s *(nyaya panchayat)*. The village *panchayat* was to implement the plans and decisions authorized by the assembly, while the justice *panchayat* performed the task of deciding petty civil, revenue, and criminal cases.

The Constitution of 1950 also acknowledged the need for a social and economic transformation of India's hundreds of thousands of villages. Under the First Five Year Plan (1951), community development was regarded as the method to bring about such a transformation. The first series of pilot projects to study what would be involved in a nationwide program were launched in 1952 by an agreement with the Ford Foundation. In 1958, a committee investigating the effectiveness of subsequent development programs reported a general failure due to the lack of association of the people with the projects; they were imposed from above instead of from within. The committee then recommended that the existing structure of Local Self-Government through *panchayat*s be altered into a three-tiered system upon which all development work in their jurisdiction would devolve. It was found necessary to have two *panchayat*s at the village level, as the traditional function of *panchayat*s was primarily that of dispute settlement. The justice *panchayat* would carry on this old function of conflict resolution (see later), and the village *panchayat* would deal with the new tasks of social reconstruction. The report of the committee in 1958, which studied the progress of community development, suggested an even more radical departure for the village *panchayat*s; they were to implement development work and promote self-motivation for these programs at the grass roots.

The new three-tiered system which the committee recommended was to be matched at every level with a complementary one in the Community Development administration. Thus, at the bottom tier the village *panchayat,* consisting of an elected village head *(pradhan)* and approximately ten to sixteen *panchayat* members, is to deal primarily with agriculture, sanitation, and provisions for village wells. The Village-Level Worker is the Community Development liaison.

The second level of local self-government is formed by a *panchayat samiti,* which corresponds to the Community Development Block of 100 villages under a Block Development Officer (BDO). The *panchayat samiti* consists of all elected heads of villages and the BDO. They elect one among themselves to be the head *(pramukh),* and this appointment is usually made on political party lines. The second tier is to concern itself with the development functions of the block, namely that of improved agriculture, cattle, promotion of health education, and industries. There is often much competition and ill feeling at this level between the administrators of the Community Development program (the BDO and his

FIGURE 5. A Community Development worker helps a villager sign his name in the registry during a village meeting in which the possible installation of a government tubewell in Kusampur is considered.

government officials) and the implementors (the *pramukh* and his village representatives).

The *zila parishad,* at the highest level of the Local Self-Government system, coincides with the administrative boundaries of the district. It consists of all the presidents of the *panchayat samitis,* members of the State Legislative Assembly and National Parliament from that constituency, and the District Collector. The *zila parishad* has only a planning and supervisory capacity with no direct powers of execution and taxation.

Although *panchayati raj* may have been born of a marriage between community development and rural local self-government, it has generally "not taken any effective part in planning from below" (Narain 1969:24). The Arunpur *panchayat* takes no part or initiative in development work and is completely inoperative at the present time. Because of factional divisions and a general lack of interest, the villagers believe that it cannot really achieve anything worthwhile. In interviews with each of the fourteen *panchayat* members, we were told that none of them had contested the post in the last *panchayat* election held in 1963. The present Pradhan chose the members he wanted when he won the election. Men from several castes were selected (six Bhumihars, four Chamars, one Brahman, one Kurmi, one Nai, and one Kahar) who were either his firm supporters or else were equally friendly to both village factions.

The *panchayat* has met only two or three times since 1963. Almost all of its members said that they had wasted five rupees to obtain a useless post and would not do the same again. When one of the Chamar *panchayat* members was asked if he would like to hold that post when the next elections are held, he replied:

> Whether or not I am elected next time—I don't care. What will be my loss? It [the *panchayat*] has not been of any use the past six years. I was never called and I was never with Amar Singh [the eldest male in the Pradhan's household] or the Pradhan in the last six years. Last year Amar Singh called me and said, "Give me the five rupees fee for being a *panchayat* member." And I yelled at him, "Look, you made me a member, but I never worked as one. So burn your file, because we never acted as *panchayat* members. So where are they and where is the *panchayat*? I am not giving five rupees."
>
> Amar Singh got mad, but I never gave the money because I knew I never worked as a *panchayat* member. So why should I give—so they can eat it up? It is clear that these high-caste *pradhan*s are useless and can't work. I dream that a man from the Chamar settlement will become the *pradhan*. I know he won't be the real boss; they will be some of the Bhumihars. But never mind, at least we will have the chair [i.e., post]. At least people outside the village will know that there is a Chamar *pradhan*. I don't care who is boss.

The *panchayat* secretary, a government appointee in the Community Development administration, serves several villages and is supposed to supervise much of the paper work of the *panchayat*s. The Arunpur secretary was suspended for incompetency in 1966 and there has been no replacement for him. The Pradhan has not succeeded in collecting the taxes that are to aid in village development work. Any land that was previously owned in common by the villagers has long since disappeared. The possession of a remaining pond is currently being contested in court by two Kahar brothers who say that the pond is theirs because they have cultivated fish and water vegetables in it and have paid the taxes for the last twelve years.

In 1957, a two-room *panchayat* house was built in Main Pura, but neither the Chamars nor the faction which rivals the head of the village can make use of it. While I was there, the house was let rent-free to a

Brahman teacher at the Intercollege who came from another village and was close to the Pradhan's family.

NEW ALTERNATIVES FOR CONFLICT RESOLUTION

The second arm of local self-government is the statutory justice *(nyaya) panchayat* that was imposed upon the village to aid in settling disputes previously heard by big men *panchayats* but now increasingly finding their way to the district courts. Any dispute involving less than fifty rupees is supposed to be settled by this *panchayat*. The justice *panchayat* of Arunpur includes its eight neighboring villages. Each village sends representatives from their own elective statutory village *panchayat*. The representatives of these various villages then choose one among themselves to be the head. The head of the justice *panchayat* in which Arunpur participates comes from the neighboring village of Ramapur and is the brother of Krishna Singh, a powerful local big man.

The fact of the matter is, however, that the statutory justice *panchayat* is also virtually ineffective. People complain that (1) it works in the same manner as the courts and takes a lot of time; (2) it does not meet regularly or discharge its duties properly; (3) the men who sit on the justice *panchayat* are elected (not selected) members who do not necessarily represent the wisest and most respected men; hence, (4) they do not act impartially; and, (5) because they may not be men familiar with the village in which the dispute occurs, they may more easily be fooled by false evidence. The two major reasons for the failure of the justice *panchayat* seem to be that villagers do not have the same trust for elected officials as they do for those chosen in the traditional *panchayats* and that they still prefer to take their cases to the courts. Even where the Pradhan has the opportunity to settle quarrels and fights, it is said that he does not want to involve himself. A dispute that eventually ends up in the court would prove too time-consuming and bothersome for him.

The lack of confidence in elected village officials, which applies to the justice *panchayat* as well as the village *panchayat*, stems from the feeling that the truly good and wise man will not demean himself by contesting an election. He will accept the position only if he is unanimously chosen. In the majority of cases, then, the man who assumes office after being elected over other candidates is one who is pursuing his own self-interest and wants the post to benefit himself and his supporters. A contested election, villagers say, creates at least two parties—that of the elected and that of the defeated. Each contestant will remember who stood for and against him and thus in his official capacity will always show favoritism and partiality. Most men also complained that village elections were a major cause of dissension and increased factionalism.

Distrust for elected local officials has, among other reasons, led people increasingly to prefer the alternative structure of the court system to that of the new statutory justice *panchayat*. That the traditional *panchayats* have also been bypassed as a mode of conflict resolution can readily be seen by the number who have been concerned with legal tangles in Arunpur. At least sixty heads of families have been involved in one or more (and as many as thirteen) court cases. With the exception of six instances—two concerning the ex-zamindar Babu Sahib, two that involved land in another village, one against an employer for loss of work, and one against a merchant for fraud—all the litigants were from Arunpur. The majority of the cases involved disputes between unrelated parties for land (often neighbors). Disputes between *pattidars* (patrilineally related kin) over divided property were less in number. Occasionally a case went to court that involved beatings, destruction of property by an animal, or an accusation of murder.

There are two main reasons why villagers prefer this alternative structure for conflict resolution. First, there is the general decline in adherence to and respect for traditional *panchayats* based on the desire for a favorable, rather than just, decision (see Chapter 2). When this is combined with a lack of faith in the statutory *nyaya panchayat,* then recourse to the courts may be seen as a default. Certainly the drawbacks of appealing to the courts are clearly recognized. It is an expensive, time-consuming process which protracts the enmity between disputants while they await a decision. Yet despite the great expense involved and the lengthy waiting period, even penniless Chamars have initiated legal proceedings. Several factors specific to the village form a crucial part in explaining this. There is the close proximity of the courts in Banaras as well as the opportunity this provides for becoming sophisticated in such matters. In addition, Arunpur has men with the time, education, and money to indulge in such affairs. It seems that the stronger party (in terms of money to bear legal expenses and bribe officers, and power to occupy property by force while the case is going on) has the most to gain by initiating a legal struggle, judging from the fact that quarrels over land most often find their way into court. Such struggles often seek to wrest property from its rightful owner.

The willingness of village big men to stake their fortune and prestige on the outcome of a legal contest is also implied in the following statement by a Bhumihar: "If the dispute is between us [relatives or faction members], we settle it ourselves, but if it involves our rivals, we go to court." The courts are regarded as an extension of the village political arena where fights for prestige over one's caste fellows and lower-caste men can also take place (see also Cohn 1959:90, 93).

A similar situation has been described for the village of Senapur, twenty-five miles north of Banaras in Jaunpur District. Previously, most disputes were settled on a local basis by the dominant Rajput caste. Power and prestige, law and judicial proceedings were all bounded by the "little kingdom"—a local area in which "all the villages were 'owned' at one time by one lineage of Rajputs, locally termed 'Thakurs' " (Cohn 1959:80). The establishment of a legal system in India based on British procedural law conflicted with the local law ways. Likewise, the introduction of electing village *panchayat* officials presented an alternative to the traditional mode of selecting decision makers. Villagers have been quick to react in both cases. "Indians in response thought only of manipulating the new situation and did not use the law courts [in this case, statutory *panchayats*] to settle disputes but to further them" (Cohn 1959:90).

While the legal system of the courts is not in itself new, it is (along with the *nyaya panchayat*) an example of the alternative structures that are becoming increasingly available to the villagers of Arunpur and whose appearance has brought about changes in their lives and outlook. The government administration offers other alternatives, specifically through the Community Development and Local Self-Government *(panchayati raj)* programs. It also offers a choice of channels by which new resources can be brought into the village and has added a new dimension to the relationship between villages and outsiders, especially government officials.

New Resources and Relationships with Government Personnel

Most new resources that come into the village are from Community Development funds and materials, which are distributed through the Local Self-Government institutions. For example, the Community Development Block receives government aid and grants in five areas: public health, road construction, help for Untouchables (mostly in construction of wells), industrial grants, and animal husbandry. The Village Level Worker (VLW) informs village *pradhan*s of what aid is available and who can apply. He also processes applications for a specific item and forwards them to the Block Headquarters for approval. New seeds and fertilizers received by the Block are distributed at various rural centers. Loans for these agricultural improvements are also available on a short-term (usually seasonal) basis. Once again, the VLW is the intermediary between the villager, who wishes a loan, and the Block officials, to whom the application is made. There are also cooperative societies that will make loans to their contributing members.

Arunpur has received money to build wells, construct drinking water taps from the tubewell, pave streets, and build a *panchayat* house and a house for some Chamars. All of this was done by the Pradhan, in the name of the village. These resources actually were used as a form of patronage to repay party men for their support, and villagers now refuse to pay the *panchayat* tax because there was such an obvious bias in the distribution of these favors. Because new projects must be matched by funds available in the village, primarily through the collection of this tax, it is not possible for Arunpur to receive any more government aid at the present time.

With the entire area of panvillage development in abeyance, the only other government resources available to villagers are those that are applied for and distributed on an individual basis. They are primarily new seeds, fertilizers, government loans to cover their cost, and the installation of pumping sets for irrigation. As these resources are distributed to the villagers by government agents, the relations between these two groups form an integral part of this discussion. The most important official at the village level is the Tubewell Operator (see Chapter 9), and secondarily the VLW and Seed Store Inspector, the latter in charge of distributing the actual supplies of seed and fertilizer.

The VLW for Arunpur had been transferred to this area only two months before we arrived in the village. He is a thirty-five-year-old man who comes from a district near Banaras. He served in another area for eight years and since his transfer has made his home in the city. He said that his position initially required him to act as a multipurpose social worker in the rural communities and to provide the link between the Community Development program and the village population. Since the major emphasis in development has turned to agriculture and irrigation, however, he spends most of his time dispensing information on new techniques and innovations in that field.

The VLW is also responsible for propagating the government family planning program. Block officials exert pressure on him to fulfill certain quotas and threaten to jeopardize his job if he does not meet them. The VLW even sought the aid of Mohan Ram, a Chamar leader whose own son is also a VLW. Mohan promised to help him find at least four men who would submit to vasectomies, but most men are reluctant to go through with the operation.[1]

The VLW is also pressured by his superiors into obtaining a minimum amount of orders for new types of seeds and fertilizers that the government wants agriculturalists to use increasingly. He, in turn, then makes fulfillment of a specific order contingent upon the buying of these new types as well. A concomitant of the fact that certain targets are set for the

VLW is that he spends less time among the poorer landowners, who (he says) are "uneducated, inexperienced, and always doubt new information." He finds it necessary to go to the big farmers who are "educated and experienced" because they are ready to innovate and take risks. The VLW understood that this preference for the already rich was not good. On the other hand, he stated that it was important to go to the big men first, for it is only after they have tried new seeds which succeed that the smaller farmers will be convinced. The favored big farmers will be the first to receive a highly desirable seed available only in limited quantities. Others are forced to buy it on the black market, if they can afford to do so.

The preference for big farmers is a bias built into the system and the nature of personal relationships. The VLW had his own stereotypes of the different people that compose a village, and to him all small-scale cultivators are ipso facto "uneducated." Certainly, barriers to communication do exist. When the VLW goes into the Chamar Pura people begin screaming and yelling at him, trying to attract his attention; at the same time they are suspicious and perhaps abusive. He is not, then, very likely to go back there and have much interest and care in their welfare. He finds it more pleasant to go to the houses of the rich and to sit quietly chatting, take their orders, and enjoy a hot glass of milk as well!

Whereas his predecessor came to the village perhaps two or three times a year, the present VLW comes at least once or twice a week. He was always in a rush and complained of constantly being harassed by his superiors at the Block Headquarters. He also said that they make his job more difficult. There are so many administrative departments that nothing really gets done. The higher officials do not care about their work, and although he is required to attend all meetings, they rarely come. Inefficiency at Block Headquarters can often have disastrous results for cultivators. When the latter's application for grain, fertilizer, or loans, for example, is forwarded there, the request is often not filled in time. A man may order seeds and irrigate his fields in advance only to find that the seeds come at a later date and the fields have already dried up. The VLW did not find, however, that factionalism hindered his work. He was friendly with both sides and stood aloof from their feuds. He said that no villagers wanted to lessen their agricultural output because of disputes; rather, competition in agriculture was marked between the two parties.

Orders for seed and fertilizer given to the VLW are processed at the Block office, and the cultivator goes to a government seed store to obtain what he needs. Before 1967, they had to go to Banaras, but now there is a government storage depot just opposite the village on the main road. The Seed Store Inspector lived next door to us, and we saw him daily and observed his interaction with the villagers. He was always rude and blunt to smaller cultivators and showed marked deference toward the richer ones. On one occasion, the Inspector refused to sell anyone fertilizer which had been stored there for a week. However, when the brother of Krishna Singh (a big man from neighboring Ramapur) came, he sold him whatever fertilizer he needed.[2]

The Seed Store Inspector, like the VLW, also regularly takes bribes. Often, if people do not have enough money to pay this extra charge, some of the seed or fertilizer is kept back by the Inspector, who then sells it at black market prices. He said that he shares his extra money with his assistant and the VLW. The latter, in addition to taking money for himself, also takes money from the villagers to distribute to other officials who have a hand in processing any particular application and claims that this is necessary to get work done.[3] Bribery and general corruption in the official world are well known and accepted by villagers as part of the way the system works.

The village record-keeper of property and revenue *(lekhpal)* also receives bribes in connection with determining ownership of disputed land or giving preference in informing someone of land for sale. A messenger from the Banaras court who brings a summons for an Arunpur Nai waits for some extra money for his "pocket expenses." At the local police station, the taking of bribes is rife. The results range from letting people go who have committed crimes to having to pay for the innocent to be released. One Arunpur faction leader was reported to have given a 300-rupee bribe when he called the police to Arunpur during his dispute with a rival (Case 17, Chapter 7). Villagers who want an electrical connection for their pumping sets must bribe a multitude of officials before their work is done.

In cases where money was received by the Pradhan for the village, such as loans and money for well or house construction, some amount was siphoned off. This general state of affairs existing between the village and the official world has led the villages to be very distrustful of the latter. Perhaps the saddest part of all is how far this mentality has seeped down into the perception of village life itself. Some Chamars and others said that whenever they get into trouble with the police or courts or need to contact officials, they always go to their Bhumihar patrons, who can more easily approach outsiders. But, they say, no influential Bhumihar ever accompanies them without charging a certain amount of money for his services.

Expansion of Government Administration and the Political Arena

The extension of government administration and resources into the village has had two main effects. It has reinforced a continuation of the traditional concentration of power. Specifically, the failure of the statutory village and justice *panchayats* to become meaningful bodies in Arunpur, as well as the inability of the Community Development program to reach a significant proportion of truly needy villagers, has resulted in a perpetuation of the status quo in political and, to a large extent, economic power. The individuals who have played an important role in Arunpur history and those who continue to do so today as big men in the village political arena are all primarily from a few select and wealthy Bhumihar families. It is these men (or their families) who figured importantly in the British administration and in the present government's statutory *panchayat* system, as well as in the meetings of the traditional *panchayats* to settle local disputes. The big men of Arunpur participate most in the new structural alternatives present in Independent India, especially through the courts and by their control of statutory *panchayat* Community Development resources within their power. They have also become middle men who mediate between the villages and important outsiders.

At the same time, the introduction of new resources and new forms of conflict resolution has had the effect of widening the field for political activities. The political field of an enterprising big man now extends way beyond the confines of the village arena, and even for the "little man" it has opened up. Previously, the distribution of resources was fairly well established in a set pattern and any disputes over this were settled by the British-appointed headman. Competition for resources took place within a rather confined group, that is, the dominant caste. Now, however, new resources have become available in the village, and they exist in an unstructured zone of competition where the old rules are in flux or do not pertain, and the new ones have not yet been established. This unstructured competition is further complicated by the fact that a man now has an increased range of choice regarding structures that may be of use to him. The political arena itself has altered because of these many changes.

The effectiveness with which a big man competes in the village arena is determined and manifested not only by his power and control over resources, but also by his family name, prestige, and caste status. The next chapter describes these relationships so that the connection between caste, kin, and power may be better understood.

NOTES

1. Until the time I left the village in May, 1969, I knew of only five men who had vasectomies (four Bhumihars and one Chamar) and three who were "thinking" of having operations. Seven men said that they practice "natural" forms of birth control (unspecified) and one used condoms. Only one woman had ever tried using the pill.
2. Krishna Singh owns the Seed Storage building as well as the one in which we and the Seed Store Inspector lived.
3. He also spoke of people in government service giving bribes in order to be transferred or to obtain a position they desired.

CHAPTER 4
Caste and Kin: The Network of Social Relations

The village represents a universe of social action for the people of Arunpur, where behavior is governed by rules pertaining to caste and kin. The rules of caste define one's position and rights and duties in relation to other castes, as well as denoting the appropriate behavior for that specific status in a ritual hierarchy. The rules of kinship delineate the categories of consanguineal and affinal relations and their behavioral components. They also account for the ties a person has outside his natal place, for in north India the village is an exogamous unit. Although these kinship rules still appear to be strong and binding on the individual and are heavily considered in any specific decision into which they enter, the same does not seem to be true of rules governing caste relations. There are a number of areas where caste has adapted to new situations in changing India.

Symptomatic of this response to change is the increasing tendency for villagers to make the distinction between two societies *(do samaj)*, one of the village *(ganv ka)* and the other outside the village *(ganv ke bahar)*. It is this sort of distinction that is implied when a man says:

> I can eat and drink with anybody, of any caste, if he is from outside my village. But not in my village, because here I have to consider some of the things which may affect my family. . . . But all those who have fought any court case must have cleaned the officer's pot [*lota*],[1] and many times the officer may be of low caste.

Similar explanations are given to justify other seemingly contradictory behavior. A Nai related that he could not shave the beard or cut the hair of an Untouchable and requested God never to give him any such occasion in his life. Yet his sister's husband and son have opened barber shops in a small town and in a village-cum-bazaar where they cater to all. The Nai believed that

> If we shave the hair of Chamars, we are violating village rules; but not [if we do so] outside, because that is the territory of the shop *[dukan ka desh]* and *biradari* [caste] is not there. Inside the village, caste is above all; but outside, man is highest.

Another person said that village society is native *(deshi)* while that outside the village is foreign *(videshi)*, the rules for the two societies also differing. It has been pointed out that this process of compartmentalization, a separating of "two spheres of conduct and belief that would otherwise collide," is an old one. It is also an adaptive process that enables people to express behaviors that actually belong to distinctive ways of life and thought (Singer 1972:321–325). This compartmentalization of behavior applicable to inside and outside the village (or "native" and "foreign") is not only basic to operating outside the kin world, but also to reducing the conflict between recent changes and traditions.

It would seem that greater mobility is going to increase both the range of society outside the village and the number of people who will participate in it. This will increasingly demand some readjustment of cultural rules to actual behavior. Women, who have less mobility than men, are more conservative in maintaining rules regarding commensality outside the village. More occasions arise for men, however, when it becomes necessary to ignore the rules, such as "cleaning the officer's pot" while pursuing a court case, or eating the molasses of a Chamar (see later) while pursuing election votes. Even within the village, and especially among younger men (those under forty), there seems to be some relaxation of certain rules regarding eating, drinking, and deference behavior among castes.

Formal Relations among Castes: Dominance and Jajmani

There are two sides of the coin to relationships that castes have with one another within the village context: dependence and interdependence. The formal political relations among castes involve a differential access to power and are governed by the idea of dominance, while the ritualized economic interaction of *jajmani* relationships mutually binds individual members of one caste to individuals in another in an exchange of goods and services. Inequality and the differential access to power and ritual purity are delineated by *jajmani* relations as well and find concrete expression in the deferential behavior shown to the Bhumihars by lower castes.

If someone is sitting on a cot when a Bhumihar walks by, he will immediately stand up. Kurmi and other Touchable caste men will either squat on the ground, or, depending upon the Bhumihar in question, sit on a separate cot in his presence. An Untouchable will never sit before him but always squat on the earth. The Bhumihar has the right of way on a narrow village path. Within the rules of ritual purity, he can also command anyone of lower caste who happens to be near to perform services such as drawing water, washing dishes, and bringing tables, chairs, or tea.

Before discussing dependence and interdependence among castes, however, we must say something about what is meant by "caste." Like so many other translations, the use of the single word "caste" for *varna, jati,* and *biradari* is both inadequate and misleading. *Varna* is a Sanskrit term found in classical Hindu texts and usually means a "class" (or "color"). There were four such groups in ancient India: the *brahman* (priests and intellectuals), *kshatriya* (rulers and warriors), *vaishya* (artisans, merchants, and farmers), and *shudra* (servants). The Untouchables are often considered as constituting a fifth class or as being outside the *varna* system altogether. *Varna* does not have any effective usage or meaning within the context of social relationships for Arunpur villagers.[2] It has become a significant referent for caste in those situations where a group is upwardly mobile and claims a higher status (Rowe 1968; Lynch 1969), or in the case of socially or politically active caste associations where *varna* then takes on meaning in a political arena that is larger than a single village (Srinivas 1962:15ff; Béteille 1969:163ff).

Jati (literally "race," "genus," "species"), a much later Sanskrit term for caste, denotes the largest endogamous unit which we may call a caste and is generally used to refer to castes other than one's own. If a man speaks of his own *jati* or caste fellow, however, he will use the Hindi term *biradari* ("brotherhood" or "community"), translated as "subcaste." The latter is the smallest endogamous group representing the meaningful unit for marriage ties and dispute settlement (Mayer 1960:4ff, 153). Thus, many subcastes make up a caste and the distinction between the two is made on the basis of internal (kin) and external (intercaste) relations (Mayer 1960:9; Ghurye 1950:20; cf. Béteille 1969b:152ff).

Looking at caste relations within Arunpur, I found that the Bhumihars exert what Srinivas has termed "decisive dominance," that is, the distribution of wealth, power, and numbers coincides with their high ritual status (Srinivas 1959:2). Although for the most part they ranked themselves lower than Brahmans on the caste hierarchy, Bhumihars maintain that they, too, are of the priestly caste. They say that it was through their association with the Banaras rajas, who were also Bhumihars, that they gave up their traditional religious functions and began to engage in *kshatriya*-like activities. They took to hunting, eating meat, and drinking, and also became landlords and hence involved with the land and agriculture.

Practically all Bhumihars use the *kshatriya* surname Singh, although three college-educated men gave the Brahman appellation Sharma.[3] Other castes in the village refer to them as *thakur*, meaning "chief," "lord," or "master," and usually a referent for a *kshatriya*. A common attitude, even among Bhumihars themselves, is that theirs is a caste in which most of the offspring were produced by illicit unions with lower-caste women. There are histories of this in almost every major family group, and it is usually traced back to service in the Maharaja's court. The most common sort of slander among feuding Bhumihars is to accuse the other faction of such a bastard origin. Yet even the sure knowledge of impure ancestry is not an impediment to marriage seekers if the family in question happens to be wealthy.

There was a poor "outcaste" Bhumihar in Arunpur—outcaste in the sense that no one would marry into his family nor openly eat in his house (although he eats in the house of others). His father had kept a Kohar woman and he was produced from this union. His own marriage was arranged with a Bhumihar girl only because his neighbors and fellow caste men were willing to support him at the time and deceived the girl's father about his true ancestry.[4] The villagers contrast this case of a gentle man's helpless situation with that of a big man in the area whose house contains a similar scandal. Although the latter is not well liked, "everyone runs to eat in his house" because of his great wealth, and he was able to marry his daughter into a good Bhumihar family.

Among themselves and others, Bhumihars also have the reputation of being an unusually prestige-conscious group harboring immense feelings of competition. Most often, this takes the form of trying to appropriate the best lands, appear as the best men (e.g., in marriage alliances or expenditure, house construction, material wealth, and education), push down others who would rise up, and maintain rather poor relationships with the lower castes both in thought and practice.

The Brahmans do not effectively enter the political arena in Arunpur because of material poverty as well as poverty of prestige. They are highly untypical representatives of their status group. All but one group of related households *(khandan)* are notorious for entering into illicit unions. It is difficult for their sons to marry and they must "purchase" (pay bride-price for) wives, which further perpetuates their notoriety. Even though other villagers do not approve of their behavior, however, they are not outcaste in the sense that all services or social intercourse are

FIGURE 6. A Brahman from a nearby village performs traditional priestly functions during the naming ceremony for a newborn Bhumihar.

withdrawn from them. To become outcaste means, as in the elderly Bhumihar's case, to be put out of one's *biradari* for marriage and commensal purposes and not to lose one's caste *(jati)*. Even if a Brahman is outcaste in this sense, he is still considered higher than a Kurmi and all other castes, and so he will continue to be served by his clients *(prajas)*. This was acknowledged to be a rather recent definition of "outcaste" and villagers regarded it as reflecting the weakening of caste sanctions.

In addition to their illicit unions, Arunpur Brahmans also eat meat, drink, smoke *ganjha* and one of them has taken on the job of goat slaughterer. One *khandan*, consisting of the separate households of five brothers, is well known for their practice of buying wives. The latter practice no form of purdah (seclusion and covering of the face) and openly help their menfolk in the fields.

The Kurmis are not a political match for the Bhumihars, either. Known to be traditional agriculturalists whose men, women, and children are extremely hard working and industrious, they take little part in village feuds and are not consulted for effective dispute settlement. Practically all Kurmis own some land or have a cash income from other jobs. Even the heads of the two largest and wealthiest households make no attempt actively to enter the political arena. For the most part, they feel that the Bhumihars are not to be meddled with and that, since Kurmis are economically independent and not tied to any particular faction, it is better to concentrate on one's own affairs to achieve greater prosperity. On certain occasions, especially the *panchayat* elections, they will support one or the other Bhumihar party.

There is one older Kurmi who is trying to raise his caste's status by advocating that others follow his example by praying daily and refraining from meat and drink. A few others have adopted the surname Singh and have begun wearing the sacred thread *(janeu)* previously forbidden to castes included in the *shudra varna*. The Kurmis do not actively follow him and he is considered less educated and generally more conservative in his beliefs. He often complained that the Kurmis are not united and that this inhibits them from putting up a candidate of their caste, or even lower, to stand against the Bhumihars in the *panchayat* elections. He believes that the strength of the Bhumihars lies in their unity as compared to other castes and their success in dividing others by flattery and fear.

The economic independence and ethic of hard work for which the Kurmis are noted has inspired a rather grudging respect among the Bhumihars. Just how grudging it is was uncovered by the feelings expressed during the statewide midterm elections (February, 1969). Then the high castes chided Kurmis who thought their caste man would win because of their greater numerical strength in the area but who lost nonetheless.

Other castes present in Arunpur either own little land or engage in some occupation that does not provide them with a thriving livelihood. The one exception to this is a comparatively prosperous and large Kalwar family, but they, too, take pains to avoid crossing the Bhumihars, whom they both fear and respect. Some lower-caste families are personally bound to different Bhumihars by a *jajmani* relationship or by indebtedness for money or favors received in the past. Yet only when one speaks of the Untouchables (primarily the Chamars) is the absolute dependence upon the upper castes so clearly revealed. The type of conflict and friction that this position entails is important in village politics, and the situation is more fully explored in a later chapter. Suffice it to say here that the Untouchables are overwhelmingly landless and there is little scope for them to pursue any occupation other than that of agricultural laborer. This is due both to their situation of poverty, which has reduced their opportunities to practically nothing, and to the pressure exerted by the Bhumihars.

Traditional relationships between master and servant still survive in the village. Chamars who are ploughmen or agricultural laborers are the most subordinate workers. As Cohn notes for a similar village just north of Banaras, "members of other caste groups in the village also do agricultural work, but since the Chamars are the most numerous of the impoverished lower castes, an employer talking about his 'laborers' *(mazdooras)* is most likely to be referring to his Chamars" (1955:56).

The distribution of political power in Arunpur still coincides with the distribution of economic power, even though the traditional ordering of economic relations through *jajmani* ties has considerably altered. *Jajmani* makes use of hereditary personal relationships to express a division of labor and regulate the flow of goods and services from one caste to another according to custom. In this way it acts to preserve ritual purity by delegating polluting tasks to lower castes (Gould 1967:36ff; see also Kolenda's discussion of Wiser, Beidelman, and Leach, 1966) and is intrinsic to the hierarchical nature of caste. Traditionally, each caste was accorded a particular occupation and a person became a "client" *(praja)* when he performed that service for a specific "patron" *(jajman)*. Payments were made in kind and took the form either of biennial presentations of grain, of the use of a piece of land, or of separate payments for participation in individual ceremonies.

For the most part, the patron-client tie was a hereditary one, and the patron could not arbitrarily change a traditional worker. Similarly, no one other than the hereditary worker could perform such services. Although the roles of patron and client are ideally interchangeable, the former on one occasion becoming the latter on the next, it is the *ksha-*

triya or dominant landowner who is recognized as the patron par excellence. The royal court with king and retainers is reproduced in miniature by the dominant caste and its clients in present-day Indian villages (Hocart 1950:79; Dumont 1962:52-53; 1972:205-207; Pocock 1962:79; cf. Gould 1967:40-41).

Of the sixteen castes present in Arunpur (excluding the ex-zamindar Babu Sahib, who belongs to a merchant caste), only the Bhumihars and Kurmis are always in the position of patron. These two groups are still primarily engaged in agriculture, although today they follow a variety of other occupations. The remaining castes each formerly had a traditional service occupation which they exchanged with one another but mostly rendered to Bhumihar families. The Brahman is the epitome of a religious specialist in *jajmani* relations, and he has no economic service or commodity to offer at all (Pocock 1962:85, 91-92). Because of their low status in the village, however, no Bhumihar employs an Arunpur Brahman to perform any ceremony or ritual. These Brahmans perform rituals for Chamars instead, contrary to a taboo on the offering of their services to Untouchables.

Some members of the Nai and the Dhobi castes are still strongly involved in *jajmani*. As there is no one of the Dhobi caste in Arunpur, Bhumihar and Kurmi families employ those from another village to clean their clothes and annually pay them fifteen to twenty *sers* (one *ser* = two pounds) of grain per household. In 1948, Opler and Singh found that no villager of Senapur (twenty-five miles north of Banaras), "no matter how low his social status, cuts his own hair or shaves himself" (Opler and Singh 1948:486). More than twenty-five years later, a different picture is presented in Arunpur. Here, many of the younger men avail themselves of the razor blade or prefer to have a haircut and shave at an outside barber shop. Yet though the razor may take away the barber's daily work, it does not destroy his *jajmani* relationships. The economic services that the Nai and his wife perform, like those of the Dhobi, are intimately embedded in the ideas of purity and pollution and are integral to all rituals. From shaving and hair and nail cutting to acting as a messenger, painting the feet of patrons with henna dye on auspicious occasions, and giving massages, they are present at every extraordinary occasion taking place in a Bhumihar's life.

Even among the Nais, however, the traditional rules regarding hereditary arrangements between patron and client have given way to a more flexible arrangement that takes into account the situational factors affecting the persons involved. In one case, a Nai left a patron when the latter became the rival of another patron with whom the Nai had extremely strong ties. The Nai told me:

Jajmani is a matter of love. If there is no love, there is nothing like a patron. Narain Singh was my patron, but he lost my love, so he lost his *jajmani*. *Jajmani* is not an imposed bond . . . . I left Narain and then he called upon a Muslim Nai—but his wife [the Muslim's] cannot go into the house, so he is in trouble. Narain requested many times that I again become his client, but I cannot. This *jajmani* is a matter of love, but it is such a stupid thing, that if one who has served all his life [as client] becomes old, he will be thrown away. Nobody will ask about him.

It is not clear whether or not such infractions of *jajmani* rules occurred in the past and, if they did, with what frequency. Yet there seems no reason to think that people could not have adjusted to a new situation as their changing relationships warranted. Similarly, the Nai also said that the Bhumihars paid him less and expected more service than the lower castes. Although descriptions of *jajmani* stress the element of reciprocity and the stabilizing and integrating aspects of the system, an equally strong element is the asymmetrical nature of the power relationships discussed earlier.

The Kahars are another caste in Arunpur who still refer to themselves as clients serving particular patrons. Their traditional occupation was to draw water, roast grains, and act as general servants on any occasion when a large number of people gathered at a Bhumihar's home. Today this is confined to grain parching by the women and participation at weddings, births, deaths, and other ceremonies and feasts. They can also act as messengers at such times and accompany their patron when he goes to attend some function in another village. But their main source of income now is from the cultivation of fish and a form of water chestnut in the two village ponds. The Kahars complained that the confined area of their *jajmani* relationship has now become an unprofitable one and that only fear of what the Bhumihars and other villagers would say and do makes them continue the work. They receive payments for individual occasions on which some service is performed. Although the presence of Kahars was required on all ceremonial occasions, they seemed to perform no function that was integral to the ritual aspect regarding purity and pollution—unlike the Nai and Dhobi.

The Lohars as a whole have not participated in *jajmani* relationships for the past thirty years. Like the village Telis who used to be involved in oil pressing, they found less and less of a demand for their services as new machines and parts became available in the city. Only three elderly men (aged fifty, sixty, and seventy) continue to do this work in the village. One said that he receives two maunds (one maund = eighty pounds) as the total annual payment from all his patrons. The second receives pay on a seasonal basis; for each plough that he services, he

FIGURE 7. A Lohar works on a plough.

receives twelve *sers* at each of the two harvest times and five *sers* at the time of planting. The third Lohar works in the neighboring village of Ramapur for part of the year, and in the remaining six months takes work on a cash basis. One young man, who tried to perform his traditional occupation in the village and could not get enough work, has been engaged in making bicycle bells for the last three years. He occasionally works in the village on Sundays as a laborer, at the rate of three rupees per day. Another young boy, aged sixteen, does carpentry work in Arunpur and nearby villages for a daily wage of three rupees.

The Telis, Kohars, Noniyas, and Kalwars do not participate in any sort of *jajmani* relationship with the Bhumihars or any other caste in the village today. Two Kohar men follow their traditional occupations but require individual payment for each one of their products. The Chamars no longer perform the polluting tasks—once considered their most important functions—of removing dead animals and leatherworking. Unlike the Telis, whose work was taken away from them by the introduction of machines that press the oil seeds, the Chamars gave up a traditional occupation which they felt was more degrading than profitable. They are now engaged in many different occupations but work primarily as unskilled laborers. Only the women continue to act as midwives at childbirth and assist the mother and child while they are in a polluted state. The Untouchable Musahars prepare leaf plates that are used on the occasion of every large feast and also remove the used plates when the feast is over. In the cases of both the Chamar women and the Musahars, payment is made to them at the time service is rendered.

In trying to understand the nature of *jajmani* as it survives in Arunpur today and the way in which it has changed, we need to distinguish it from the more generic patron-client relationship as well as to examine the extent to which it may constitute a system that includes the landlord-laborer bond as well. Patron-client contracts, a characteristic of all peasant societies, bind people of significantly unequal economic statuses who exchange different types of goods and services. The tie is vertical and asymmetrical and the exchange between the two is based on moral paternalism (Foster 1963:1281). Among the several different kinds of patron-client ties in an Indian village may be found: rich man and dependents, creditor and debtor, landlord and tenant, faction leader and follower, landlord and laborer, and *jajman* and *praja*.

The bond between the *jajman* and *praja* expresses the ritualized economic interaction among castes that anthropologists have formalized into a system, and is the prototype for all other patron-client relationships. As Pocock points out, however, there is a difference between the dependence of a landowner upon labor and the dependence of the same

FIGURE 8. A Musahar gathers wood.

man for the performance of a marriage (1962:82). *Jajman* (or *yajman*) literally means "the one who gives the sacrifice," that is, the person employing a priest. Its meaning is extended to include those who employ others and give remuneration for services performed. The opposite of *jajman* is *praja* (or *kamin*), denoting a "dependent" or "subject"—from the raja-*praja* dyad. *Praja* also refers to those castes whose hereditary specialization derives from the basic opposition of purity and impurity and, by extension of this idea, encompasses what may seem to be purely economic activities. Villagers used the term *praja* to refer to both relationships, that of *jajmani* and that of the more general political domination by the Bhumihars.

It seems a moot point to debate whether *jajmani* is based on reciprocity or on dominance (e.g., Wiser 1936; Ishwaran 1966; Beidelman 1959; Orans 1968); it is based on both. While there is little doubt that the surface relationship belies a reliance on dominance and coercion, a deeper, underlying meaning lies in the legitimation of unequal relations through the hierarchical values of caste. Not only can we assume that these values were generally subscribed to, even by clients on the bottom end, but the advantages of the system must have acted as an incentive to patrons to meet their moral obligations (Epstein 1967:233; Scott 1972:8ff; Moffatt 1975; see also Mencher 1974a).

There is no unanimous agreement regarding the extent to which the landlord *(malik)* and laborer *(mazdur)* tie may be considered as part of a *jajmani* system. The more general view is to include all village economic relationships within the purview of *jajmani* (e.g. Breman 1974:13ff). On the other hand, Epstein speaks of two separate types of links with a *jajman*—that of their functionnaires and that between peasant masters and Untouchable agricultural laborers (1967:232; also Cohn 1955:56; 1965: 88; Harper 1968). Pocock recognizes that "hereditary specialization is an 'organizing principle' of the caste system" (1962:89) but disputes that it constitutes a single system of relationships and argues forcefully for a separation of the services of the unskilled laborer from inclusion in *jajmani* (1962). There is, however, the difficulty of deciding to which category (i.e., specialization intrinsic to the caste system or that relating to purely economic activities) castes belong. Pocock considers the Untouchables, for example, as part of the category where ritual activities predominate. Yet they provide, and provided, the majority of agricultural laborers. The Untouchability of the Pasis, Dharkars, and Musahars (until recently, when they began to remove used plates at feasts when Chamars refused to do so) also seems to be more strongly correlated with the food they eat (e.g., pig, mouse, frog) than any ritual services they perform (see also Opler and Singh 1948:488).

A way out of this dilemma is to turn the argument on its head and use the category, not a particular caste, as the independent variable. In this way, a continuum may be devised showing the extent to which a caste: (1) traditionally incorporated different types of relationships, and (2) has moved into new categories. A comparison of these two points would enable further analysis of which castes (i.e., in terms of their occupations and functions) are integral to the caste system as a system, as well as providing a baseline from which to determine how much change can occur before the structure of caste has been left with a name alone.

It is necessary, therefore, to separate out those aspects of traditional caste specialization inherent in a single caste (i.e., removal of dead animals, haircut and shave, washing clothes, and so on) and those activities into which any successful or unsuccessful caste member may have partaken (e.g., landholding, agriculture, or labor). Insofar as Chamars undertook their traditional services of a polluting nature for customary payments, we may see them as operating in *jajmani;* insofar as they were engaged as agricultural laborers, whose exact conditions of labor involved them in a purely economic relationship that was often on a contractual basis (Harper 1968:46ff), we may see this as a separate relationship. In addition, low castes are more numerous than those of the strictly service castes, and the carting away of dead animals, leatherworking, and midwifery chores could not possibly have supported a large number of Chamars (Harper 1968:45, fn).[5]

The similarity between the landlord-laborer bond and that of *jajmanpraja* may now be seen. Both are based on a moral and paternalistic patron-client dyad in which the weaker party exchanges security for inequality. The differences are, however, significant. Associated with the variations in terminology applied is the fact that a laborer is usually completely dependent on only one master, while other castes serve many. Such complete dependence of the former does not leave much assurance that the moral obligations of the landlord were always carried out fully in the past. Laborers do not necessarily come from any single caste. Although in Arunpur, as throughout most of India, they are predominantly Untouchables, there are many instances where tenants of other castes have been reduced to laborers, especially after zamindari abolition and the more recent advances in capitalist agriculture. Relations between landlord and laborer are, moreover, more on a contractual basis and there is evidence that they were like this in the past as well.[6]

Since 1947, when occupational mobility became more marked, there has been a greater dissociation of caste, occupation, and involvement in *jajmani* relationships in Arunpur (see Table 4, Chap. 2). It would not have been difficult to predict that those castes which performed a greater number of functions intimately tied to ritual activities would remain closer to the system through time. Others, such as the Kalwar, Noniya, Lohar, Kohar, and Teli, whose participation in these activities is less required and who can shift more easily to a cash market economy, have tended to drift earliest from the traditional form of exchange. With this increasing participation in nonhereditary occupations and a cash economy, marked by a general decline in traditional relationships, the tendency is to equate *jajmani* more and more with the purely ritual-ceremonial occasions and less with the economic exchange of services.

Several factors have led to this lessening of *jajmani* ties in the village. First, there is the existence of nearby bazaars and, in Banaras city itself, other alternative means of obtaining services. A person who works in the city or a young man who fancies himself smart may find it more convenient or prestigious to use extravillage facilities. Second, many functions have been displaced by newer modes of production, while the changing economic scene has also created entirely new opportunities. For instance, some forty-five village men now work outside Arunpur and commute daily—mostly to Banaras. A growing number, now thirty-two men, are

FIGURE 9. A Kohar sits before his potter's wheel. Pandeyji is behind him.

also employed at places that are distant enough that they are required to live there. In most cases, a man leaves his wife and children in the village and returns to Arunpur during his vacation time. There is a greater tendency on the part of those who increasingly participate in cash-producing occupations to make monetary payments on the specific occasion a service is rendered. This is especially true of those castes that are primarily nonagricultural and thus cannot pay in kind. In addition, some people feel that they no longer wish to perform certain demeaning jobs required of their caste.

The Chamars, for example, have given up removing, skinning, and eating dead animals, and eating the leftovers at feasts. The latter job is performed by Musahars, while Chamars of other villages perform the former tasks. In several other ways, the ties they now have with particular Bhumihars and Brahmans differ from that of the traditional *jajmani* relationship. For one thing, being a ploughman or an agricultural worker is not a hereditary occupation but is due to the economic exigencies of a man's life. Some Chamars, who have a little education and initiative and are not bound by indebtedness, do gain other employment as daily laborers in Banaras, as rickshaw drivers or even as officers in the government Community Development program.

There are limits, however, to the new occupations upon which villagers will embark. Agriculture is open to all castes, but a barber will not take on a washerman's work in Arunpur, or vice versa. There is a wider range of positions that men of all castes can hold outside the village. Even this has limits, however. For example, primarily because the job of pedaling a rickshaw has fallen to the lot of Chamars, many Kurmis believe that such work is below their status and would not do it even if there were a promise of greater economic gain. Here, people's behavior is still regulated by what they feel are the rules proper to village society. On the other hand, a Bhumihar told me that he has no objection whatsoever to starting a shoe factory in some large city, providing he could be sure of a profit.

INFORMAL RELATIONS AMONG CASTES: FRIENDSHIP AND SEX

Hierarchy, and its expression through patterns of deference, does not present the complete picture of intercaste relations in Arunpur. Rules regarding hierarchy, deference, or commensality are adapted by the people to fit their own particular pattern of relationships and iodiosyncrasies. As I observed village life, I was struck by two major areas that provide exceptions to the accepted rules of behavior: friendship and illicit sexual relations.

Friendship is formed on the basis of variables other than caste status, such as personal preferences or proximity to one another, and often involves breaking certain caste strictures. There are close relations between one Brahman family and the Lohars, whose houses are adjacent to one another. A Brahman woman of the same household sits on the ground with a Chamar woman who often visits her and each one uses a kinship term for the other. Similarly, some Brahmans who are supposed to eat only fried *(pakka)* food of non-Brahmans, would eat boiled *(kacca)* food at the homes of their Lohar and Kurmi neighbors. Bhumihar children ate boiled food at a Nai's marriage party and little Brahman girls aided in the construction of a Kurmi men's sitting place *(baithka)*. The children did this because the Kurmis often gave food to their poor families.

A particularly close friendship also exists between a Bhumihar and a Kurmi. The latter was invited to a small feast for intimate friends at the former's house and ate in the same line as other Bhumihars and Brahmans. An older Bhumihar woman could squat on the ground in the Chamar *pura* and chat with the men and women there; and I have even seen Bhumihar men sit on the low side of the cot with other castes.[7] Perhaps

FIGURE 10. Villagers participate in wrestling matches and feats of strength on the festival of Tij.

the most striking contravention of caste rules is the sharing of the earthen *ganjha* pipe *(chilam)* by all castes, including Untouchables.

Behavior regarding eating, drinking, smoking, sitting together, and having friendships across caste lines seems to depend on the personal preferences and choices of the individuals involved. The powerless and poor Brahmans, for example, do not have much to lose by exhibiting friendship to others beneath them. Nor do they feel any pressure from their caste mates to act differently, since caste control among this group in the village is ineffective. Though such feeling is strong among the Bhumihars as a whole and their sanctions are forceful, there are those among them whose circumstances do not necessitate such strict adherence to behavioral rules to maintain their prestige. The college-educated young men, those who work outside the village or those whose caste is high but whose economic position is lower could manipulate the rules with a greater flexibility. But there were certain Bhumihars, usually the older and more powerful men in the village, who would never exhibit such behavior and tended to guard closely the activities of their family members. They sat as equals only among their (caste) equals. Those whose prestige was high enter only into relationships which would either maintain or enhance their perceived prestige.

The matter of illicit sexual relations should also be viewed in this context. I refer not to those stable unions which result from the infraction of marriage rules, as among the Brahmans, but the more furtive affairs between people of two different castes. The majority of these involved Bhumihar men and lower-caste women (especially Chamars) and thus connect sex to dominance and inequality in the distribution of power.

One affair involved a Bhumihar boy and a Kurmi girl—both of whom were married. The girl's father informed the men of the boy's family several times of the matter and asked them to intercede. Another situation involved a rather notorious Parihar girl who had affairs with Bhumihars, Brahmans, and Lohars in the village. Similar stories were confirmed about the behavior of Bhumihar girls in a neighboring village. One of the sisters of an Arunpur Brahman family was said to operate a house of ill repute in Banaras where several of her brothers' non-Brahman wives had stayed.

There were also cases involving Kohar women and Bhumihars. One married girl conceived a child and was sent back to her husband's village when she was five months pregnant. They did not accept her in that condition and so she was returned to her father's house, only to be remarried after the birth of her child. While we were in the village, we were told of another ongoing liaison between a Kohar girl and a Bhumihar. Two Bhumihars also told of having affairs with Brahman girls in their youth, while a common sort of factional slander was to accuse the other party of having had sexual relations with women in their own *patti* (i.e., women considered to be their "sisters").

As mentioned, the most common occurrences of these relations were between Bhumihars and their female Chamar workers or dependents. Men of all castes openly acknowledged this. Often it was revealed to illustrate the point that while higher castes would not touch or drink the water of a Chamar nor sit on the same cot, they did not hesitate to touch their bodies. At other times the topic would come up when villagers asked whether my assistant and I had accepted the blessed offerings of sweets *(prasad)* of a Chamar, or whether we had taken food and drink from them. In one particular case, my assistant became angry with a man who was arguing loudly on this point, and said: "Okay. I ate there. What did I do wrong? It makes no difference. We are still better than those who have made love to them in the fields." Upon hearing this, the man in question left immediately without a word.

This situation, in which Bhumihars take advantage of the women who come to work for them, had become intolerable for the Chamars. When a group of them drafted a letter to Jagjivan Ram, a Chamar who was then Food Minister in the national government, it became the issue of a major complaint (see Chapter 8). The unfortunate lengths to which affairs can go is illustrated by the sad tale of a twenty-two-year-old Musahar who drowned himself by jumping into a village well. This occurred after a heated argument with his wife in which she refused to stop her relationship with two Bhumihars for whom she worked. It was reported that she received many favors from them both in cash and in kind.

The purpose in revealing this aspect of village life has been to show that such behavior is a form of expression as important and valid as are the rules which explicitly deny such relationships. Further, it is also an example of the existence of contradictory rules to which people may refer in making behavioral choices. In this case, the rules regarding intercaste relations, which are governed by the concepts of purity and pollution, are supplemented by a rule that accepts this sort of behavior (in fact, even expects it) from the rich and powerful dominant castes. While the situations involving Touchable women seem to be random and based on the personalities of the parties to an affair, those concerning the Untouchables have this added structural variable of differential power.

Conflicts among castes, especially between the Bhumihars and Chamars, seem to play an increasingly important role in village politics. At the same time, the major political activity in Arunpur is organized by factions that cut across the dominant caste of Bhumihars. This has resulted to some extent from splits within a *khandan* (largest group of related males). The structure of kinship, especially kin groups in the village, is crucial to an understanding of this intracaste cleavage.

Kinship in Arunpur

The most notable variations in kin groups of different castes are those relating to family size and the position of women. These, in turn, correlate highly with economic position. Arunpur is typical of the rest of In-

FIGURE 11. Men of all castes share the *ganjha chilam*. From left to right: a Brahman, two Dharkars, and a Bhumihar enjoy a smoke while sitting along a tubewell canal.

dia where the size and extension (both generational and collateral) of a joint family are contingent upon its wealth; the biggest families are the wealthiest. The largest joint family in the village consists of forty-four members; three elderly Bhumihar brothers and their offspring (married sons with their wives and unmarried sons and daughters), grandchildren, and great grandchildren. They feel, however, that the family has become too large and unwieldy to continue living together amicably and are preparing for an eventual friendly division of property to prevent bitter conflicts. To this end, they are systematically acquiring more land until they have approximately one hundred fifty *bigha*s. At that time, all land and other assets (including a family brick-making business and pumping set) would be divided equally among the three brothers. This is in strict adherence to the rule of equal distribution of joint family property regardless of the number of offspring involved. The eldest brother has sixteen dependents (males and unmarried females), and the two younger ones have nine and three respectively. This decision regarding property division has been accepted as fair and inevitable by all concerned.

As can be expected by referring to Tables 2 and 3, wealth correlated positively with rank in the caste hierarchy and thus the largest families are found among the wealthiest of the Bhumihars. Among other castes, only three Kurmi families and one among the Kalwars are wealthy enough to support families numbering sixteen to twenty-four members. The most highly educated Chamar family, with 1.25 *bighas* of land, consists of nineteen people: two brothers, their wives, and the three sons of the younger brother and their wives and children. Economic pressures account for the tendency among Chamars and other Untouchables for married brothers to split apart even while their father lives. In other castes, this usually occurs after the father has passed away and when respect for him and his wishes no longer keeps the family together. Despite such divisions, new joint families quickly spring up as soon as a man's eldest son marries.

Family size is an important factor within the arena of village politics for, more often than not, decisions reached are backed up by the implicit or explicit use of force (see also Béteille 1969b:188). The success of this threat depends upon the number of men one can call upon for support who are willing to engage in open conflict (with bamboo poles, sticks, spears, and fists) if necessary. Many past cases of conflict over property involved the use of force, and force figured prominently in the disputes over water we observed or heard about during our stay. The primary level for the recruitment of support is thus the undivided family. At this level one refers to the *parivar* (family), which is either nuclear or joint *(sanyukt)*. The latter consists of lineal or collateral male kinsmen (or both), their spouses, and unmarried females sharing one house, one cooking place *(chulha),* and maintaining undivided property and household expenses.

Villagers put most emphasis on the maintenance of joint property in their discussion of the meaning of *parivar*. They see the major advantages as economic, for by pooling resources, more money is saved and manpower is consolidated for work and use as a pressure group. No less important is the fact that the social life of an Indian is intrinsically family-centered and that the sense of security and well-being that comes from being among one's own far outweighs any advantage that may accrue to the single nuclear family. The word *bans* is used to refer to a man's male offspring and the value placed on the continuation of the *bans* is often an important reason for the existence of large families.

We were told that to succeed in joint family living, the following principles must be enjoined: (1) There must be no favoritism within the family—every other child is to be treated as one's own, and you must always consider the other person. If anything is to be bought, for example, for one's child or wife, it must be presented equally to all. (2) All must contribute their total income to a joint account. The man with one son and a large income should be treated no differently than the man with a smaller income and many children. (3) There should be a single, powerful decision maker whom all must obey.

The essence of this formula seems to be the stress on unselfishness and equality. But despite the almost universal preference for the joint family, it is recognized that there are many tensions within such a group; sometimes they simmer below the surface so that members only grumble about the arrangement, but often they explode to the surface and end in a definite rupture. In the following discussion, I shall try to give some idea of the nature of conflict that can arise at the level of the family and reserve for the next chapter elucidation of case histories.

In a large family with a wide generational span, compounded by differential access to education, there is often conflict between the elders and the younger men. The former feel that they are not respected enough, nor are their opinions actively sought and heeded. The latter, more educated, wish to implement their ideas, which often represent a change from established patterns. Those in large families sometimes expressed the feeling that their life had become depersonalized and that the scale of living in a household of many persons was like that of a "hotel" or "factory." People complained of not receiving enough individual attention. One man said that this was a constant source of friction in his life. His wife was ill and weak from many pregnancies, yet no one in the family would look after her properly or see that she received medical attention. When he finally took it upon himself to do so and diverted some of his salary to pay the bills, an open breach occurred. Conversely, the same man was accused by another family member of being too selfish and of caring for his wife more than for the family or the money he spent.

Another area of dissension arises from the inequality of labor and wage contributions, despite the second injunction just given. We were told that the joint family is a system which breeds many parasites and cripples. The necessity to support a noncontributing member rankled others. The head of the family may also feel himself overburdened because he is the only one who properly cares about the family and must arrange everything. Connected with this sore point are the disputes which arise from the maintenance of a joint family account. Some people do not adhere to the first stipulation cited and keep separate items for themselves or hold back part of their wages to be spent on personal items. The greater availability of, and emphasis upon, the acquistion of material goods has often increased desires to a point beyond which the economy of a joint household can survive. Disputes also arise over the

FIGURE 12. Bhumihar children from Narain Singh's house.

priorities of expenditure: whether a boy should be sent to college or another *bigha* of land purchased instead.

Finally, a whole area of conflict and tension arises out of the clash of individual personalities with the roles they are supposed to enact. Quarrels among women were given as a major reason for the disruption of a joint family. It was mentioned that there are caste differences in the position of women. Generally, the upper castes keep their women in purdah, while the lower castes let their women work freely in the fields, and, as in the case of the very poor or the Untouchables, they may also work for others. The independence of lower-caste women results from their greater freedom of movement and earning capacity and contrasts with those higher in status. There are also differences among families of the same caste who observe purdah. One family may be stricter than another and a young bride will never show her face or speak directly with elder males. Or they may observe the custom of covering the face and slightly turning the head while still speaking directly to a father-in-law. We likewise observed differences among individuals in the same family. Still, the major contrast lies between the Bhumihars on the one hand and the lower castes on the other.

When a young bride first enters her husband's family, she is in an unenviable position of alienation and subservience. The newest entrant, after an initial period when she is treated as an auspicious guest, must do the most labor and show the greatest respect to others in the house by her obedience and quiet demeanor. The new bride is often extremely depressed if, in addition, her husband works outside the village and spends only brief periods visiting her and his children. In rare cases, she may even return to live with her parents. Some women are known to be quarrelsome and argue with all. Some fight only with the other women in the household or have specific grievances against their mothers-in-law, whom they may accuse of favoring other sons' wives.

Although a woman seems to have no real escape when the pressures of family life become too great, a skilled man may leave the house for a period of time and engage in outside employment. Quarrels between brothers are said to be incited usually by their wives and more rarely arise due to fundamental differences between male kin. A man may also be on poor terms with kin whose role expectations would otherwise denote friendly relations. A joking relationship should exist, for example, between a man and his elder brother's wife, but this may not necessarily be the case. Or a man may feel pressure to conform his behavior to ways that the family demands but with which he is unable to comply. One woman was perpetually pregnant and had only once brought forth a full, healthy baby that survived. Consequently she feels weak, unsure of herself, and unhappy. At night she dreams of all her lost children, and, tortured by the sight of them before her eyes, wakes up agitated and disturbed. For this reason her husband sleeps in her room every night instead of staying outside the house with the other men.[8] This created problems and disapproval in the joint family, for such a sleeping arrangement is not their custom and they feel it will be a bad influence on the younger boys and girls.

Above the family, the next level of kinship is represented by the *khandan*, a kin group consisting of all the male descendants of a common-named ancestor, and their wives and unmarried daughters. Within this

FIGURE 13. Giving an oil massage to newborn infants is a villagewide practice.

group there is a special term, *pattidari,* used to refer to all those who had rights in previously undivided property. The place where *pattidars* live is called the *patti.* They all necessarily belong to the same *khandan,* but the term seems to refer more specifically to the most recent property division among kinsmen. Thus, when the large Bhumihar family mentioned earlier achieves their property division, the three brothers and their respective offspring will become *pattidars* of one another. At present, however, their *pattidars* are the descendants of their father's two brothers, among whom the property was divided many years ago. There is often friction among *pattidars,* and when this gets out of hand, as it has among the *khandan* of Little Pura Bhumihars, it can result in the organization of conflict along factional lines. Here, every familial and personal dispute tends to escalate out of the personal arena and into the public.

The circumstances out of which a division of property grew provide a legacy of suspicion and feelings of competition even among friendly *pattidars.* Ill feelings are greatest when one of the *pattidars* seems to prosper more than another and succeeds in buying more land, building a new house, or acquiring a pumping set. In this situation, it is more likely that only a threat to the *patti* as a whole will enable them temporarily to forget their ill will and close ranks against a common enemy. *Pattidars*, however, are often mutually helpful in the matter of water distribution, lending agricultural implements, aiding in agricultural activities, and all social or ceremonial occasions.

So far, I have spoken of kin groups and relationships that are relevant to the social universe at the village level. Wider groups come into view when marriage is being considered, as the village is an exogamous unit. The *gotra*, often regarded as a clan, consists of all those who claim to be descendants of a common *rishi* (ancient Indian perceptor), and who may or may not show actual genealogical ties. Among the higher castes—in Arunpur, the Brahmans and Bhumihars—*gotras* are exogamous and a child is a member of his father's *gotra*. Among Kurmis and other low castes, marriage takes place within the *gotra*. The *biradari* (subcaste) is an endogamous group that consists of several such clans. As far as could be discerned, however, these groups played no active role in politics. Their major importance in this connection lies in the fact that further extensions of kin ties, through *biradari* and marriage connections, result in the formation of alliances with other families who may be called upon to help in any dispute.

While rules pertaining to kinship and caste exist so that interaction between people may be carried out smoothly in accordance with learned behavioral expectations, they do not preclude occasions of conflict. Not only may a person choose to disregard the rules in a particular situation, but the rules that apply in a given context may also be in contradiction to one another or necessitate decisions which choose among alternative rules. This chapter has indicated several areas in which conflict may arise. The next chapter takes a closer look, through the use of case histories, at specific examples of conflict which did not escalate to the level of the villagewide political arena.

NOTES

1. Touching (including removal of and cleaning) any food or utensil used by another is considered defiling *(jhunta)*. Although low castes perform these chores for higher castes, the reverse situation would be even more polluting.
2. That the people of Arunpur do not use the term *varna* as a referent for caste, and often do not even know what it means, is a strikingly different situation from what Miller found. He states that the distinction between *varna* and *jati* in a Haryana village "is meaningful [to villagers] . . . as a mechanism for the analysis of differential levels of inequality" (1975:59). His glossing of *varna* as "caste" and *jati* as "sub-caste" is unusual (1975:60), as is his lack of mention of *biradiri* (see Miller:71 for *bhaichara;* cf. Mayer 1960:167ff on *bhaibandh*).

3. A Nai and a Lohar also used the same surname, Sharma.
4. He was also the sole exception in Arunpur to the rule that Bhumihars do not touch the plough. Because he is also "outcaste," he most likely suffers no loss of prestige from doing his own ploughing.
5. A stimulating and provocative article by Meillassoux (1973), an Africanist, provides a radical departure from most thinking on this subject. He adopts an historical perspective and concludes that the "status system of the *varna* was an attempt to maintain class relationships as they existed during the classical period" (1973:90). Thus, both class and clientship relations exist beneath the ideological representations of caste. He maintains that the institutionalized relations of *jajmani* are essentially personalistic ones of the patron-client type, whose nature and political implications override their economic content. They are not, in essence, exploitative. Such relations, however, are dependent upon class relations that enable the patron to make use of essential goods for the maintenance of his clients. Clients profit, through the mediation of the patron, from the exploitation of laboring classes who provide the surplus to support the patron-client relation. Class relations include those between the landowner and his agricultural workers, slaves and serfs (both in the past), tenants, or wage-earning laborers, "even when they were associated with other paternalistic relationships" (1973:102–103). Meillassoux sees clientship as derived, secondary relations that are functionally dependent upon the class relations that fed them. The ideology of caste—hierarchy and purity—served only to codify and reinforce the preexisting relations of subordination and alienation.
6. Miller writes that in a Haryana village, Untouchables are separated from other *shudra*s by being collectively termed *mazdur*. He also states that the term *jajman* does not have wide usage as denoting a patron of service castes but refers only to relations with the priest (1975:65; 83; also Pocock 1962:88; Breman 1974:20).
7. Caste etiquette demands that when two men can sit on the same cot, the higher-caste man sit on the high (i.e., completely strung) side while the lower-caste man sits on the partially strung end. The same division obtains between all other nonequals (e.g., young and old).
8. In the men's sleeping and sitting place—*baithka*.

CHAPTER 5
Conflict in Arunpur: Disputes that Do Not Escalate

Many activities in an Indian village are concerned with competition for things of value, that is, command over resources or control over other men. In Arunpur there are several cleavages across which conflict could and actually did take place. Some of this political action escalated to the level of the villagewide political arena. Conflicts over certain resources, such as land on the open market or the distribution of government tubewell water, lend themselves more readily to such escalation because they are theoretically open to all and certainly coveted by all. This is in sharp contrast to the lack of disputes over the distribution of water from privately owned pumping sets. Still other disputes, such as those described in this chapter, have not spilled over into the villagewide arena and remain, so far, apart from it. Disputes within a family are less likely to involve others of the community than disputes between factions, although the latter did originate from an initial split among kinsmen. All conflicts, however, have the potentiality of entering the wider arena.

The analysis of the way in which political activity that is not part of the villagewide arena operates at different levels within the village proceeds through the use of case material relating to conflict within the family, among affines and *pattidar*s as well as that inherent within the patron-client *(jajman-praja)* dyad. The latter specifically excludes those patron-client ties between the upper castes and their Chamar laborers, as the conflicts between them entered the village arena. Generally, there seems to be a greater tendency for nonkin disputes over valued resources to escalate than for those among kin.

One of the major concerns of the fieldwork was to determine whether there are boundaries between the political activities that take place at various structural levels in the village, starting from the simple dyadic relationship within a family or between neighbors, and those reserved for the political arena encompassing the whole community. I initially struggled rather unsuccessfully with the Western concepts of "private" and "public" to equate public decisions with those of a political system. I attempted to attach the caste and big men *panchayats* to these labels, respectively, but was forced to abandon this line of thinking. It could not account for the fact that certain disputes that might be considered public (i.e., known about by all and settled by outsiders) did not enter the village political arena, whereas the reverse was sometimes the case.

It became more fruitful to classify the data the way the villagers did. Their view of the nature of conflict structured the collection, presentation, and organization of the material to a great extent. What they considered to be a family matter, so did I; similarly, what they spoke of in terms of factions *(partibandi)* or casteism *(jatpat),* or as belonging to the spheres of the caste and big men *panchayats*, I, too, will speak of in these terms. To discern their rules for classifying such events, I first put each case in the appropriate category in which they had described it. Then I abstracted from the cases in a specific category (e.g., factional, caste matter, and so on) those variables they had in common that seemed adequately to account for the inclusion of each case in that group. In this way, I also classified those cases whose categories I had not ascertained from the villagers. Finally, when I began to try and separate the political activity of the villagewide arena from other political activity, it became necessary to answer the following questions: (1) Who are the people involved, and what are the recruitment principles for gaining supporters? (2) What are the the alternatives for action present in the situation, and how are these valued? (3) What are the cultural constraints upon, and incentives to, alternative actions? Although there remained certain ambiguities in the attempted classification, a pattern did emerge that distinguished between conflict among individuals and the larger villagewide conflict.

CONFLICT WITHIN THE FAMILY

The preceding chapter outlined several possible areas of dispute within the family. Actual case histories will be discussed here to illustrate conflict at this level.

Cases 1 and 2: The Wayward Sons c. 1966-1969

1. A Brahman man constantly complains of his only son, who is sixteen years old. The boy was supposed to be enrolled in Arunpur Intercollege and took his school fees from home every month. But he never attended classes and instead used the money to run away to Bombay with the ruffian son of an outcaste Bhumihar from Arunpur. After traveling there without a ticket, he could find no work and so returned home. He goes often to Banaras to see films and visit prostitutes; he eats betel, polishes his nails, keeps "long" hair, and takes money from his parents on false pretenses. Both of his parents are afraid that if they beat him or try to hold the boy in check, he will either beat them in return or run away and desert them. They also fear that if he continues this way, with his bad habits and not studying, no decent Brahman girl will marry him and he will have to purchase a wife like his other relatives. The boy's major complaint is that he is not married.

2. A Nai widow has great hopes for her only son which seem doomed. The boy was admitted to Banaras Hindu University after graduating from the Intercollege with a first class in his high school examinations. Although he was already married, while living on the campus he met and fell in love with a rich girl of the Khatri (scribe) caste who was also attending the University. One day the boy's maternal grandfather saw the two walking together and asked them what they were doing. The boy replied that the girl was his beloved and that he couldn't live without her. She responded similarly. The elderly Nai returned heartbroken to the village and proceeded to arrange for his grandson's second marriage ceremony *(gauna)*. At that time his young wife would come and live with her husband and consummate their marriage. After the bride came, the grandfather told her to go to the University and warn both her husband and the Khatri girl to discontinue their relationship.

The boy failed after his first year at the college and was readmitted to Arunpur Intercollege. The Khatri girl came to meet him there many times. The Intercollege Principal also advised the girl to forget the boy, but she refused to listen. When the grandfather was informed of this, he went to the school and beat his grandson with a stick before the other students and the girl. The boy's wife was also there and she managed to stop the beating after the boy promised to forget his beloved.

Two years passed and the boy was again readmitted to the University where the Khatri girl was doing her M.Sc. The two began to meet once again. The boy's wife went to the University one day and started pleading with him to stop seeing the girl. Nonetheless, the relationship continues and the Khatri girl says that she will remain unmarried if she cannot marry the boy.

Conflict arose over the behavior of an only son in both of these cases. Sons are in an exceedingly important position in Arunpur, as they are almost universally in India. It is they who remain with their parents and support them in their old age; they continue the family line *(bans)*. The position of an only son is clearly more crucial and is supplemented by the cultural norm of respect and obedience to one's parents and elders. The major issue of conflict pertained to the question of marriage. In India, marriages are arranged by two families when the boy and girl are still quite young. The actual consummation of the marriage follows upon a second marriage ceremony (the *gauna*), which takes place soon after both reach puberty (about thirteen to fifteen years for a girl and fifteen to twenty years for a boy). Given the strict segregation of the sexes and the practice of purdah among upper-caste women, the early first marriage is regarded as a necessity to ensure both the purity of the girl in her virginity and the psychological satisfaction of the boy in the allure that his marriage will eventually be consummated.

The Brahman boy complained that his parents had not even arranged his marriage. The actions of his other kinsmen who had "purchased" wives presented him with viable alternative modes of behavior with which to handle the situation, albeit such behavior is generally not condoned. The fact that he felt no constraints is clear from his parents' fear that to discipline him would mean to ultimately lose him. The boy has also threatened to throw his father out of the house once he does get married. On the other hand, the conflict for the Nai boy revolves around the question of arranged marriage versus "love marriage." He had seemingly respected the role expectations for himself of his mother and grandfather, up to the time I left Arunpur, by choosing to remain within his previously arranged marriage. Both disputes, however, have stayed within the family level and there was no recourse to an external decision-making body (e.g., a caste *panchayat*).

Cases 3 and 4: The Jealous Wives c. 1953–1969

3. Some fifteen years ago, an elderly Brahman woman, reputed to have been a go-between in the purchase of girls for marriage, had arranged the marriage of her husband's younger brother with a Nepali woman. The latter bore three children while the older woman had none. The Brahman woman feels that her husband does not care for her and that he lavishes all his affection and concern on his brother's children. She said that they

all abuse and beat her and that she has no satisfaction in life. Because of the constant fighting between the two women, the brothers have been forced to divide their households and live separately.

1968

4. Raju, a Chamar rickshaw driver, was living in Banaras in a Chamar woman's house. He formed a liaison with her solely for the purpose of ultimately acquiring her property. She had a daughter by a previous marriage and now had a son by Raju. With a wife and four children in Arunpur, Raju kept the two "wives" separate for a couple of years. Then he brought the Banaras woman and her two children to live with his wife and family in the village. The two women fought and Raju beat his first wife. The situation had become so unbearable that Raju's father decided to call a *panchayat* meeting of village big men to settle the dispute.

The major conflict in the Brahman family seemed to result from the competition between a man's wife and his brother's children for his affection. As already stated, children are an important asset in a man's life, and the lack of them in this case has triggered the dissension. Additional conflict also arises from the proverbial antagonism prevailing between the wives of two brothers, which leads villagers to say: "A hundred mustaches can live peacefully under one roof, but not four breasts." The jealousy felt by the Brahman woman over this displacement of her husband's affection and wealth was too strong to be overcome by his own feeling of responsibility toward continuing the joint household. Hence, they ultimately decided to divide. The poverty that exists among the Chamars, however, does not permit the luxury of maintaining large joint families, and they quickly break up at the first signs of pressure and tension. Raju's father had requested the big men (i.e., Bhumihars) of Arunpur and neighboring villages to sit in a *panchayat,* and he hoped that they would tell his son to take the Banaras woman away so that the wife could live in peace.

This case, along with Case 9 that follows, presents an interesting example of the decision to call a big men *panchayat* to deal with an affair that normally comes under the jurisdiction of caste *panchayat*s. Presumably Raju's father felt that if he could get these powerful men to sanction his decision to return the second woman to Banaras, his son would be bound to obey. When I arrived at the scene of the *panchayat* with one of the Bhumihars who had been called, we found only the Chamars of that *pura,* Raju's sister's husband, and an Arunpur Kohar there. Raju told us that he had succeeded in convincing his relatives to discard the idea of calling a *panchayat,* as that would mean "throwing mud over our faces." In other words, he felt the necessity to keep this conflict from escalating to preserve his *khandan*'s prestige. When I asked why they had not called a caste *(biradari) panchayat,* which usually treats such matters as the infraction of caste rules and disputes involving marriages and divorces, they replied that it is ineffective these days. "Today there is no moral duty *(dharma)* and that is why the *panchayat* is not obeyed." When the *panchayat* of the British-appointed village headman of old used to settle all disputes, the opposing parties quickly forgot they had been adversaries. Today, in the Chamar's opinion, the present *pradhan* has no comparable power. If consulted, he probably would have advised them to go to court. There a dispute becomes more entangled and can smolder for years. Yet even though a poor man of low caste can ill afford to do so, he will often follow this advice and seek to imitate high-caste people by taking his case to court. The Chamars realized that the presence of this alternative method of dispute settlement was drastically affecting the structure of their traditional caste *panchayat.* At the same time, the formality and expense involved in actually calling a caste *panchayat* may also have influenced the Chamar's decision not to do so.

Case 5: The Disaffected Son   1967-1969

Satya is a young (age thirty-six) teacher in the Intercollege who comes from a large and influential Bhumihar family. About a year before I had come to the village, his wife became extremely ill during pregnancy. He did not mention anything to his other family members, who all knew of her condition, as it is expected that they will take up the responsibility of looking after others and not only "care for the accounts or the farm." However, as no one seemed to be concerned about his wife, Satya finally took her to the hospital in Banaras himself. She stayed there about six to eight weeks. He was the only person who went to visit her daily and bring her food.

Satya had the huge expense of paying for her medicines and other bills after her return home and therefore could not give any money from his salary (250 rupees per month) to the joint family account. The second month, he had some money left after the expenses and he gave it to Chandra, the family member who kept the accounts, through a boy in the family. Chandra became angry at this and told the boy to return the money to Satya and to tell him to give it to the family head instead— Satya's elder brother. Satya kept the money. The account-keeper then complained to the family head: "Your brother, Satya, not only takes his wife to the city, which brings a bad name to the family, but he won't account for his money. How am I to manage and know where money is coming from and going to?"

Satya's elder brother confronted him and demanded an explanation of his behavior and expenditures. The family had spent thousands of rupees on Satya's education, his brother continued, and it was expected that he would contribute to the household purse. The two brothers exchanged hot words and Satya threatened to leave his wife and children in the village and depart from the house if he was not wanted there and was to be accused of breaking up the family. The elder brother was not happy with this, and after that, they stopped speaking to each other. For three to four months, Satya spoke to no one, neither his elder brother nor even the women and children in the houshold. He would go early in the morning to teach at the Intercollege and come home only late at night to eat and sleep.

Satya remains bitter about the treatment that his wife has received in the family. He says that everyone knew she was ill and could have died; but nobody cares for her, "as they care for their cows." He is disillusioned with his life and dissatisfied with living in his family. But he finds it difficult to make an actual break and take his wife and children away.

This case is important because it most clearly illustrates the type of power conflict that can usually arise in a joint family, as well as reveals the alternatives for, and constraints upon, action. Each of the three people primarily involved—Satya, his elder brother as the family head, and Chandra the account-keeper—has a certain position in the family and in relation to one another that has brought about a conflict of interests. Each felt that in some way their power was being co-opted by another. As a son of the family, Satya has a duty to honor the interests of the group first and to contribute his entire earnings to the joint account. He also is not expected to be seen escorting his wife in public. The Principal of the Intercollege had once even commented to Satya that it was not becoming for him to go to Banaras so often with his wife. A man is not to speak of his own needs in the family, for it is the responsibility of others to take note to them and do what is necessary. Caught up in the complexity of running such a large establishment of forty-four household members, however, the elders were not responsive to the requirements of Satya's wife. Satya decided to act for himself because of the gravity of the situation.

Chandra is Satya's "nephew" (father's elder brother's son's son) and is expected to accord him due respect. But there is only a small difference in their ages, and the account-keeper is a B.Sc. and teacher at the Intercollege in his own right. Furthermore, as the eldest son in his immediate nuclear family, Chandra became its "head" when his highly regarded and influential father died. Thus he feels he is his "uncle's" peer, not subordinate. He also has the additional prestige and power that comes from keeping the accounts of this large family with its huge and varied income. The individual personalities of these two further complicate the issue. Satya is easygoing and carefree, and when he became disaffected with the family earlier, he gave up keeping the joint family account. This duty then passed on to Chandra, who takes his task seriously and is hard working and sensitive in everything he does. The two never got along well before.

The family head, in both this position as well as that of elder brother to Satya, is a man to be doubly looked up to and obeyed. As effective head of the family, he has the power to make all authoritative decisions and to expect complete compliance with them. Hence, he responded angrily to the words of his younger brother. His reference to spending thousands of rupees on Satya's education with the expectation of return reveals the way in which education is regarded as a precious investment for a family's future and is one of its most important resources. Education means power for a family: the power to make strategic decisions that involve intricate knowledge of agricultural innovations, the official world, and the court system. The power to gain prestige for the family name, and the power to be able to make good marriage alliances that provide a constant pool from which to recruit supporters and strengthen a family's bargaining position in any conflict that may arise, are also boons of education.

Satya's two major alternatives of action were either to stay with the family or to leave it; this latter choice being subdivided into leaving with or without his wife and child. He could not decide to leave without taking his wife, for on previous occasions when he had taken up jobs in other cities, he always had to leave his service and return home. His wife was constantly ill and unhappy when he was gone. The decision lay between the alternatives of either staying or departing with his family. Though Satya is extremely unhappy at home, he finds too many constraints on leaving. His wife, an illiterate village woman, would be miserable in the city away from other family members. Used to the security and confinement of life in purdah, she could not manage on her own. Satya himself, for all his talk, admits that he fears what others will think of him and that he does not want to be regarded as the one who broke up the family. The unity of his family has also been a great source of prestige and strength in the village and he is loath to put that position in jeopardy. His only solution was to remain at home, the aloof, seemingly uncaring and disaffected family member. While we were in Arunpur, two other men belonging to different Bhumihar families had disputes with their family members. In both instances, they decided to leave the household for a certain period of time and seek employment elsewhere, leaving wives and children behind.

Case 6: Forbidden Love   1968–1969

In a large Brahman house consisting of the separate households of five brothers and a sixth household of a deceased brother's two sons, a dispute arose between the latter two. The younger brother, Mohan, is a rather slow and plodding individual and is married to a girl from Banaras. The elder brother, Daya, remains unmarried.[1] He is a notorious figure in the village and known to be a gambler, drinker, "stud," and thief. When Mohan went to work in Calcutta, Daya lived with the girl in his absence. She was six months pregnant when her husband returned from Calcutta, and shortly thereafter went to her father's house in the city.

Meanwhile, Daya took a gold chain and a transistor radio received by Mohan as a part of his wife's dowry and sold these. Then he tried to sell the land in which Mohan also had a legal share. Finally, he locked Mohan out of their joint room in the house and a physical fight followed. Mohan ran and brought a knife with which to kill his brother, while the latter fled to his beloved's house in the city.

Mohan then called upon his wife's father, who knew of the affair, to come and settle the dispute. But both the girl and her parents preferred his brother. Many times he also requested that my assistant and myself go to Banaras to speak with his wife and her father. We never went. The Pradhan (elected village head) once tried to settle the dispute, but to no avail. Daya continues to claim all the things his brother received in the marriage, including his wife, plus all the land shared by the two.

The normal posture between a woman and her husband's elder brother is that of complete avoidance. There is no other alternate rule for behavior, and as a desired "resource," the girl clearly belonged to her husband. The conflict, however, has its roots in the peculiar fact that Arunpur Brahman women do not observe purdah and in the personal predilection of the girl and the elder brother. Because of his cleverness, the brother has also succeeded in winning the affection of her parents. None of Mohan's attempts to settle the conflict succeeded. Nor would Daya listen to the advice of the Pradhan, who suggested that they divide all their property equally. When he finally returned home from Banaras, he suggested that they all live together again, but his younger brother was warned that the arrangement would mean Daya would again start staying with his wife.

Mohan said that he had another alternative, to sell his share of the land, nine *bise* (one *bigha* = twenty *bise*), for 5000 rupees and then go to a place where land is cheaper and settle there. He also thought of starting some business in Banaras. But Daya would not permit this sale. Mohan was unable to act and went to Banaras again to implore his wife's parents to support him. There he discovered that his mother-in-law had sold some ornament he had presented to his wife and this made him even angrier. His relatives blamed him for his inaction, while he said that his wife, who had meanwhile given birth to a baby girl, was the guilty party. Daya was entirely to blame.

Mohan was too weak to stand up to his clever elder brother and, despite the fact that the latter was so completely in the wrong, people tended to support him more. I had the feeling that Mohan's indecision added to his loss of respect in the eyes of others. Daya felt absolutely no constraints on his actions; he neither listened to his other relations, his friends, the Pradhan, or us. He wanted his brother's possessions (wife included), and the single-minded strategy he followed was that of winning over the people most concerned, that is, the girl and her parents. The fact that the Pradhan was called upon to intervene was not enough to escalate this dispute from the family level, for nothing came of his decision. The Pradhan is an extremely busy man, looks after a large amount of family land, and is engaged in his own business. He had little interest in or time to give the matter. Further, the Brahmans in the village are not people of importance, and these two brothers were conspicuously lacking in property and prestige. There did not seem to be any gain for a big man in the village to exploit this affair for his own ends. As the following chapter will show more clearly, this case reveals that it is not so much the nature of the dispute as the people who become involved which determines the escalation of conflict from the family to the villagewide arena.

Recourse to dispute settlement was made on the level of the immediate family in almost all of the foregoing six cases. The conflict remained localized even when outsiders were consulted. Thus, at the level of the family, people are engaged in competing for property, women, affection, and prestige.

Conflict among Affines

Disputes can also occur between two families united by marriage, and for the most part this type of conflict remains an affair between the affines concerned and the relatives who acted as go-betweens. It is entirely to their advantage to see that the conflict does not escalate and terminates quickly, for the marriage contract is regarded as forging a permanent alliance between two families.

Case 7: Dispute over the Giving of Marriage Gifts *(Tilak)*[2]   1969

Nagesh, a Bhumihar boy, was to be married at the beginning of June. The girl's family was to send several people to take part in the customary presentation of gifts before the marriage *(tilak).* Nagesh's family also planned a marriage for one of their daughter's, to take place May 10–12. Wishing to avoid the extra expense and bother of having to make separate plans to receive and feast the party of gift bearers (which was to be about fifteen to twenty men but would expand to several hundred when Nagesh's other relations and villagers were included), they requested his future wife's family to present the gifts on May 11, when their daughter's marriage would be in progress.

The girl's side said that they could not possibly arrange all the purchases and the necessary people until June. This incensed Nagesh's family, and they were ready to send a letter saying that there would be no presentation and that the gifts previously sent by the girl's side to signify the bond between the families would be returned.

Nagesh prevailed upon his family to keep to their previous bond and ultimately the ceremony took place in June, with marriage several days later at the girl's home.

This conflict arose because of a cultural rule which states that a boy's family is supreme and all-powerful in a marriage, while the girl's side must comply with their wishes. The refusal of the girl's family to cooperate added insult to the injury which Nagesh's family already felt, for they had been doing everything that their daughter's future affines were requesting. They expected at least as much in return from Nagesh's prospective in-laws. They constantly compared the 3,000 rupees they received for expenses in Nagesh's marriage to the 6,000 rupees they planned to spend in their daughter's marriage.[3]

Nagesh's decision not to break a marriage contract that had been agreed upon some three years earlier is interesting when compared with the possible alternative of breaking the alliance. As a student at Banaras Hindu University, Nagesh had met a Bhumihar girl and professed to have grown most fond of her. He used to visit her and her widowed mother often at their home in the city. The mother also grew fond of Nagesh and wished him to marry her daughter. He refused because his engagement had already taken place, and he felt that to break it would be a blot on the family name. Further disgrace would come when people dis-

FIGURE 14. Women gather in the Pradhan's house to bid a sad farewell to a daughter who is leaving for her in-laws' house, after the *gauna*.

covered an engagement was broken so that a "love marriage" might take place. Nagesh's first concern was for his family's prestige (cf. cases 2 and 5). Now, when his family wanted to break off the marriage of their own accord, thus possibly paving the way for his marriage with the other girl, Nagesh again appealed to the propriety of the situation. His elders listened and the wedding took place, even though the gifts did not come when they desired.

Case 8: The Second Marriage Ceremony *(Gauna)* Fight   1969

A second marriage ceremony was taking place in the home of Krishna Singh from the neighboring village of Ramapur. Krishna Singh is one of the most powerful, wealthy, and influential Bhumihars in the area. As Secretary of Arunpur Intercollege and *pramukh* of the Community Development Block, he is one of the leaders in his caste, active in politics and an expert in affairs of both the courts and *panchayat*s. The dispute took place when the groom and his party reached Krishna's village quite late in the evening. Their taxi got stuck in the dark and muddy narrow lanes leading to the house, and the boy refused to get out and walk to the door. He insisted upon being driven there. It took one and a half hours to free the taxi and finally reach that destination. This was the beginning of what seemed a deliberate attempt by the *gauna* party to embarrass their hosts.

The party was requested to come and eat when dinner was ready. They refused, saying that first they would like five cups of tea. When these were brought and drunk, they asked for another four, then followed this by a request for four more cups. The third time the hosts refused to bring any more tea and again requested that the party come and eat. One of the guests then said that he had to go to the toilet and the rest insisted upon waiting for him to return. He came back from the fields after some time and everyone finally ate. When dinner was over, the groom said that rather than sleep in the garden, where arrangements for them had already been made, they would sleep near the house. The hosts finally agreed when they persisted in this matter. Just at the point of agreement, however, the party decided that they didn't really want to stay there after all and started to retire to the garden area. While one of the guests was putting their things in a suitcase they had brought along, he also picked up a jacket and scarf belonging to the son of Krishna, a lecturer in an Intercollege.

A fight followed the quarrel and verbal abuse over whom the jacket and scarf belonged to. It is said that Krishna's son landed the first punch and that the guests (with the exception of the groom) were badly beaten. They left the house in anger and walked to the main road. There they stopped a truck, explaining that they wanted to take one of their friends to the hospital. One of Krishna's acquaintances, who learned what had happened, reached the scene and requested the driver not to take the boys. The whole group then began to walk toward Banaras. When they were near the city station, seven miles from Ramapur, Krishna and some others caught up with them. They persuaded them to return to the village, where an informal, on-the-spot *panchayat* of the family members and guests concerned was held. Although Krishna and others apologized and expressed their deep regrets, the groom remained angered.

The following morning, the groom entered the house alone and asked for his bride, instead of coming with several others of his party as is customary. He refused to participate in the farewell ritual in which money and gifts are presented by the women of the house to the groom. Nor would he partake of the yogurt and sweets which are considered important to ensure an auspicious departure. Only when one of his close relatives implored him to comply with this did he accept the things given by the women as well as the other gifts which were part of his wife's dowry. These were all loaded in his taxi and a truck and finally the entire party departed without having taken food. When they reached their own village, some forty miles away, the women of the house became furious upon hearing what had transpired and they became determined to return the girl. The elder men's decision to let her stay prevailed and saved the situation, but the women decided, in turn, that they would never let the girl visit her natal village.

The people involved in this conflict situation, the decisions that they made, and the results of these choices are all interrelated. As mentioned previously, not only is the boy's family considered superior in all marriage-making decisions, but they are also highly critical of the reception they receive every time a visit is made to the girl's home. There is an element of testing the extent to which all of one's whims can be satisfied by the hospitality offered. The groom and his party, however, were acting entirely unreasonably and greatly taxed the patience of their otherwise accommodating hosts. The decision to remain at the house and sleep there, for example, was an impertinent and discourteous request. Women in the house must observe the strictest purdah before affines, and the thought of a large number of mischievous college boys in front of the home, when there were young girls within, caused much dismay.

The position of a new bride in her husband's home is an unenviable one. Any conflict that would serve further to depress her position there is to be totally avoided. It was with this in mind that Krishna and the son who was involved in the fight profusely apologized afterwards. There is a custom in this region (more common among higher castes) that a girl can return to her natal village only after she has spent at least a year or two at her new home; it is possible that Krishna's daughter will be penalized and could spend up to five or more years at her husband's home without ever returning to Ramapur. At the same time, villagers generally feel that it is best to get wives from poorer and lower families, as they will not show off and will more easily accept their subservient position in the family. Krishna's house is wealthy and influential, and it was perhaps the need to assert themselves in a big man's house that led the boy and his party of college friends to act as they did. It should also be noted that although a boy has little or no say at all regarding his own marriage arrangements, his wishes are prominent at the time of the actual marriage and second marriage ceremony. In many ways, he is treated like a prince and behaves accordingly.

The hosts decided to comply with all of their guests' demands while stifling their own anger. The fight which ultimately erupted represented a serious breach of etiquette. I was told by one of Krishna's close associates: "I am convinced that Krishna's son hit first, and though the guests behaved obnoxiously, it was at their [i.e., Krishna's] house and they must have given a better account of themselves. It was absolutely wrong on their part [to act that way]." The result of this over-hasty behavior is that the girl will always suffer in her husband's home, although the scandal would have been greater had she been returned to her natal home.

Case 9: The Branded Daughter   1968–1969

Three years before my stay in Arunpur, a poor Teli married his ten-year-old daughter to a twenty-two-year-old boy from a nearby village. The second marriage ceremony *(gauna)* occurred when the girl was twelve years of age. Her mother-in-law did not let her cohabit with the boy, as she had not yet reached puberty. The following year, when the boy came on his vacation to the village from Calcutta, he attempted to have relations with his wife. She would not cooperate with him. The boy started to beat her in anger and then took an iron bar from the fire and branded her on the face. The father heard of this, took his daughter home to Arunpur and then called upon the big men of the village to come and settle the dispute.

This situation is similar to that of Case 4 earlier, where a matter considered within the realm of a caste *panchayat* is referred instead to that of the big men. The Teli said that he had gone through the village and requested all the big men (in this case, the wealthy Bhumihars as well as two wealthy Kurmis) to come; most told him that they would, but only two came, along with a few observers. When asked why he did not call a caste *panchayat,* the Teli said: "What do you talk of a caste *panchayat*? Even the Pradhan, who is an officer in this village and knew of this, couldn't dare to come. So what big man in my caste will come to decide this? Jai Singh [the Bhumihar who settled the dispute] is our friend, even though he is a loudmouth. We will marry our daughter somewhere else this year, if possible."

It is the custom of all caste *panchayat*s to impose some fine on the guilty party (usually in the form of a feast for *biradari* members), as well as take some money from the supposed victim to give to the *panchayat* members. It seems likely that the Teli made his unusual decision to call the village big men to settle the affair because of his extreme poverty. To call a caste *panchayat* is a much more formal matter and he could ill afford any expense that might be involved in this. Even to appeal the case to a caste leader would have involved the initial expense of traveling to see him, plus the subsequent arrangements that must be made.

During the *panchayat,* Jai "called for both sides to present their cases. When the boy first appeared to state his story, he seemed quite fearless." Jai threatened him, "If you do not listen, I will sell your whole house. Remember that I am a Bhumihar." The decision of powerful Bhumihars carries the same weight as that of a caste *panchayat.* The boy subsequently calmed down and said that he had acted out of passion. He was fined 1,095 rupees (465 for breaking the marriage, 565 for marriage expenses, and 65 for his behavior), although I do not know if this enormous sum was ever paid. The Teli who called the *panchayat* was charged 100 rupees, but Jai forfeited this amount because he was so poor. The other Bhumihar who was also present, an irresponsible drunkard, demanded 50 rupees as his half share but was eventually satisfied with 5 rupees. Jai's decision was written down, officially stamped, and a copy was given to each of the disputing parties.

CONFLICT WITHIN THE KHANDAN

The decision made by family members to divide themselves and all their property is a painful one, often accompanied by great conflict over who gets what from the common pool. Unfortunately, I have no examples of such disputes. In many instances, however, even after a division does take place among brothers (or including their father) and they become *pattidars*, some dispute usually remains that can drag on for years. The following two cases present examples of such disputes that continued after a family had been divided.

Case 10: Competition for a Deceased Man's Land   c.1943–1950

This case describes a breach that originally arose between two Bhumihar *pattidars* in Little Pura who disputed the property of a deceased third party. It is also a conflict that figures in the subsequent history of Arunpur factionalism. About twenty-five years ago, land that had been held jointly by two brothers was divided. The younger brother, Hans Singh (see Chart 2), died leaving only one son. This son, in turn, died with no issue and, because he had been a minor, his wife had no claim to any share of the land. The widow went to live with Jai Singh. The elder brother, Buddhi, had three sons. The middle son, Kesar, died with no issue and his widow went to live with Chandra Singh. This son (Kesar), however, had been legally entitled to a one-third share of his father's property, and upon his death this right devolved upon his widow. The entire land, for practical purposes, however, was equally divided and cultivated by Kesar's two surviving brothers and their respective offspring, Chandra and Jai.

Sometime later, c. 1950, when Kesar's two brothers had passed away, Chandra tried to get the entire one-third share of the widow who was living with him legally registered in his name. Until that time this land had continued to be cultivated by Chandra and Jai on a half-share basis. Although people advised Chandra against his action, he went to the court to register his name on the land. Jai appealed to his other *khandan* members, Cheddinath and Rampat, to help him in opposing Chandra's move. They succeeded in calling a *panchayat* of the local big men which decided that Jai should get half of the land registered in his name. And so it was done.

The sequel to this event is Case 11. It should be noted here that the people who had a right to compete for this land were clearly delimited, that is, they were the descendants of the three dead brothers, Rajan, Kesar, and Lalji. Since Chandra and Jai could not settle the dispute between themselves, they decided to appeal to a higher body of adjudication, the big men *panchayat*. This appeal made the dispute a matter of public knowledge but did not necessarily move it over into the village political arena, which was then still under the control of the British-appointed village headman. At the present time, however, Jai is allied not with Rampat and his *pattidar*s, but with the man he fought against—Chandra. The latter never forgot how a section of his *khandan* went against him, and what began originally as a conflict within a kin group exploded to engulf the entire village. Disputes that were once exclusively among kinsmen now claim to attract supporters along diverse lines of recruitment (see Chapter 7).

Case 11: Disputed Ownership of a Pond   c. 1950–1958

This case involved the entire *khandan* of Little Pura Bhumihars. As their ancestors had been collecting the land revenue for village zamindars (see Chapter 2), Babu Sahib offered to sell them a twenty-five-*bise* pond near their *pura* shortly before Zamindari Abolition. The price was low, and Cheddinath went to Chandra and Jai to request them to become partners with him and his *pattidar*s in the land the zamindar had offered. They both refused, and only Cheddinath and his *pattidar*s purchased it. Several years later, after Cheddinath died, Chandra claimed to be a partner in the pond. He called a big men *panchayat* and pleaded that Cheddinath and his *pattidars* had deprived him and Jai of their rightful shares. The *panchayat* decided in Chandra's favor and this decision was obeyed by his other *khandan* members.

The *panchayat*'s decision was an oral one. By fraud and with the help of the village record-keeper *(lekhpal)*, Chandra subsequently got the entire pond registered in his and Jai's name. It was perhaps out of gratitude for their support in Case 10 that Jai informed his other *khandan* members (notably Rampat Singh) about this. He also requested them not to implicate him in any court case but to only involve Chandra. A suit was duly filed, and four years later the court awarded a one-fifth share in the pond each to Chandra and Jai. The latter, knowing the actual situation, still accepted this share. He became allied with his *pattidar*, Chandra, and from that time onward "all men who criticized Chandra and Jai became their enemies."

Although Cases 10 and 11 may be seen as marking the beginning of *partibandi* (factionalism) in Arunpur, the actual disputes took before its inception and the personnel involved remained confined to the *khandan*. This is a far cry from what we shall see happens in the present day; any conflict between the Chandra-Jai and Raj Kumar parties now immediately escalates. As it is, these two disputes illustrate that the most common resource for which kinsmen compete is land, especially land previously held in common (i.e., by the joint family). Such disputes used to be settled primarily by the big men *panchayat*, like the one that originally convened in Case 11, and the villagers felt bound to abide by the rules of their decisions. No other recourse was readily available to them.

People go directly to the courts today or may decide to use them if they are not satisfied with the decision of the traditional *panchayat*. A court appeal means that villagers are burdened by the cost of conducting such a dispute and, worse, that the case can drag on year after year while enmity between the parties hardens. During the process of shuffling a dispute from one court of appeal to another, the land is usually controlled by the stronger party, who is not necessarily the rightful owner. The courts do, however, present a structural alternative to the traditional *panchayat*, and the options offered by these two structures refer to contradictory sets of cultural rules.

DISPUTES WITHIN JAJMANI RELATIONS

Before concluding this chapter, I should like to mention briefly another form of almost institutionalized conflict, the "ritualized conflict" that is always present in patron-client *(jajman-praja)* relationships. Despite the fact that each participant knows what is expected of him and what he will receive in return in the ideal of *jajmani* (see, for example, Wiser 1936), there is actually much scope for disagreement and dispute.

The statuses and behavioral expectations of each person in the *jajmani* dyad are set, much like that of kinsmen. There is a certain continuity of personnel who are involved, because these are mostly hereditary affiliations and almost always last for a lifetime. The closeness that often develops between a patron and his client is similar to the feelings that bind kinsmen together, and kinship terminology is extended to these relationships. It is expected that the patron and client will support each other when the need arises, and the relationship forms one of the lines of recruitment into different factions (see Chapter 7). This type of conflict is also mentioned here to avoid the impression that the only type of political activity that exists outside of the villagewide political arena is the struggle that takes place among kinsmen for the scarce resources in their possession. Disputes among kin are more likely to arise, however, because they share more resources in common, but this is not to the exclusion of other types of conflict.

In the majority of *jajmani* disputes, it is usually the client who is dissatisfied with the payment received for services rendered. At a wedding that took place in a Bhumihar's household, fierce haggling went on between one of the men and a Nai woman who demanded more than the sari and two rupees (in addition to food for three days) which were offered to her. I have seen similar types of arguments when a drummer was being paid for playing during the singing to celebrate the birth of a child, or when money was being paid to a Kahar client for her services during a Nai's marriage. There were huge fireworks on each occasion, resplendent with curses on both sides, but there seemed to be no hard feelings after an agreement was finally reached. Indeed, this is the expected sort of behavior.

Many disputes also took place over the amount of daily wage to be paid to field laborers by the farmers for whom they were working. This usually occurred during the harvest season, when each laborer is paid a specific, previously defined share of the crop being cut. Conflict then arose when the laborer felt that the farmer was cheating him of the rightful amount. These conflicts always involved Chamars and their primarily Bhumihar masters. Although often the disputes did not escalate beyond the parties concerned, they are representative of the class conflict that is part of the villagewide arena and will be discussed in a later chapter.

CONTAINMENT OF CONFLICT

From an analysis of the nature of political activities excluded from the villagewide arena, several points can be made. By far the most important fact in discerning the difference between this and the villagewide type of conflict over resources seems to be the matter of how wide the breach becomes and in what way the dispute is resolved. In most of the examples given, only the people immediately concerned were involved in settling the matter. When an external adjudicative party, such as the Pradhan, a local big man, or a *panchayat,* mediated the dispute, the event did become a matter of common knowledge. The arbitrators, however, no longer involved themselves in the matter after decisions were reached. They remained disinterested parties. In other words, no one tried to benefit by widening and expanding the original breach to involve other people in the conflict.

This type of disinterested involvement in settling a dispute is markedly different from what occurs in village factionalism. What identifies the latter are the contestants involved and the power they wield. Taking a case to one or the other of the village big men may embroil the affair in village *partibandi;* the decision to go to court rather than to a *panchayat* also moves the dispute into a wider arena. Similarly, every incident that occurs between opposing leaders, even so small a matter as two dogs fighting, is regarded as fuel for the fire, and a major confrontation results. In her study of the political activity of the Reddi and Kamma castes in South India, Elliott finds that disputes among the lower castes tend to escalate to the public arena of the village only when "they are adopted by the dominant caste leaders as their own"; this is because such conflicts do not initially affect the relative statuses of those holding power in the village (1970:134). As the following chapters will reveal, conflict escalates to a wider political arena when a powerful man exploits and manipulates a dispute to his own interests and advantage.

Although all of the case histories presented in this chapter are examples of political action insofar as they involve competition for things of value, they have the following characteristics in common which set them off from the villagewide conflict: (1) the main disputants, who were related to each other through either kin or *jajmani* ties, came into conflict on the specific issue involved and were otherwise on good terms with each other; (2) the conflict remained localized and only those who were involved parties concerned themselves in the matter; (3) the conflict was resolved by recourse to decisions by either the parties concerned or to external arbitration by the Pradhan, a local big man, a *panchayat,* or the courts. The major concern of each of these arbitrators was to settle the dispute as objectively as possible and end the matter there.

NOTES

1. I never learned why Daya remained unmarried. Given his personality and resourcefulness, however, it seems certain that the choice was his.

2. *Tilak* is one of the rituals that accompanies the long marriage ceremony. This ritual takes place some time before the actual marriage. The main portion consists of either the father or brother of the bride-to-be placing a *tilak* (auspicious mark) on the forehead of the boy to be married. Then he is presented with presents (clothes, jewelry, sweets, fruits) and gifts of money previously agreed upon.
3. In north India, hypergamy is practiced in the sense that a girl is married into a "better" (more prestigious or wealthy) family than her own.

CHAPTER 6
The Anatomy of Leadership: Big Men of Arunpur

Every village has a number of men who, because of their power and influence, make decisions affecting others in everyday affairs. Power and influence are based on a combination of caste, wealth, and personal qualities. The few men who have both the desire and means to compete actively in the village arena are the key to its political activity. In Arunpur, those known as "big men" figure in its factions and in the disputes between the landed and landless. They control whatever resources enter the village and make decisions regarding their distribution. Without such men, there would be neither faction rivalries nor any sort of cooperative venture. They are the chief organizers of the political arena and stamp it indelibly with their activities. This chapter will approach the subject of leadership in two ways; through a cultural definition based on terms villagers use and through an analysis of leaders in both the pre- and post-Independence eras.

CULTURAL CATEGORIES OF VILLAGE LEADERSHIP

The people of Arunpur speak of four different types of leaders: *neta, agua, rais,* and *bara admi.* Each of these terms refers to a cultural category perceived and verbalized by villagers that is more or less representative of the qualities of actual influential men. The first, *neta* ("leader"), is reserved for important men (or women) in one of the national political parties or in the government. For example, members of the State Legislative Assembly and National Parliament or national figures (such as Gandhi, Nehru, and those in power at present) may be referred to as *neta*. A local man who has a wide network of followers organized through his allegiance to a particular political party will also be called *neta* by his supporters.

Disappointment with the actions of politicians has given this term the second derogatory and often sarcastic meaning of a hypocrite, liar, or cheat. "A *neta*," I was also told, "is the man who defeats others [in elections] by wearing homespun cloth *[khadi]*. But this is only the sign of a leader. This type of leader *[neta]* is a gift of the British. Before that, no one heard of this kind [of leader]." A *neta* of this sort is generally regarded as acting without principles to achieve his goals and without the good of the people or the village at heart because he works for a particular political group. A *neta*'s first interest is to involve himself in power politics and win an election. He thinks in terms of his own caste and how he can win its support to advance himself and his party.

The second term, *agua*, is seldom used. It may be translated into English as "foremost" or "leader" and carries the connotation of the leader who is actively followed and respected and is foremost among his peers. The head of Arunpur under the British *(mukhiya)* and the present *pradhan* are sometimes referred to by this word. Members of different (non-Bhumihar and non-Brahman) castes would also speak of their caste leaders *(biradari agua)*, outstanding men chosen to be spokesmen and followed by all.

The word *agua* was also used, however, to identify the heads of the two different factions in the village. When we first asked villagers who belonged to these factions, we were told the names of certain men and that they were the faction *agua*. The men who are considered leaders *(agua)* in Arunpur are thus the heads of factions. Each has a core of followers and concerns himself with attempting to increase his network of supporters by offers of mutual gain. It is the leader as faction head who most commonly enters the political arena in village India. By contrast, when reference was made to the general status of these and other influential local men, they were called *bare admi,* big men. The faction head and other types of leaders may thus be regarded as the activization of big man status.

By far the most important terms for an influential man at the village level are those of *bara admi* and *rais*. Although the former is sometimes used as a cover term for both of these types, further questioning revealed that a distinction was made between the two in terms of style and quality of leadership. A *rais*, best translated as "noble man" or "aristocrat," is a man of affluence whose primary virtue is that of generosity.[1] Wealth is of great importance, since the key function of the *rais* is to help the poor without considering his own interests or ends. Should such a man's fortune decline and he become increasingly concerned with making ends meet, his *raisat* (nobleness) will correspondingly decline. I was often told that despite this pragmatic requirement, it is one's style of life and not one's money that makes a man *rais*. But this style, it must be noted, is very much that of lordly grandeur.

Raisat is inherited and reveals itself in the virtues, behavior, and character of a man. It is for this reason that a low-caste man—a Chamar, for example, or even a Kurmi—cannot be considered as such. The traditional virtues of a *rais* are not regarded as a part of their heritage.[2] The following qualities were most often mentioned as integral to this ideal type: gentility, traditional heritage, honesty, generosity, and wisdom.

The *rais* acts disinterestedly and without jealousy in helping the poor, even though it may involve some personal loss. In this way, he is often compared to a mango tree, which provides both shade and fruit, whereas a big man *(bara admi)* is like the palm, which is so high and lofty that it can provide neither. In return for his benevolence, the *rais* wins the trust, respect, and obedience of all around him. Of course, a "poor" *rais* may not always be obeyed because "money is sometimes the most important factor that makes one man listen to another." No one in Arunpur was considered a *rais*. From the one man in a neighboring village who was so named, I understand this to be a position of passive leadership whereby a man is more often requested for help and advice but does not pursue an active political role. This is notably different from the style of a big man *(bara admi)*, who is concerned solely with his own self-interest.

The chief quality of the big man is that he has wealth, although education is regarded by some as being a secondary feature. I was told:

> Suppose a man has only crude power—he may suppress two or three persons and may stop them, but others will oppose his views or secretly abuse him. But if he has power and intellect, then he will play such a game that no one will understand that he is doing wrong.

Intellect in a big man does not mean the ability to counsel wisely but rather to deceive others in order to further one's own ends. When he helps the poor, it is with the idea of some return, either to take what belongs to another or to utilize the advantages of the accumulated favors he has bestowed upon them. By being big, it is said, a man "collects the blood of the poor." Power and strength (in the sense of physical might) are a correlate to wealth and enable this type of influential person to exert pressure over men and control available resources. Although a big man can help one who pleases him, he can crush those who would rebuke or go against him. Others will always obey these men out of fear. A big man is considered to have the following qualities: wealth, influence, power, shrewdness, and physical strength. His behavior is characterized by feelings of self-interest and enmity.

While the presence of another aristocrat or big man does not lessen the influence of the aristocrat, the power of the *bara admi* is strongly affected if another seeks to share in it. The power that can be exercised in a village or local area is regarded as of a limited quantity, and a big man's sphere becomes smaller by the presence of other competitors. Because of this, there is tension even among members of a coalition faction; big men say that they, like two lions, cannot live together in the same forest. It is this factor that makes a man strive to crush others who would be his equals. The characteristic of competing for power and crushing others is regarded as typical of Bhumihars (or any other dominant caste, for that matter). A man of that caste, speaking about a deceased Bhumihar and his family in the village, said:

> Raja was really like a Kurmi because he was a hard-working and soft-hearted man. He gave money to anyone in the village, without interest. But now his family members are not respected because they try to be real Bhumihars—they want to rule over others by force—and to be a real Bhumihar means to be a cheat.

Caste does not ordinarily enter into the consideration of what makes a man big, for each caste can have its own such representatives. Caste, however, is an important determinant of big man status in the village-wide political arena. It is more likely that these big men will belong to the caste that is dominant in a village or in a local area. Bhumihars were in this position in Arunpur and the surrounding area, and it is not surprising that the village big men all came from this caste. It is also for this reason that, from the perspective of a lower-caste man (i.e., Kurmis and below), the term "big man" has two dimensions. At one level, all those of high caste, especially the Bhumihars, are regarded as big men. When pressed further about who are the truly powerful and influential men, however, the Kurmis and others would name specific people.

Compared to the aristocrat, the big man is seen as one who is actively involved in village politics, leading men and competing for control over them and their resources. The major distinction between these two cultural types seems to rest on their different motivations for helping others. It is possible for a big man to become an aristocrat if he takes on the qualities of the latter, although this must usually be carried on for several generations.

If the cultural definition of leadership, in terms of big man and aristocrat, is compared to the qualities villagers think a leader *should* have, an interesting discrimination results. To a sample of thirty-six literate men of all castes in Arunpur, we gave twelve cards on which different attributes were written. These were: speak well, settle disputes, introduce change, give benefits, help others, honesty, education, impartiality, family position, age, wealth, and caste. I had arrived at these specific attributes by analyzing the criteria that enter into culturally defined as well as actual leadership. They were requested to rank the attributes in the order of importance they should have for determining actual leaders. The most striking result of this poll was that those qualities considered most important for the aristocrat and big man, that is, helping others and the possession of wealth, were relegated to secondary positions. Honesty and education ranked highest. This can be regarded as an expression of dissatisfaction with the way in which leaders were serving the present needs of villagers in a changing environment.

The criterion of honesty is explained by the fact that there is an increased number of occasions for a leader to be dishonest, specifically in the distribution of new resources that either come to the village from outside or are only available from within. The villager's contact with the official world in which the bribe is "king" (discussed in Chapter 3) has greatly reinforced the desire for honesty. All too often, people have been promised and led to expect much, only to be sorely disappointed. Water from the government tubewell is not distributed fairly; the government Seed Store Inspector takes bribes and often gives bags of seed and fertilizer mixed with stones and dirt; officials in the police, court, and the Community Development administration all demand special favors before looking at a petition or deciding a case; the politicians promise one thing and then deliver nothing; and even money which comes into the village is greatly reduced after passing through many hands.

The desire for a leader to be educated as well as honest expresses the villagers' recognition of education as an important resource in itself and one that can lead to the acquisition of other resources (see also Srinivas 1959). A village can ill afford to elect one of its members as *pradhan* who has little or no education. How will such a man know how to articulate village needs and communicate with officials; how will he know his way around the labyrinth of obtaining permission to install a pumping set or applying for government funds and loans? The rapidly expanding world of the villagers requires the presence of educated middle men who can help others to cope with such changes. These people will be able to advise how to get what, when, and from whom. Similarly, education is necessary to farm more productively, and a village leader is one who can advise about and show the way in accepting agricultural innovations and a more prosperous lifestyle.

This last point, regarding the connection between education and agriculture, is something inferred from the behavior of the villagers and not from how the card attributes were ranked. The wise practice of agriculture (including giving aid and advice to others), as opposed to simple concern with gaining more money and property, is something that is respected and admired. Most of my sample, however, agreed that wealth alone was of no importance in determining good leadership, or ranked it low. Almost all also rejected caste as an attribute deserving consideration. But when asked which qualities most leaders of today actually possessed, my informants replied that wealth, dishonesty, and caste considerations were of primary importance (see also conclusions in the study by Oommen 1969).

Big Men in Arunpur before Independence (1947)

The cultural definition of leadership can be compared with a description of men who entered the political arena of Arunpur in the past and play such a role at present. The situation in the village before Independence (1947) was different than it is today. Although the account I have been able to draw is sketchy, since people told us different things about these big men depending upon their personal allegiances, the degree of repetition in their stories leads me to feel that the broad outlines of the picture can be presented.

The foremost leader in the village at that time was the British-appointed headman, and for two generations headmen came from the *khandan* of Little Pura Bhumihars (see Chart 2). We were told most about the last headman, Cheddinath Singh, who served for thirty years and was also the revenue collector for the zamindar. In addition, he became the head of the British *(amin) panchayat,* which included Arunpur and the surrounding villages. Backed by the special powers that the foreign government bestowed upon him, Cheddinath ruled the village effectively and would rarely let a dispute reach the courts. He decided all cases while sitting as the head of the village and local *panchayat.* Cheddinath also received large sums as bribes (as much as 100 to 200 rupees per day, it is said), especially when he decided who was the rightful owner of disputed property. Even his own descendants admit that he did many wrong things in these matters, but no one dared to oppose him because of his great power.

He lived in a grand style, surrounded by his admirers, and spent not less than 2,000 to 3,000 rupees per month. He visited prostitutes, was fond of young boys, and often held large parties with dancing girls at his house. A four-horse carriage took him to his varied destinations. For four to five years, Cheddinath continued in this manner and in the process spent not only all the money he received as bribes or "gifts" (his salary being negligible), but also started to sell part of his share of the joint family land. His father's brothers, who were still alive, decided that the only way to save the family fortune was by partition of the joint household.

Cheddinath's father, Chand Singh, had also been the headman and was reputed to have been of similar character. He, too, lived in a grand manner, and it was from a mixture of fear and awe that he was obeyed and respected. It is said that a Brahman committed suicide on Chand's doorstep after the latter had refused him a loan of money and insulted him.[3] A government official came to investigate the matter, but no one would testify against the powerful headman. Even today, however, this family scandal is remembered and whispered about.

The British learned of the unjust behavior of these two headmen but did nothing, since both remained obedient and loyal to the alien rulers. Cheddinath died in 1950, three years after his office was abolished. A few years later, the system of elected village officials through Local Self-Government *(panchayati raj)* was introduced throughout the State.

Another big man of the pre-Independence generation, and a contemporary of Cheddinath, was the zamindar Babu Sahib. Before 1950, he was a powerful figure and his office conferred high status upon him. Since the abolition of zamindari, however, his fortunes have declined considerably and he has retired completely from the village scene. Much of the land he had held previously was given as payment to servants instead of cash. That is how the Bhumihar who was his accountant and his Arunpur Nai received their lands. Land was not worth much at the time and Babu Sahib did not foresee that it would so increase in value. Today, he is left with only twenty *bigha*s within his walled compound.

The following story, emotionally recounted by the Arunpur Nai who still serves the ex-zamindar, reveals just how much Babu Sahib's position has declined.

> The days go by, but not all are equal. Early in the morning I was called by Babu Sahib. I went there and found him sitting under a tree looking depressed. I greeted him and asked why I was called. Babu Sahib apologetically said, "I am becoming poorer and I don't have money to please and pay all the men who lived with me and helped me in my good days. Now I request that all of them do not kill their time remaining with a poor one like me, who cannot give them food to eat." Then he also requested me to leave his service.
>
> I told him, "Babu Sahib, you are right. This type of thinking is good for a big man. I know that time is a changing process—a king of yesterday may be the beggar of tomorrow. But I don't care. I will not leave you, because you

have helped me in my bad days. I am yours. I got much from you and now I will render my services free of charge."

The descendants of the Bhumihar who founded the village some hundred and eighty years ago, Arun Singh, have also been highly esteemed (see Chart 1). Ganesh Singh, who died in 1931, was known for his learning and wealth and was a renowned astrologer. His younger brother and one of his grandsons, Ajay Singh, became active in the Independence Movement; the latter also founded Arunpur Intercollege. His son Amar was highly respected as well, although age and physical ailments now restrict his activities (see later).

Only one Kurmi was considered a leader and respected man in the village at that time. Sita Ram, the elder brother of the father of the two richest Kurmi men in Arunpur today, was named as influential in all the surrounding villages. He was an essential member of the village and local big men *panchayat*s, and it is said that even Bhumihars would go to him for advice and obey his decisions. The thirty *bigha*s of land he amassed, in addition to starting an iron and cycle repair shop in Banaras, made him quite wealthy. He died in 1948. Though his descendants are hard-

FIGURE 15. Present descendants of Arun Singh, the elders of the Pradhan's house, husk corn. Amar Singh is at the far right.

working and honest, they do not command the respect that he did. They are interested only in advancing the prosperity of their respective families.

The personalities of the heads of these two wealthy families, moreover, seem to be the biggest drawback to their assuming active leadership roles. Both are heavy drinkers, deferential to the upper castes, and spend most of their time at work in Banaras. Perhaps they feel that the prestige of bigness and the involvement in village quarrels are not worth the economic loss that might result. As long as they are able to go about their own business, they seem ready to show outward deference to the Bhumihars and leave them free in the political arena. The wealth and manpower that these two Kurmis command place them in an ideal position to assume the leadership and direction of their caste. Had their personalities been different, they could have proved a definite threat to the Bhumihars.

A number of points emerge from the information we have been able to gather about village leadership in the pre-Independence period that can be contrasted to the picture today. During this time, the major source of prestige lay in the status of specific castes and certain families and in the respect traditionally due to positions of authority. People belonging to influential families were primarily concerned with maintaining their social status and not solely with increasing material gains. Agriculture was not a capitalist venture, nor was there any involvement with outside business activities. In addition, the two major power figures in the village, the headman and the zamindar, were appointed by the British and were hereditary positions, while the men who served on the village *panchayat* were selected by villagers. The source of power for both the headman and the zamindar came from holding a position of authority which had the effective backing of an external source, the British Raj.

These positions of authority were also more effective in gaining compliance with their decisions than are the positions of the present-day big men. Pre-Independence leaders were said to be rarely opposed, and the headman settled village disputes so that few reached the courts. The result of this was that, although there were other influential men in the village, the positions of the headman and zamindar remained unquestioned, if not unchallenged. They provided the basis for a panvillage leadership that most obeyed. Others who would challenge them were to a large extent dependent upon the zamindar; the basis of their power lay in holding land, and land derived from the latter. Villagers maintain that the opposition which sometimes arose against these men was not of the same intensity as the present factional conflict which divides the village.[4]

While a change has taken place in the type of leadership at the village level, there is a certain amount of continuity between the leading families of the past and the present-day big men. Neither the descendants of Sita Ram Kurmi nor the only son of Cheddinath Singh have the personalities or interest to follow in their forebears' footsteps, but the big men of today still come from other families that were highly regarded in the past. A particular family may rise or fall on the wealth and prestige scale as the years go by, but this is a slow process rather than a sudden change. Money and prestige are hard to come by and take time to accumulate. The only family in the area which may be considered nouveau riche is that of Krishna Singh, the most powerful local big man from the neighboring village of Ramapur.

BIG MEN IN ARUNPUR TODAY

The men who are considered big in Arunpur at present are all Bhumihars concerned almost exlusively with advancing their own families' position through the acquisition of material goods, and whose major source of power and influence comes from their wealth.

The new formal, state-administered system of Local Self-Government through elected officials has replaced the old village head and his *panchayat*. Although one of the big men has become the elected head of the village (the *pradhan*), and this does add a certain amount of prestige and power to his present bigness, the other elected council members derive no influence from their position. The post is a meaningless honor since the statutory *panchayat* never meets.

Today, the villagers say, no one obeys anyone. All think themselves big. If some listen to the elected village head, it is because of the office, not the man. When I inquired about why one or two big men were obeyed in the past and now no one is obeyed by all, I was told:

> It is the age of money and labor, so every man is influential now and there is competition to see who is bigger and who is to be followed more. Formerly, men were interested in prestige—now all run after money. Previously, there was a direct exchange of goods [via *jajmani*], and now there is an indirect exchange based on money. So people now run after money.

The Pradhan put it this way:

> In the old days there were only one or two influential men in the village. Today there are more, but they don't command the same obedience. Today everyone considers himself big. Several families in the village own about equal amounts of land and money. If there was only one with more wealth than the rest, the situation would have been different. But now we think in terms of not letting another achieve more than us; so we compete to keep the

same distribution of wealth and influence in the village. It is [this way] because of education and wealth.

People in Arunpur said that this represents a great change in the administration of village affairs since Independence. They alternately give the reasons as the decline of morality *(dharma)* or the lack of fear for authority on the part of the people. They also cite the distrust of elected officials to account for the downgrading of authority. Because of this, disputes can no longer be settled within the village, and the slightest provocation results in a court case. It is also the explanation given for the fearless behavior of faction leaders, who will listen to no one in settling their grievances.

The political arena of this village has changed to the point where leadership or big man status is no longer inherent in any position but is now a commodity on the open market and something of value for which many can and do compete. Previously, the British-appointed headman was the acknowledged chief of the village. Today there is no such position of authority to which all will accede, and in its place have emerged new big men who are organized into two competing parties. Other people who could possibly be leaders, by virtue of their caste rank or education, do not enter into the picture. The Brahmans in Arunpur, for example, do not command respect and they have neither the knowledge of religious matters nor the prestige that usually adheres to this caste. The highly educated B.A.'s and M.A.'s in the village take no interest in community affairs. To some extent, their education and exposure to city life has alienated them from their neighbors. Those who live in the village and work at the Intercollege restrict their social intercourse to their fellow teachers and *pattidars*. Others who work outside come home only on annual leaves. Furthermore, in almost every case these educated men belong to one of the big village families and are themselves swept up by factional rivalry. At the same time, little opportunity is left for the younger, educated ones to assert themselves independently when one of the older men fills the position of family head.

The abolition of zamindari has also had several important effects that can be related to the rise to preeminence of the big men. While land reform did little in the way of conferring ownership on the landless (see Chapter 2), it did confirm the Bhumihars as absolute owners of land they previously held as fully secure tenants with fixed rents. Those large pre-Independence families that had enjoyed privileged relationships with the zamindar (i.e., the *khandan*s of the village founder and of the *mukhiya*) and had held a higher proportion of large landholdings now gained absolute control over most of the principal means of production in the village. The richer landlords were then able to purchase land that came onto the open market and to direct any surplus into economic activities, especially business. Their success as entrepreneurs has accelerated the economic disparities within the dominant caste, and these rich Bhumihars are able to expand their economic and political control of the village (see Wood 1973 for a similar case in Bihar).

There are five men in Arunpur whom the villagers and local people consistently named as big men and whom we observed to be the most powerful and active in making decisions that affected others. This was corroborated by noting to whose door outsiders, such as the Community Development Village Level Worker and election candidates, would consistently go. These big men came from Bhumihar families in the two main *puras*, and certain events over the years have resulted in the formation of alliances among them. The big men of Arunpur are, at the same time, considered the leaders of the two village factions.

The Pradhan of the village, Prasad Singh (age forty), is the head of one of the oldest and most respected families in the village that is descended from the founder (see Chart 1). He is considered one of the main leaders of one faction. Amar Singh (his father's elder brother) was also highly regarded, but his active participation in these matters greatly decreased in the past few years, due to advanced age and ill health. Still, he was greatly respected and his advice always sought. He died in 1970, after I left India.

The Pradhan comes not only from a distinguished line of ancestors, but his joint family household of forty-four members is the largest in the village. They own much land, have a half interest in a brick and truck business, and can boast of the many educated boys in their family. Their fortunes are on the rise. The Pradhan's *pattidars* also include people of some importance. One was the previous *pradhan* of the village for ten years and is the most knowledgeable man in the village in religious matters, village history, and local customs. Another relative was the chauffeur of a high State Congress Party leader for many years. The Pradhan can make use of a large number of contacts outside the village through his family and kin, ranging from the District Magistrate and Collector and members of the State Legislative Assembly to the Block Development Officer, the local Police Sub-Inspector, and a whole variety of minor government officials.

The Pradhan has a quiet, unassuming, yet firm manner and is respected by all, even members of the opposing faction. Before starting his brick and truck business with Krishna Singh of neighboring Ramapur village, he worked for ten years as a distributor for a textile cooperative in

FIGURE 16. The Pradhan.

Banaras. He says with great pride that he never accepted any bribes during that time, nor as village head will he now give bribes to officials to receive money from the government for village use. The Pradhan rarely has time to perform his official duties, however, and feels that it is best to refrain from attempting any pan-village program that might further enflame party rivalries. During his term of office, he received government aid to help two Chamars build their homes and to build a drinking well near his Nai's house.

Through partnership in the brick business and by his past friendship and close association with the family of Krishna Singh, the Pradhan can always call upon the latter for help in any factional dispute. Many villagers, and especially the opposition, think of Krishna as the real head of this faction. Krishna, the Pradhan, and another Bhumihar from Little Pura, Raj Kumar Singh, are three allied leaders.

Raj Kumar Singh (see Chart 2) is a thirty-two-year-old man who, though not the eldest male, is the head of his joint family of twenty-two members. He is outgoing, hard-working, and passed his high school examination from Arunpur Intercollege. His family connections are also prestigious, for he is a member of the *khandan* that originally populated

FIGURE 17. Raj Kumar Singh.

his *pura* and from which the village headmen came. His family is doing extremely well in agriculture and is in the process of building the largest brick house in the village from the profits they have made. Some 40,000 rupees have already been invested in this project, and another 20,000 will be needed to finish the job to their design and satisfaction.

Perhaps because he is the youngest and most educated of the village big men, Raj Kumar is cultivating a certain style of politeness and sophistication in manner and speech. Like the Pradhan, he is equally fluent in Hindi and Bhojpuri. One of his admirers, an elderly Brahman, stated:

> Raj Kumar is walking on the path of nobleness *[raisat]*, and all are watching him. He helps the poor. He brings seeds from the city and tells others about these new types. If people want to obtain some to sow themselves, he will even take them to the office in the city. He has prestige [and not his rivals] because when the Police Inspector comes he always stays with Raj Kumar.

The faction that opposes Raj Kumar and his allies in the village is led by Chandra Singh (age fifty-two), who belongs to the same *khandan* (see Chart 2). When Chandra was eight years of age, his father died, and as the eldest son he assumed full responsibility for his family. After struggling for several years to make farming a going concern, Chandra finally met with success. His next project seemed to be an involvement with the smuggling of *ganjha* from Nepal. It used to come to the nearby railroad station and other village stations, and from there distribution was made through his agents. Both the station master and one of the Pradhan's *pattidar*s used to make some share of the profits. It is said that money made in this way was used to finance the construction of his large house (the first brick house in the village) and later to start a lucrative cold storage business dealing with potatoes.

Many people in the village and surrounding area are indebted to Chandra for either money or grain, and many fear his power. In the past, he was known to be a vengeful person who would stop at nothing to achieve his goals. People often accused him of "making the village burn" with rivalries and disputes.

Today he has abandoned what even he refers to as his past "bad ways" and laments that he wasted so many years of his life in a mood of anger and revenge. Chandra now devotes most of his time to buying potatoes at a low price and reselling them after they have been kept in cold storage in Patna while the price rises. This business brings an annual profit of about 50,000 rupees. His youngest brother looks after the farm work at home, while a second brother is in the army and lives in Delhi. However, he still considers Krishna Singh of Ramapur to be his archenemy and would do anything to belittle or humble that man and his

FIGURE 18. Chandra Singh, drinking tea while campaigning for the Jan Sangh, is flanked by a Saranpur supporter on the left and Lalji Singh standing behind him.

family. Chandra also regards the Pradhan's family as foes because of their close association with Krishna and because of several disputes with them over land.

After his initial conflicts with the Pradhan's family, Chandra stopped going to their *pura,* where most of the people support his rivals. He visits only the house of his ally there, Narain Singh. Otherwise, Chandra's most frequent companion is a fellow Bhumihar from the nearby village of Saranpur. He said that this man used to be his bodyguard, and people say that he still performs this function.

Chandra was on guard whenever we met him and seemed to act stiffly, in an affected manner. His speaking tone was soft, but more like that of a man who is revealing some intimate or hidden information. On every occasion he would say that he wanted to compromise and forget the antagonisms of both parties. But, he would continue, the other side was not willing. Chandra always asked what his bad points were and what other people in the village thought of him. He was particularly concerned

FIGURE 19. Jai Singh, on the left, and his staunch Arunpur supporter campaign for the Jan Sangh in the constituency.

about the opinions of his rivals, Raj Kumar, Krishna Singh, and the Pradhan and his family men.[5]

The second man in this party is Jai Singh, a forty-four-year-old *pattidar* of Chandra. He is by far the most colorful man in the village. Tall and very fat, with a loud raucous voice full of good humor, he is easy to make fun of. At the same time, for our purposes he was the most open and best informant in the village. Whereas most of the other big men were to some extent always on their guard, Jai was fully relaxed and could say anything that came into his mind. Of course, he does this with others as well, and it has earned him the reputation of being a kind-natured, slightly foolish loudmouth, who is basically good but is being misled by the evil Chandra.

Jai compared himself with his ally:

Chandra is too formal a man. He is a polished man, but inside his heart is not so plain. Not only Chandra but many others are of his kind. I vomit anything I feel; I never hide it. I am like a sleeping lion and these polished men are snakelike and poisonous. I don't care if a man disturbs me a little, but if somebody goes beyond his limit, I can never excuse him.

Jai was also most fond of boasting how he could make big men small—the Police Sub-Inspector, the Intercollege Principal, or Krishna Singh—or how he had the most contacts with important men outside the village. He would repeat the fact many times that he was educating and also bearing the cost of marriage of his sister's son. He said his purpose in doing this was to show his fellow *khandan* members and the other villagers how wise and prosperous he was. He hoped they would respect him more for it.

Jai is considered a big man because he thinks himself big and, by his actions and participation in village affairs, has made others regard him as such. Compared to the other *bare admi,* however, his wealth appears negligible, and there are no other adult men in his household upon whom he can call for immediate support. Yet he is still the man most often called upon to participate in big men *panchayat*s and to settle the internal disputes of low castes, which might otherwise have to be heard in a caste *panchayat*. One reason for his popularity may be that, while other big men spend much time outside the village, Jai remains mostly at home and has more free time to devote to such activities. Jai's good nature has kept him close to all, while the others have lost contact with the people, have no interest in them, or feel that it is beneath their dignity to meddle in low-caste disputes unless it provides some advantage. In turn, villagers feel the distance between themselves and these big men and have lost faith in the latter and their concern for the well-being of the village.

Only Jai talks of doing good for Arunpur as a whole. The Pradhan has this desire as well but readily admits that he has no time for such a pursuit and says it is best to let factional enmity die down before attempting any new plan for village improvement. Jai's feeling may be seen from the following remarks:

> I have an idea, a map in my mind, that if I am *selected* [not elected] *pradhan* I will try to utilize all the help gotten from the government to uplift the Chamars and other poor people.
>
> I have the idea to send my son for higher education abroad, and I hope he will be the first man in the village who will help me in abolishing all the conservative ways and style of life, such as casteism and creedism.
>
> I try to help others, but because you know a man can do what he likes only if he has power, and power can be obtained by position, I became the *thokdar* [in charge of tubewell water distribution]. I had a good, big dream of making Arunpur a good village. . . . That is why I requested the engineer, who was originally fixing the [government] tubewell near Main Pura,

to fix it near Little Pura, so that I might succeed in utilizing my power in the impartial distribution of water to rich and poor, high and low castes. But after that I wasn't successful, and my dreams remained dreams.

Jai says that he contested the last election for *pradhan* in 1963 for the reasons stated and succeeded in becoming the person in charge of water distribution *(thokdar)* solely for his *pura* when the government tubewell was constructed in 1953. Even though the Pradhan is theoretically responsible for the distribution of water in the entire village, most low-caste people still go to Jai with their requests.

Like Chandra, Jai is not often seen in the streets of Main Pura. He occasionally sits there, in the hut of an old Brahman, but is most often at the house of the third member of their party, Narain Singh (age fifty-three). The latter belongs to a Main Pura Bhumihar *khandan* which settled in the village several generations after it had been founded and is not related to the village founder's descendants. His ancestors came to Arunpur about one hundred years ago and today most of his other *khandan* members live either in Banaras or in Calcutta. His closest *pattidar* in the village is related to him through a common ancestor of three generations ago.

Narain spends most of his time in Calcutta, where he owns a cloth shop and some property, and is rarely in Arunpur. His wife and children, however, remain in the village. A younger son, who is an M.A. from Banaras Hindu University, joins him in the city part of the year. The farming of the joint family land, shared by Narain and an elder brother, is looked after by one of this brother's sons. I met Narain on only half a dozen occasions. Though he has only a primary school education, his long residence in Calcutta has made him well versed in state and national politics and in the changes that are occurring in Indian society. He has hopes of highly educating all the boys in his family. He speaks with admiration of the way in which girls in Bengal study through high school, but believes that this would not suit life in the village. Like most of the other big men who talk of changes that they think are drastically needed (e.g., the end of casteism and Untouchability, education of women, higher age at marriage, and lessening or abolition of *purdah*), Narain is not willing to adopt any of these measures on his own. For the most part, he successfully keeps his life in Calcutta and in Arunpur separate. His influence in the village derives mainly from his wealth and alliance with Chandra Singh.

Chandra, Jai, and Narain on one hand, and the Pradhan and Raj Kumar on the other—these are the big men of Arunpur who, through a series of past events, have allied themselves into two opposing factions.

Before closing this section, however, something must be said about the influence of Krishna Singh in Arunpur and his involvement in the politics of this village. His activities show the way in which the village political arena is not tightly bound but expands to include the bonds of friendship or enmity across village lines, much as kin and economic relations do. Krishna has been closely associated with the Pradhan's family for many years, and it is this alliance which led him to intervene in Arunpur politics. He is one of the wealthiest men and the most powerful man in the area which extends to all the villages around Arunpur and even beyond.

Krishna is regarded as one of the more spectacular examples of a man who has greatly increased the wealth, power, and prestige of his family, all within the last thirty years. Born into a comparatively poor Bhumihar family sixty years ago, Krishna and his brothers have had to live with the rumor of a tainted family ancestry. Villagers constantly juxtapose this to Krishna's present wealth and influence to underline the fact that he is a *bara admi* par excellence; his origin and high-pressured tactics can never earn for him the *raisat* he so desires.

In his youth, Krishna was a primary school teacher and became friendly with Ajay Singh of the Pradhan's family, who was active in Gandhi's Non-Cooperation Movement. After leaving his teaching position to help

FIGURE 20. Brahman priests officiate at the ceremony to sanctify the land upon which Krishna Singh's house will be built. Krishna's two brothers are standing, while a third squats with his wife behind him.

raise the family's fortunes, Krishna continued his close relations with Ajay. The latter also increased the social standing and network of Krishna's connections by his friendship and help in arranging well-placed marriages for Krishna's family members. Finally, when Ajay had the idea of founding the Arunpur Intercollege, Krishna was also asked to join in the task and, by clever means, succeeded in wresting much of the land on which the Intercollege stands from some Kurmis. He was also able to convince others to donate money and worked through all the legal tangles of getting the school established, although it is said that he never gave a *pie* himself.

I was told that Krishna's father used to lend money and that often Krishna would take an unpaid debt to court and contrive to have the security (usually land) fall into his hands. By 1947, he had considerable property as well as experience in court matters. Others, especially those who had *rais*-like qualities and shied away from court dealings, would employ him to act on their behalf in legal affairs. As his father grew older, Krishna took his place in attending *panchayat* meetings. But whereas the father was known to act impartially to end disputes, the son sided with one party and sought to intensify the conflict.

A shrewd and capable man, Krishna has earned a reputation for knowledge of legal matters along with an ability to acquire another man's land and to cause divisions between men. In this way, he succeeded in breaking the unity of the Kurmis in his village who were numerically predominant and dared to oppose this Bhumihar. As a personal favor in return for Ajay's friendship, Krishna is also credited with creating two factions within the *khandan* of the last British *mukhiya* at a time when they were all united against the house of Amar Singh (Ajay's father) and the Pradhan. Krishna has also increased his family's property from 15 to 200 *bighas*.

During the year we were in Arunpur, a number of events occurred that adversely affected the social standing of Krishna's house and seemed to have brought what prestige he previously had to a new low. His son was involved in an embezzlement case with the government; his new house that was being built on another's property with stolen material was begun with inauspicious omens (the foundation was built on an old Muslim burial ground); he falsely accused a worker at the government Seed Store of stealing from his supplies; and the *gauna* of his daughter was marred by conflict and dissension (see Case 8).

Arunpur villagers speak of Krishna as a big man, but one to be especially feared rather than respected, who has gained his present power by the use of force and foul means. They do not have much to do with him personally. If they need help in some matter, they go to one of the leading Bhumihars in their own village. Krishna's link with Arunpur is through his close association with the Pradhan's family. He has done many favors for them, especially in the purchase of land, and they, in turn, have added some respect to his family's name. He wields influence not only because of his wealth, but also because of the positions he holds and the contacts he has. As Pradhan of his own village, *pramukh* of the Community Development Block, and an executive of the Intercollege, he has a wide, strong network of influential contacts that was crystallized in the machinery he set in motion to free his son in a court case. He is close to members of Parliament and the Legislative Assembly from his district and to State Congress Party leaders. He has influence with civil servants in the courts and the administrative service, and especially close contacts with the local police station, as well as elsewhere. His relatives are in positions of importance ranging from a younger brother who is the *sarpanch* of the statutory *nyaya panchayat* to an affine who is a judge.

Krishna is disliked and envied by most villagers and only grudgingly respected by a few other big men. His power and ability to crush others make people fear to cross him or utter a bad word against him. Even the Pradhan once severely reprimanded his younger brother when he learned that the brother had been speaking about Krishna to us. "You have to live in this place," the Pradhan said, "and so long as you do, do not speak against Krishna." Because his power is so great and he does not hesitate to use it to achieve his ends, Krishna is considered to be the real leader of the Pradhan and Raj Kumar faction. It is specifically he who has antagonized Chandra, Jai, and, to some extent, Narain. All three are extremely jealous of Krishna and the wealth and power he has acquired.

CULTURAL CATEGORIES AND VILLAGE LEADERS

While there was no one in Arunpur who was considered a *rais,* other powerful men did conform to the cultural definition denoted by *bara admi.* This type is best recognized as the village politician who takes an active role in local affairs and characterizes the influential men in Arunpur. Villagers clearly articulated that when a man becomes a *bara admi,* it is because of his ability to control other men and resources by sheer power, force, and deceit.

Big men remain big because of their power, irrespective of whether or not people like them or actually receive benefits from them. An individual cannot actively change the status of a big man simply by withholding support from him. I used the word "leader" to denote a person who is voluntarily followed and whose support is based on mutual aid, rather than on fear or domination. A person can make a deliberate choice among existing big men, often the heads of rival factions, in selecting whom they wish to follow and support. Thus, I use the word "leader" (in the sense of *agua*) in referring to Arunpur big men in their active role as faction heads with a specific following.

A number of characteristics are shared by all of the big men of Arunpur, despite their personality differences. Although their age varies greatly (thirty-two to fifty-three years), they look like other villagers in their outward appearances and manner, albeit somewhat more prosperous. None wears the Western clothing so popular with the younger generation. All wear the traditional *kurta* (long, loose shirt) and *dhoti* (long piece of material wound around the waist and between the legs). The most important ascribed qualities are that they belong to the dominant caste of Bhumihars and to families who had a recognized status in the past. Each of them is also the sole effective head and decision maker within his own family. In addition, all have achieved wealth by making agriculture a profitable venture and in some cases by involvement in outside business as well. To this extent, they are innovative in accepting new seeds, machines, and other changes which will increase their productive output. They have also fully accepted material betterment as one of the ideals (if not the major one) in their lives; bigger and better houses, better clothes, education, and marriages, and a general higher standard of living. Their families' wealth varies from the seventy-five *bigha*s of land and approximately 60,000 rupees annual income of the Pradhan to the twenty-four *bigha*s and 9,000 rupees received in produce sales by Jai Singh. Chandra, Raj Kumar, and Narain follow the Pradhan in land and other income, respectively.

Although their education varies from just primary school for the older ones to high school for the younger, all big men are convinced of the importance of education and are sending their sons on for higher studies. An added factor in the complex scene of rivalry and enmity between the two factions of big men is that one side is more conspicuously highly educated than the other. The Pradhan and Raj Kumar party has a greater number of intercollege students and graduates in their families. The leaders themselves are more educated than Chandra, Jai, and Narain. The consciousness of a feeling of inferiority in this respect has led to such comments as the following, made by a member of Narain's family and a close associate of Jai:

> I know that you [myself and assistant] are research scholars, but I know no less and I will make you dance. Look, don't think that Jai is a stupid one. He knows more than anybody knows in the village. For example, in *that* house [the Pradhan's] there are many B.A.'s and M.A.'s, and whenever

they come here to take water from the tubewell, Jai "teaches" them how to take water. So? He permits them to take water and tells them how many hours should go to whom.

In their capacity as faction leaders and brokers, the big men act as mediators between the villagers who need help and the officials or other outsiders with whom contact must be made. Each one, therefore, takes care to extend his network of contacts with important people outside the village through whatever ties he can utilize. Ultimately, a man's contacts are his most important assets, and it is they, not his wealth, which really buttress his position. Wealth, of course, is an invaluable means of gaining such contacts. To boast of how many influential people one knows and can depend upon for support is common. Big men also have an active concern and stake in controlling what goes on in the village, as well as a personality suited to accomplishing their ends.

None of these big men, however, is a leader in the sense of a person whose foremost concern is with the welfare of the village. Nor does any actively involve himself in social service or the promotion of the type of change that the Community Development program thinks village leaders should bring about. Although all recognize the need for change in society, they are not interested or willing to take on the role of the social innovator, except where personal advancement is concerned. These men are the leaders of factions that are concerned with organizing the competition for resources and power. The next chapter will deal explicitly with the organization of factional activity and discusses the ties that bind followers to their leaders.

NOTES

1. *Bhargarva's Dictionary* (1964) gives an additional gloss of "rich person."
2. A low-caste man with the qualities of a *rais* will be referred to as being "like a *rais*."
3. To insult and be involved in the death of a Brahman is regarded as a critically grave sin.
4. The position that a major aspect of leadership has changed is not to be mistaken for the view that there was no conflict in the past. Granted that enough ambiguity in the village authority structure and political system of pre-Independence India was present for considerable conflict to take place, other studies emphasize the unique roles of the *mukhiya* (village headman) and zamindar. Mayer points out that as the only villager with statutory authority until 1950, the *mukhiya* was the chief representative of the British Raj in the rural communities and a leader of the villagers in dealings with officials. He was not, however, a despot. His status was shared with other members of his caste and he had also to reckon with leaders of other castes (Mayer 1960:93ff; also Retzlaff 1962:1-26). Nor was the position universal (Miller 1975:114).

THE ANATOMY OF LEADERSHIP 133

The zamindar is pictured as having even greater power (Islam 1974; Rangnath 1967:269). A recent study by Chakravati (1975) documents, with fascinating case material, how the abolition of *jagir*s (large landholdings) and subsequent land reforms in 1954 provided the basis for the redistribution of power in a Rajasthani village. Information relating to the past histories of two Bengali villages also point to the preeminence of British-appointed leaders (Nicholas 1968a:253, 256–257).

While both positions ended abruptly with legislation leading to their demise, there was probably a more gradual reduction in their actual exercise of power. Mayer states that the years before Independence saw a gradual decrease in the influence and power of the *mukhiya* in Malwa region until he was reduced to the level of mediator (1960:96). Doubtless the position also depended upon the personalities involved. Headmen in Arunpur are presented as having been particularly strong individuals.

5. I have since learned that Chandra died in an unfortunate accident. I have also been told that *partibandi* has considerably abated following his demise.

CHAPTER 7
The Political Arena in Arunpur: Factions

The villagers' term for factionalism is *partibandi*. *Parti* is the English word which has become a part of their vocabulary ever since national political parties were introduced. On the local scene, the word refers to a cluster of people who have some common interest for a particular purpose, and who can stay together if it is to their advantage. It is a voluntary association of men. *Bandi* means a "prisoner" and comes from the verb *bandhana*, "to bind" or "to enslave." In conjunction with *parti*, *bandi* are the people who are bound together by a particular interest into the same party (see also Bailey 1968:281).

As Bailey notes, village people usually speak of "parties" or *partibandi* (his *doladoli*) in a derogatory sense (1969:51) and blame it for the increase of conflict since Independence and the ensuing disunity in community life. Narain Singh, one of the Bhumihar faction leaders in Arunpur, explained his opinion of the connection between the changes that have occurred since Independence and the increase in factional conflict.

> Since Independence, every man has been given individual freedom to rise as much as he wants. Thus every man has a competitive feeling and his own way and style of life. No one has faith in others. Every man is a separate faction now, and men of similar views are forming larger factions—though everyone is still conscious of his own self. This *partibandi* has given birth to selfishness in the village, and that is why sticks are brought out daily, men are being abused and trust is changing into distrust. No one looks for a *panchayat* decision, for they fear the partiality of the judges. . . . *Jajmani* relations are also losing their stability. See, Ashok the Nai was our *praja* [client] and has now left us. The Chamars have stopped taking away the dead animals.

Factions, however, are not permanent groups. Not only do the personnel shift according to the issue in dispute, but the multifaceted links between leaders and their individual supporters, rather than between these members, are primary. As is evident from the cases to be discussed in this chapter, factions are organized for conflict and engage solely in political activity.[1]

ORIGIN OF PARTIBANDI IN ARUNPUR

The history of the present factional alignments consists of a number of events which reveal different cleavages that have occurred in the past. The first of these relates to the original conflict that existed between the two groups of Bhumihars who live in separate *puras* in the village. From the beginning, when the first settlers came to Little Pura and allied themselves with the zamindar by becoming his revenue collectors, the descendants of Arun Singh opposed them. They were joined by most of the other Bhumihar *khandans* in Main Pura. The leading families in this earlier *pura* fought against the British during the Independence struggle, whereas the Little Pura group did not.

Crosscutting this original breach between these two *puras* was the cleavage that later developed within the single Bhumihar *khandan* of Little Pura. Cases 10 and 11 earlier outline disputes in which two men stood together against their other *pattidars*.

Amid this background of preexisting tensions, the year 1952 seems to mark a watershed in the history of Arunpur politics. India had gained Independence just five years earlier, and this was quickly followed by the Uttar Pradesh Abolition of Zamindari Act (1950). Cheddinath Singh, the last person to be headman and powerful on a panvillage basis, died in 1952. In the same year, the new system of Local Self-Government by elected councils *(panchayati raj)* was introduced, and one of the *pattidars* of the present Pradhan became village head. The Arunpur Intercollege was also founded at this time, by the joint efforts of one of the Pradhan's family members, Ajay Singh, the ex-zamindar Babu Sahib, and Krishna Singh of Ramapur. Ajay Singh died a few years later (1957) but his relationship with Krishna Singh had already been cemented into a firm alliance between the two families. *Partibandi* is said to have started in Arunpur due to this alliance and the indebtedness of Krishna to Ajay.

Relations between the Pradhan's family and the Little Pura Bhumihars deteriorated rapidly after Independence. The latter reportedly were responsible for a number of thefts that took place in Main Pura. Krishna Singh, already known for his ability to make two men fight and for his cleverness in legal matters, set out to divide the Little Pura Bhumihars and succeeded in doing so extremely well. The following dispute was mentioned by all the leaders of the two factions as being the cause célèbre for village *partibandi*.

Case 12: Competition between Little Pura Bhumihars
for a Kurmi's Land　　　　　　　　　　c. 1952–present

A Kurmi in Arunpur wanted his four *bighas* of land to be registered in the name of his only offspring, a daughter living in her husband's village. Chandra Singh helped the man remove the legal claim his mother's brother's son also had on the land. After this, Chandra began to cultivate the land for the Kurmi on a half-share basis.

Krishna Singh encouraged Raj Kumar Singh, a member of Chandra's *khandan* whose house bordered on the land, to attempt to gain control of that property. After the Kurmi died in his daughter's husband's home, Chandra got the woman to agree to sell him the land. Krishna heard of this only a day before the transfer was to be concluded. That night he went to the woman's village with the Pradhan and asked her to sell the property to them and Raj Kumar. They managed to get her to agree to this and the deed was duly registered in the District Office the next day. She, in turn, received 2,000 rupees as advance payment for the land.

When Chandra heard of this, he filed a suit against the three parties—Raj Kumar, the Pradhan, and Krishna. He then approached the Kurmi woman and offered her 4,000 rupees if she would testify in court that she was not the true daughter of the Kurmi man and that, indeed, he had no offspring. If she did this, Chandra said, then she could keep the money already received for the land from Krishna et al., plus the additional 4,000 rupees to be paid by him. The land would then come to Chandra by default as he had cultivated it for the true owner, the deceased Kurmi.

The woman appeared in the Banaras Lower Court and kept her statements vague. Ultimately, though, the case was decided in favor of Krishna and his friends. Chandra then appealed to the High Court in Allahabad to get the decision reversed. The Commissioner in charge of reviewing the case accepted a large bribe from Chandra and it became known that he would decide the case in his favor when it came up for review. Krishna, however, subsequently learned that this Commissioner would retire in two years and managed to keep the case inactive until then by giving occasional bribes to the appropriate officials. By the time we arrived in the field, Raj Kumar decided to take possession of the land by force. Although Chandra did not resist, he reactivated the case in the Banaras Lower Court.

Six months later, the court again decided in favor of the Pradhan, Raj Kumar, and Krishna. Twenty-four *bise* each of the land went to Raj

Kumar and to the Pradhan, and ten *bise* went to their supporters—a *pattidar* of Raj Kumar[2] and the Pradhan's barber. They attempted to give the remaining twelve *bise* to Chandra if he would agree to acquiesce to the decision. Chandra refused and was trying once again to appeal the case to the State High Court.

The most immediate result of this lengthy contest, started on the instigation of Krishna Singh, is that the unity of the Little Pura Bhumihars has been irrevocably breached since 1952. The thefts that this *khandan* had successfully carried out in Main Pura, especially in the Pradhan's house, were immediately stopped at the same time, for each rival would accuse the other of being the culprit. Thus, in order to return a favor to his old friends, Krishna created a situation whereby a single lawsuit brought about a state of permanent (i.e., until the present day) *partibandi* in Arunpur. Any disputes between two individuals in the village thereafter, especially over land, were almost inevitably caught up in this conflict. Because most villagers do not have the resources required to wage a successful contest over the possession of land (inevitably involving recourse to the courts), they must appeal to a big man for help. Once a disputant enlists the aid of a village big man aligned with a specific faction, a rival big man will enter the fray on the opposite side. In addition, if a villager should be opposed by a man or men belonging to one faction, he will ask a rival faction leader for help. Disputes are escalated to the field of factions in this way.

Leaders will help individuals by fighting or interceding with others on their behalf and by lending them money or other material aid while the dispute is being waged. In return, they will expect their supporters to remain loyal to them and to aid them as the occasion arises. If disputing individuals should belong to two separate factions in the same caste, then there is a direct connection between these factions within other castes and those of the Bhumihars. In Arunpur, this crosscutting of ties among different factions occurs in the case of the Chamars. They have opposing parties among themselves, and each member can appeal to the Bhumihar for whom he works for support.

Case 12 also makes clear that factional conflict is not solely concerned with material gains and that other considerations enter into a determination of the costs and rewards of an encounter. If material gain was the sole concern, then Chandra should have accepted the twelve *bise* offered as his share of the pie. But *partibandi* involves more than that; there is the cost (or reward) of pride, prestige, honor, family name, influence, and comparison with one's rival. Competition takes not only the form of abuses, fights, and court cases, but also generosity to friends and clients, donations to schools, giving and receiving more in marriage, and better education and jobs. The field of competition which factional activity encompasses becomes increasingly large.

Besides the greater frequency with which disputes are now escalated into the political arena via factionalism, the case points to the increasing preference for choosing the alternative of the law courts rather than the village or big man *panchayat*s to settle disputes between rival factions. As one villager put it, "When there is a quarrel in our *pura* or among our partymen, we settle it amongst ourselves, but if it involves the Little Pura people [and their ally Narain Singh], we take them to court." Cases that end up in the courtroom drag on for an indeterminate time, with the result that, as in the situation just cited, opposing parties remain so for the entire period. This adds a quality of permanency to village *partibandi* alignments (see also Nicholas 1965:30). At the same time, any other dispute arising between these parties while the initial conflict continues is immediately escalated to the villagewide political arena.

In 1965, there was a meeting of the statutory judicial *(nyaya) panchayat* that attempted to reach some compromise in this matter of the Kurmi's land. Ten *panchayat* members from seven villages around Arunpur were invited, and Krishna Singh represented Ramapur. Chandra Singh said that he presented the head of the meeting with a petition in which the following points were made:

> I have no trust in Krishna Singh, the present *panchayat* member, for the following reasons:
> 1. He has defrauded two Banaras merchants of their land.
> 2. He has played a bad role in Mohan Ram Chamar's land dispute [see Case 18 following].
> 3. He is partial to the Pradhan and his family.
> 4. In addition, he still owes me some crops dating from my grandfather's time which now comes to about 100,000 rupees with interest.

The meeting was adjourned after the petition was read. Krishna asked the head of the *panchayat* to call another meeting to protest Chandra's behavior. The head refused because, although he agreed that the petition was in poor taste, all the accusations were true. The key point of the issue was the public announcement made regarding Krishna's indebtedness to Chandra, which explains much of the latter's antagonism toward the former. Everyone knew of this fact already, but Chandra utilized the occasion to make a public announcement on the matter and thus strike at Krishna's "bigness" and prestige.

The situation arose some sixty years earlier, when Chandra's grandfather lent fifty maunds (4,000 pounds) of grain to Krishna's father, who never returned the amount. The interest on this debt now comes to some 100,000 rupees, as Chandra will not accept a return of only the basic loan. Krishna cannot and will not pay this amount and it remains a blot on his family's name. The opposition often taunt Krishna behind his back for being unable to perform the ancestor sacrifice performed every year at sacred Gaya in Bihar. One of the prerequisites for performing this sacrifice is for a man to announce, with a drum, that if anyone has given him or any of his ancestors something not yet returned that person must come and take it back. "Whenever Krishna will play his drum," Chandra says, "I will put my palm before him and say, 'Give it back.'"

Thus an outside man, Krishna Singh, has become inexorably tied up with Arunpur *partibandi* because of his previous relations and present closeness to the family of the Pradhan. In return for the respect and added prestige that Ajay Singh, the founder of Arunpur Intercollege, gave to Krishna's family, the latter helped him and his family to get land and to oppose Chandra on several other occasions. The initial cleavage between the Pradhan's *khandan* and that of Chandra Singh in Little Pura during the Independence struggle accounts for the origin of *partibandi* in Arunpur. Krishna came to the aid of the former and caused a split within Little Pura which also added Raj Kumar Singh to their coalition. Jai Singh followed his close *pattidar* Chandra (see Case 11, earlier) and subsequent developments added Narain Singh to this second faction.

Case 13: Narain Singh Cheats a Brahman of His Land
(before Case 12 Started) c. 1952

Narain Singh was a friend of Amar Singh (then the head of the Pradhan's family) as well as of the united (i.e., nonfactionalized) *khandan* of Little Pura Bhumihars. A Brahman who lived next to Narain agreed to sell him five *bigha*s of land for 1,700 rupees. Narain bought the land on the condition that he give 250 rupees in advance and the remaining money at the time that the transfer of ownership was registered. The Brahman accepted. After the deed of sale was registered, Narain said that he had left the money in the village and would give it to him there. The Brahman believed him, but upon reaching Arunpur was unable to get his money.

The Brahman owed 200 rupees to a Little Pura Bhumihar, Rampat Singh (uncle of Raj Kumar Singh). Someone, perhaps Amar Singh of Main Pura, told the latter that as the Brahman had sold all his land he was going to leave the village without repaying this debt. Rampat called the Brahman, who explained that he had received only 250 rupees and not the full amount. Rampat advised him to ask Narain once again for the remaining money. When the Brahman did, Narain replied: "I know that you are being backed by Rampat Singh. I have so many rupee notes that I can buy him, too." Word of this boast was carried back to Rampat, who became so angry that he bought the Brahman's land himself. Then he took some laborers to the fields and started to cut down the trees standing there.

When Narain heard of this, he ran to his friends and relations (some of whom were also related to Rampat) and asked them to help him fight against the Brahmans. People came with sticks, swords and spears and camped near Amar Singh's house. However, when they went to the "battlefield" and discovered that the opposing party were not the Brahmans but some of their own kinsmen, they refused to fight. The land remained in the hands of Rampat Singh.

Case 14: Amar Singh Backs a Brahman Against Narain Singh   c. 1958

Another young Brahman sold his land to Narain Singh under some sort of pressure or deceit. After this sale was registered in the court, Amar Singh (then head of the Pradhan's family) suggested to this Brahman that he file a suit against Narain saying that his land had been occupied by force. The Brahman's case was lost after three to four years, although Narain later gave him 1,100 rupees as compensation for the original low price.

In both of these cases, Narain Singh obtained land from the Brahmans and his supposed friends (Rampat Singh and Amar Singh) sought to create trouble. According to Narain's version of Case 13, Amar Singh acted as a middleman between himself and Rampat and Amar was the one who inflamed Rampat against Narain with false words. Narain also says that Amar was jealous of the fact that he (Narain) could be friendly with the Bhumihars of both *pura*s and hence sought to harm him. What finally seemed to ally Narain with Chandra Singh was Amar's position in Case 14, in which he tried to turn the Brahmans against Narain.

Every big man in the village seems to have his own sphere of influence, which extends over his neighbors in the immediate vicinity. One *khandan* of Brahmans lives just next to Narain Singh's house and they are often forced to sell their land to meet expenses. Narain feels that he can exercise the most pressure in obtaining their property at low prices because he lives the closest. Since he and Amar Singh have parted company, Narain accuses the latter of attempting to create obstacles in the way of such purchases.

The final breach between the two men occurred in 1966, and since that time relations between their entire families have been severed. This dispute concerned the ownership and rights to use a village pond and the land near it. A Kahar who has cultivated the pond to catch and sell fish for the past fifteen years claims that payment of rent on this property entitles him to enjoy complete possession of it. The Pradhan, of Amar Singh's house, says that the pond belongs to the village and this has forced the Kahar to file a court case against the Pradhan and the village *(gram sabha)*. There are some mango trees located on land just beside the disputed pond which are also considered to be part of the public property. Narain has claimed them as his own and has clashed with the Pradhan and his family and supporters. In the ensuing fight, Narain received several severe blows on his head. After that, however, he successfully claimed the mango trees as his own.

FACTIONS AND THE ORGANIZATION OF CONFLICT

The origins and subsequent development of *partibandi* in Arunpur reveal how the major families of Little Pura and Main Pura Bhumihars have become divided among themselves. Before going on to discuss how *partibandi* has extended to encompass other villagers in this conflict, I will present several additional case histories. They reveal two main points: (1) that factions are a convenient and suitable way to organize competition arising from conflict of interests, in the absence of any other group capable of mobilizing support for political action, and (2) that there is a tendency for all disputes between key faction members to escalate to this field in the political arena.

Case 15: The Village *Panchayat* Elections   c. 1952–1963

After zamindari and the office of the British-appointed headman were abolished in 1952, there was talk of the new statutory *panchayats* that were going to be introduced in the villages. Baljit Singh, a deeply religious man who is a *pattidar* of the present *pradhan,* called a meeting of the whole village at Narain Singh's house. *Partibandi* had not yet started and the last British headman was already dead. Baljit explained that the new *panchayats* were being created for the uplift of the villages, that there should be no disputes over the elections, and that a unanimous choice of a man who will do good for the community was preferred. Someone suggested his name and he became the first *pradhan.*

Baljit Singh served two terms in office. People say that he did nothing that was either good or controversial. The only material achievement of his term was the construction of a village council house *(panchayat bhavan)*. In 1963, elections were held a third time for a new *panchayat* and village head. *Partibandi* was deeply ingrained among the Bhumihars and, as Baljit Singh was not a favorite among the low castes, the faction of Amar Singh decided to support one of their family members, Prasad Singh. He was perhaps the only man respected by all for his honesty, humility, good nature, and kindness.

Chandra Singh knew that he was too unpopular in the village and asked his *pattidar* Jai Singh also to contest the election. Jai stood for the post, even knowing he would lose, because "Indian castes are like dogs. As one dog cannot tolerate the other's presence, in the same way a man cannot tolerate the rise of another caste-fellow. What big fools we are! I contested the election against Prasad Singh because he was a Bhumihar of the rival party. If he were a Kurmi, I would never have fought against him. It is a question of prestige. If I should lose to a Bhumihar, it does not make that much difference because he is my equal. But if I should lose to a Kurmi, it would be the question of my life and prestige."

The election for village *pradhan* was conducted by secret ballot. Jai lost by 150 votes. Both sides had already selected their *panchayat* member running mates by a show of hands. After Jai lost the election, all of his candidates withdrew their nominations. No meetings of this new statutory village *panchayat* have taken place, nor has the *panchayat* tax been collected. The present *pradhan* has made no attempt to activate the *panchayat* because of *partibandi* and it is a completely dormant institution in Arunpur.

Although villagers think that the idea of having local *panchayat*s initiate and work for the uplift of their community is basically a good idea, the almost universal opinion of the new government *panchayat* system is that it is not working. In a questionnaire I administered to all household heads, one of the questions was, "What has the *panchayat* done for the village?" A few people listed the building of the *panchayat* house and the paving of some village lanes. The majority replied, "Nothing but cause fights between us"; "It is no good because it produces selfishness"; or "Nothing but trouble us (or bother the poor)."

Panchayat elections are not viewed as the basic cause of *partibandi* in Arunpur. Villagers, however, believe that these elections intensify factional feelings, as voting for a man is interpreted as belonging to his party. Elections are held by secret ballot, but by discussions everyone knows just how others feel and will vote. One of the teachers at the Intercollege analyzed the situation as follows:

> Previously, people could remain neutral from both factions if they wanted to. But now, in an election, both parties put up their candidates and a vote

for one or the other means you are a member of that party. [Question: Why should this be so? If I vote for a candidate in an election, no one supposes I must follow him on every point. Isn't voting separate from other aspects of life?] Things are not separate like that here. The people are ignorant and illiterate and do not understand about the vote. Therefore, if they will vote for one party, the other side will say to them, "You did not vote for me. Therefore, it means you have joined the other side." And so, the association between voting and faction membership has grown up.

By far the most pointed criticism leveled against the new government *panchayats* strikes at their very basis, that is, the difficulty of obtaining a group of respected *panchayat* members through universal suffrage. On this point I quote directly at some length the incisive comments made by the *pradhan* of a neighboring village on the ill effects of voting for *panchayats*, although he presents a rather idealized picture of days gone by.

> In the old days there was one man in the village whom all selected as *pradhan,* because in the eyes of the villagers he was the only man worthy of this place. Those days, every man had a feeling of social and moral fear, which is lacking in these voters. The old system was a closed system; it checked disputes and allowed for more peace and harmony which has been destroyed since elections were introduced. There was no rush or crowd to occupy positions. But these days there is competition for any post in the village. Naturally, the most improper and unlikely man for that place plays all types of games in order to win. Such games and activities are immoral ones. It is the election system which introduces malpractices and evil ways. Because everyone has an equal right to contest for a position, but because all are not equally qualified and able, so there is more opportunity for the wrong man to win. . . . All these factional fights and court cases are nothing but the manifestations of this conflict. I openly say that voting must be finished, but the government is not going to do this because it must eat away the humanity and peace of the nation. . . . What a strange thing that equal wise men elect those of unequal qualities. It usually happens that the man who is not wise gets the position and the wise man is thrown away. Even wise men become unwise at the time of election because they are carried away by feeling of prestige. To be elected or to elect a particular man becomes a question of prestige. Suppose a big man suggests that his dependents vote a certain way and they don't. Then the big man is no longer wise and human. He takes a stick in his hand to break his dependents' heads. . . . Often many of the fights in the village *panchayat* are a result of what has happened two years back. Even I feel uncontrollable anger if someone disobeys me.

Elections for the *pradhan* and *panchayat* members were to be held again in April or May of 1969, but they were indefinitely postponed. There was much talk, however, of the forthcoming contest and both factions were planning different strategies to capture the prize. Chandra Singh and his party members were determined to back Jai Singh again if the present *pradhan,* Prasad Singh, were to stand for reelection. If Raj Kumar Singh's uncle (Rampat) were to be nominated instead of Prasad, then they would back one of their Chamar supporters. The major concern of Chandra and his allies was to put down the Pradhan and his party. Therefore, they were carefully deciding whom to back and said that "one must know whom to favor in order to create a breach in someone else's group."

The Pradhan seemed willing to stand again although he knows that he will never have the time to do anything good while in office. But he is the only one who has the respect and support of so many villagers and it is likely that his family and party men are urging him to contest again. An alternative for his party would be to back some lower-caste man, yet there is a reluctance on their part to lose whatever prestige and power comes from being the backers of a *pradhan.*

The only other person who has openly made known his desire to be the next *pradhan* is a Kurmi man of little means who has passed the eighth grade and whose son has completed his B.A. Interestingly enough, both factions seem reluctant to back a Kurmi who is not obligated to either party. It would seem that their willingness to support a Chamar means that the latter can be easily manipulated and would pose no threat to the Bhumihars, whereas a Kurmi *pradhan* might not prove so malleable.

Villagers maintain that these elections are responsible for the intensification of party rivalry (see also Weiner 1965b). It seems more likely, however, that the intensity of *partibandi* is associated with the general increase of competition for new resources. Elections are, in a sense, a new resource and thus become encompassed by factional strife. One would expect that in the absence of political parties or any other politically active corporate group in the village, factions would be the most likely candidates to organize the competition for, say, an electoral contest. The leaders and their followers are already bound together in the hope of pursuing mutual self-interest and can extend their cooperation to include the struggle for any new resources which may enter the political arena.

THE DYNAMICS OF FACTIONS: ESCALATION OF CONFLICT
TO THE POLITICAL ARENA

Factions and factional rivalry also seem to expand this arena to include disputes that would normally not be considered as involving scarce goods. This escalation of otherwise "nonpolitical" events by factions seems to be inherent in Arunpur *partibandi.* If the personnel involved in such disputes are key members in a coalition (i.e., a leader or any of his family members) who can easily command the support of others in a crisis, then this type of escalation is most likely to occur. The following two incidents occurred while I was in the field and illustrate this point.

Case 16: The Molested Boy   1969

Rama Singh, one of the young (age twenty) *pattidars* of the Pradhan, was known to be mischievous, disrespectful, and often badly behaved. More particularly, he had instigated and was carrying on an affair with a fourteen-year-old boy, Mohan, from Narain Singh's house. Both families knew of this, but as it was a matter of prestige for all concerned, nothing was said and it was hoped that the situation would soon come to an end. Rama's father had even beaten his son many times in an attempt to stop such behavior, but to no avail. He continued to intimidate and molest the younger boy.

One day, after school, Rama attacked Mohan, who fought back and managed to escape to a shop on the main road. Rama caught him there and afterward Mohan came home weeping. One of the men of Narain Singh's house went to speak with Rama's father, while Narain's son went to the shop to find out what had really happened. When he arrived, he found Rama was still there and was threatening a young boy to stop him from telling about anything he had seen. Narain's son said, "You would hit the one who tells the truth?" Rama abused him and in return was beaten. Narain's son later realized that he had acted in haste but was too angered to restrain himself at the time.

That evening, Rama's father came to Narain Singh's house and called for the latter's son to come out. A *pattidar* of Rama's was also with him and advised him to return home since his son was a good-for-nothing and was probably in the wrong. When other *pattidars* later came from Rama's house and abused them, Narain's son went around the village calling many of his supporters who came to his house and stayed there with weapons (sticks, spears, sword, and so on). Finally, a *pattidar* of Narain, known to be neutral in the factional rivalries and, in fact, quite friendly with the Pradhan's family, was sent as the mediator to settle the dispute calmly.

Case 17: The Dog Fight   1968

One morning, two dogs of Chandra Singh were fighting with Raj Kumar Singh's dog and badly mauled it. One of Raj Kumar's younger brothers, hearing his dog's cries, came and found Chandra's son just looking on (some versions say that he was also pelting Raj Kumar's dog with stones). At this, he started to abuse the young boy for not stopping the fighting dogs.

In the evening, Chandra and his brother returned from the courts in Banaras and eventually learned what happened. At this point there are two different versions of the story. Chandra states: "Without thinking, at about 11 p.m., I started abusing Raj Kumar from my doorstep. I soon realized that this was a mistake but it was too late to stop. Raj Kumar and others had already run to my house—they were eight and we were two [Chandra and his brother]. Jai Singh and Dharma Singh [a *pattidar* of Raj Kumar who supports Chandra] soon reached here and requested us not to fight, for if anyone is killed it will be from the same *khandan*. But Raj Kumar would not listen and took an oath to kill me the next morning. Now it became necessary for me to call some relatives to save my life. Twelve men from my mother's brother's village came and were armed, but nothing happened and so they returned. I also sent my supporters to request Raj Kumar to compromise, but he refused saying that he would 'meet me on the battlefield.'"

Raj Kumar's version differs only in that he says that Chandra had first called the men from his mother's brother's village and only after that did he dare to abuse them. Then Raj Kumar and his men ran to Chandra's door to fight. When one of Raj Kumar's brothers was about to crack his stick over Chandra's head, Jai Singh and Dharma Singh came and intervened in the fight. Neither was willing to take sides with Chandra on this occasion. Raj Kumar, however, was so provoked that he vowed to kill Chandra and by 2:30 A.M. sent a message to the Pradhan for help. Many of his supporters assembled. The Pradhan and other elders of the village were also called to Little Pura for advice. Still, Raj Kumar would not listen. Instead he asked his men to form small groups and to approach the railroad station from different directions through the fields to catch hold of Chandra's men hiding there. But the latter, apparently, had already left.

The next morning, an informal *panchayat* was held of both factions at Raj Kumar's house which settled nothing. Eventually the trouble died down.

These two cases are good illustrations of the patterned sequence of phases which occur in encounters between factions. Such encounters are representative of a more general type of conflict, the "social drama," where marked disturbances in social life serve to make visible the existing power alignments (see Turner 1957:91–92, 131; also Swartz et al. 1966:32ff). The processual form of the "social drama," applied to these two cases, clearly reveals the dynamics of factional conflict.

First, there occurs an initial breach of a norm governing relations between persons or groups interacting within the same system of social relations. This would be the actual situations which began cases 16 and 17: the fighting dogs and subsequent exchange of harsh words between Chandra's son and Raj Kumar's brother, and the misbehavior of Rama with Mohan.

The initial breach is followed by a phase of mounting crises during which, unless the conflict can be quickly sealed off within a limited area of social interaction, there is a tendency for the breach to widen and extend until it becomes coextensive with some dominant cleavage in the widest set of relevant social relations to which the conflicting parties belong. Following the initial crises in these two situations, both sides claimed that they attempted to seal off the matter. In Case 17, Raj Kumar said that his younger brother mentioned nothing about the morning events, fearing it would only worsen matters, and that it was not until Chandra started hurling abuses that he learned of what had occurred. Chandra also said that neither his son nor anyone in the house wanted to tell him of the dispute. It was only after noticing how morose his son looked that Chandra persisted in his questions and was reluctantly told of what had happened by the women of his house.

Despite this, the conflict was not sealed off. In fact, a major quality of factional disputes which I observed in Arunpur is this very inability of people to seal off any conflict involving key party personnel. Such conflict automatically escalates and cannot be settled in any other way. Faction leaders appeal to other followers for support, and the breach widens until it becomes coterminous with faction membership. Hence, men came running from Chandra's mother's brother's village and Raj Kumar called upon his supporters from Main Pura. The breach had widened to its largest boundary. In Case 16, Narain's son reacted similarly to the threat by calling upon his men in the village to keep an armed watch at his home.

Next, redressive actions are speedily brought into operation by leading members of the relevant social group. The mediator in the Rama-Mohan case was a *pattidar* of one faction who was also friendly with the other faction. The fight between Chandra and Raj Kumar became more serious. Many more people were involved in attempting to settle the dispute and an informal *panchayat* was called on the spot. Although nothing came of the meeting, the interference of members of both factions did succeed in averting the immediate threat of bloodshed, and the matter ended after that.

Finally, there is a reintegration of parties to the dispute or a recognition of the schism. Needless to say, the parties concerned were not reintegrated after the performance of these social dramas. Indeed, it may well be that in the case of factional conflict these dramas serve the purpose of enacting a ritual of integration to symbolize the tie of each leader and his followers in opposition to those of the other faction.

RECRUITMENT OF PARTIBANDI PERSONNEL

It now remains to consider the way in which leaders recruit members to their factions. The following three cases illustrate this process.

Case 18: Krishna Singh and Amar Singh Cheat a
Chamar of His Land   c. 1953

Mohan Ram Chamar bought some land from the zamindar Babu Sahib, during the days of British rule, which had been previously cultivated by Amar Singh's family. Krishna Singh of Ramapur agreed to come as a witness for Mohan Ram in the transfer of the deed. Several years later, when Amar Singh (through his son Ajay) became close to Krishna, the latter advised him to try to retrieve this land. One day, Krishna and Amar summoned the Chamar to a *panchayat*. Krishna turned a false witness and said that the Chamar's land belonged to Amar Singh and that if the former wanted to keep the two *bigha*s, he would have to pay for it.

In the meeting, Mohan Ram showed the receipt of the original sale to the two Bhumihars, who took it and tore it up. Mohan then appealed to Chandra Singh, for whom he used to work. Chandra (and Jai Singh) helped the Chamar; they filed a suit against Amar and Krishna and after four years Mohan won back his land.

Case 19: Chandra Singh Helps a Kurmi Fight Amar
Singh's Family   1958–1962

Bhaggu Ram, a Kurmi, had some land which Amar Singh and Raj Kumar's uncle (Rampat Singh) claimed as their own. The Kurmi had planted some potatoes there and one evening Amar and his partymen uprooted them and took them all to their houses. Some of Chandra Singh's and Narain Singh's potatoes in adjacent fields were also carried off in the process. As Chandra did not want to go openly against other Bhumihars, he requested Bhaggu Ram to take action against Amar and the others. Bhaggu refused.

After some two or three months, the entire store of the Kurmi's potato crop was burned. He became angry and ran to Chandra to ask his help in taking revenge. At first Chandra refused, because Bhaggu had not helped him earlier, but eventually he agreed to help. Chandra gave the Kurmi three *bigha*s of his own land to cultivate rent free for three years, so that the man could sustain his family and fight a court case against Amar Singh. Eventually the Kurmi won back his land.

Case 20: Raj Kumar Singh Helps a Brahman and Some
Chamars Fight against Jai Singh   1966

Jai Singh was appointed to be in charge of the distribution of tubewell water *(thokdar)*. It is said that he started abusing his power and giving water only to those he liked. He also asked farmers to bring him meat, by way of bribery, if they wanted to receive water quicker. One day, one of the Brahman men abused him: "Oh yes, I will supply the meat of a he-goat's genital if you give me water quickly." Jai became angered, abused the Brahman and threatened to cut off his water altogether.

The Brahman learned that Jai was having an affair with a Chamar girl. He informed the Chamars, who caught Jai in the act. Then, backed by the Brahman and with the help of Raj Kumar Singh and men from the Pradhan's house (and his supporters), the Chamars gave Jai a severe beating. The latter filed a suit in court against the Brahman and several others, and they received jail sentences of some three to six years. The case was subsequently appealed to the High Court in Allahabad and the earlier decision was reversed.

In the process the Brahman spent about 3,000 rupees. Krishna Singh and his younger brother, together with Raj Kumar, helped to fight the case. The former gave 600 rupees and the latter gave 50 rupees. To this day the Brahman speaks of Raj Kumar Singh as his "leader," the *rais*, and the only one he will obey and follow.

As can be seen from the foregoing three cases, personnel of different factions are recruited primarily on the basis of indebtedness to a leader for aid rendered in the past. If a poor man is confronted in an encounter by one of the village big men, it is impossible for him to win the contest by pitting his meager resources against those at the command of the big man. This simple economic fact forms the major tie between a leader and his supporters. I usually found that the more severe the dispute and the greater the help received, the closer the tie between the two men. Since any man may come into conflict with another and request help from a third party, there are no set structural principles (e.g., kin or caste ties, indebtedness, patron-client ties, and so on) exclusively involved. All are potential lines of support and a faction leader seeks to mobilize any of the possible connections he may have.

One of the most direct ways to gain supporters is to activate kinship links. The Pradhan's family can count on their *pattidars*, as well as a neighboring *khandan* of unrelated Bhumihars, for support in any fight against Jai Singh, Chandra Singh, or Narain Singh. Narain is not so lucky in this way, for his sole *pattidar* in the village is known not only to be neutral in factional conflicts, but perhaps even to be closer to the Pradhan's family. The Little Pura *khandan* of Bhumihars is, of course, split. About three years ago, one of Raj Kumar's *pattidars* switched his allegiance and is now firmly in Chandra's party. In return, Chandra has helped him to start in the business of storing and selling potatoes.

The Bhumihars in Main Pura who are unrelated to either the Pradhan's or Narain Singh's family have allied themselves with different faction leaders. The elderly "outcaste" Bhumihar lives close to Narain and supports him. It appears that the Pradhan's family men, especially the elders, are more strict in applying sanctions for infractions of caste rules, and perhaps they feel that intimacy with an "outcaste" is not befitting their prestige. In turn, the old Bhumihar is probably more relaxed with easygoing Narain.

A second Bhumihar, living in his wife's village, also sits more often at Narain's place. He may have felt somewhat rejected by the close-knit atmosphere of the Pradhan's family, *pattidars*, and immediate neighbors. Narain Singh would also be more likely to welcome an outsider because he lacks the manpower the Pradhan can command.

A third Bhumihar, who is distantly related to the Pradhan (and hence in his *khandan*), was definitely allied with Narain and Chandra Singh. I could never find out the reasons for this, for he would not speak with me. On the rare occasions he met my assistant, we thought it unwise to bring up the topic. Finally, there are three Bhumihar brothers known as the Kolhas (see note 1, Chapter 9), disparagingly referred to as adroit fence-sitters who shifted their loyalties easily.

The links between the Bhumihars and the lower castes are for the most part even more tenuous. Some clients (*prajas*) feel a moral obligation to support their patrons (*jajmans*) and also realize that not to do so might be risking one source of income. Other castes, however—Kurmi, Lohar, Teli, Kahar, Kohar, and so on—are by and large independent of such disputes. The Chamars must usually follow the master who provides them with food and land in return for labor, and to whom they are also indebted.

The Untouchables and other extremely poor villagers cannot afford to remain neutral in *partibandi,* nor do the leaders permit them to remain

THE POLITICAL ARENA: FACTIONS

so. An explicit case in point is small Noniya *pura*, comprising mainly Noniyas, Kahars, Dharkars, and Musahars (the latter two Untouchable castes). Here is what an old Dharkar told us about how the poor are pressured in conflicts between the Bhumihars. The added complexity in this case is that Noniya *pura* is tied closely to Little Pura as a whole and thus crosscuts the feuds within it:

> I am so indebted to them [Little Pura Bhumihars] that though I may change my mind, I cannot change my heart. Oh, we are bound to do whatever they like or they will beat us; they will not let us go out of our houses because their lands are around the village [i.e., our *pura*]. The paths run through their fields. Their eyes are always on us as we are nearest to their *pura*.
>
> [Question: Why then don't you join Amar Singh's party? They are also Bhumihars who are equal in strength and power.] Suppose there are two suns of the same intensity and they are emitting their rays equally, but the distances are different. One is far and one is nearer. Then the intensity of the one nearer is a little more and the thing which is nearer to it will be warmer. In the same way, the people of Little Pura are nearer to us so they influence us more, even though those of the other *pura* are equal in strength. Suppose today we give our promise to those in Main Pura, but then we change our minds. How will they know? But the most secret activities of ours are open to those of Little Pura, so we cannot change from them. We must follow and obey them.
>
> The third point is because they have given us money and helped us in our bad days. Chandra Singh, Jai Singh, and Rampat Singh have given me money which equals 300 rupees. So I am bound to listen to them. And I hope they will help me until I die. Then they will give the clothes in which the dead body is carried away. So to the man who can help us from birth until death—even if he is cruel in other aspects—we are morally bound and must behave as he wants. They are rich because they have wealth, power, and means. They are everything to us because we have none of these things.

Although a man may make use of many different connections to bind another man to him, the follower does not always respond in the desired way. There are two opposing values put on the nature of the leader-follower tie: loyalty or self-interest. A leader who gives help will not forget when he is later deserted. Jai Singh once yelled at the Chamar of Case 18 for not supporting him in the village elections:

> When the bamboo stake was pushed up your buttocks you didn't dare to open your mouth then, did you? I am the man who helped you. But now you never think that I will make a suitable *pradhan* but have the idea of bringing forth a new man from the Chamar *pura*.

Similarly, he shouted at a Kurmi:

You say kind things about me to my face but you beat me on my head with shoes.[3] [Followed by a string of abuses] . . . You are dishonest. I sold you half a *bigha* of land near your house for 1,500 rupees because I had promised to do so, even though your own *pattidar* later came and offered me double that amount. But in the *panchayat* election you turned against me and voted for Prasad Singh. Not one man in your house voted for me. Whom should I trust?

One of the men whom the Pradhan can implicitly trust is a village Nai. Arunpur is this barber's mother's brother's village. Some years ago, the land that he still owned in his natal village was forcibly occupied by some men. The Pradhan and Krishna Singh helped the Nai regain possession of the land. "Therefore," he says, "if the Pradhan tells me to go out and stand in the mud, I will do so." He is known to be a blind follower, ready to beat or even kill (it is said) for his leader. He received ten *bise* of land as a reward for his support of the Pradhan's party in Case 12. The Nai not only provides physical force, when necessary, but often attends to matters in the court when the Pradhan and Raj Kumar are otherwise engaged.

Opposed to the loyal follower is the supporter who is known as a "contract witness," the person who joins a faction only because it best serves his own self-interest at that particular time. A number of people in the village are known to play this game and some of them have the reputation of being characterless men, willing to do anything to take advantage of a situation. Others, like the wealthy Kurmi berated by Jai (cited previously), try to tread a middle course between the opposing Bhumihars so that they will not suffer any disadvantage, but this is a difficult task. Men who are not that deeply involved in factional hostilities, but who may become involved on occasion, do not display the same deep-rooted enmity that key faction personnel do. The fact that the son of an elderly Brahman had been involved in a court case with Jai only two years before did not stop him from having friendly relations with the latter. The Brahman also claims Raj Kumar as his leader because he had helped in that case against Jai. Other villagers reacted against the idea of being friendly with both sides, however, and cited the Brahman as an example of a man who switches loyalties easily.

Some *pattidars* of the feuding Bhumihars also alternate between the two parties or else make an unsuccessful attempt to remain neutral. But a neutral person suffers most when he needs something from one side and is then accused of trying secretly to play both sides at once. If such an individual, for example, asks Jai for tubewell water, he is told, "Why don't you ask your party man, the Pradhan? Why ask me?" The other faction will similarly rebuke the man. No neutral man can benefit or even survive in Arunpur politics unless he is strong enough to stand against both factions and is not dependent upon either for help. When someone fights against such a neutral man, no one else will come to his rescue.

Just as the faction leaders often complained about certain villagers for their shifting loyalties, so a leader himself is often accused of not being fair to his followers. One of the notorious "contract witnesses" of the village explained his unusual logic as follows:

> This style of switching from one party to another was introduced by the big leaders *[netas]* of the country like Nehru and Gandhi. They themselves had introduced factionalism—they divided the nation into two parts, as well as 400 million of the public divided themselves into two parts. Now, even a child knows what factions are and a leader never cares for unity. He always tries to bring some men into his party to oppose someone else. In the old days, even an old man of fifty years did not know about all these things. They were gentle, but now the word "gentle" has become outdated. I never trust men like Amar Singh or Chandra Singh because they are too selfish. They never care for their party members but rather they care for themselves.
>
> As a big and fat buffalo never cares for the wooden stake that binds him and breaks it into pieces whenever he likes in order to move to greener pastures, this is the same situation with the big men. They are leaders, but when the time comes and they get a good opportunity, they will push us back and run to the spot [the advantage]. But they are not the only clever ones. We are cleverer than they; we can "cut their noses." And because I also believe in hurting others, I can beat them if they [the leaders] think themselves too big and too wise. I am their teacher and I always try to find out where there is more advantage. That is the place I like best. But above all—I believe in love. If there is a little loss, I can withstand it if there is more love.

In addition to the tension that exists between a leader and his followers, there is also strain among the big men who have joined together to become leaders of coalition factions. This is most true of the alliance between the Pradhan's family and Krishna Singh's, which came to a crisis while I was in Arunpur. At that time, Krishna's eldest son, a building contractor, had attempted to embezzle state government materials on one of his contracts. Since his business was tied up with his father's brick and truck business, in which the Pradhan is a copartner, the latter was also involved in this matter. The Pradhan's family was greatly angered by their innocent involvement in something that was going to bring a blot on their partner's name as well as soil their own prestige. A man close to both leaders commented:

> Both Amar Singh's [the Pradhan's uncle] and Krishna's families have gotten on well so far . . . and have done good turns for each other. Amar's son, Ajay Singh, by sitting with Krishna, gave him a status which his family

never had. Krishna, in turn, helped them to acquire a lot of land which they had lost previously in their bad days. This was the basis of their relationship. But now it [the mutual aid] is no longer needed. Krishna has carved out a name for himself, and Amar has enough land and money to buy more. They don't need each other so badly now.

The Pradhan and his family have come to feel that perhaps it is time to exclude Krishna from the alliance, for he is no longer needed (i.e., necessary to be a winning coalition), and the advantages gained were being diluted by the costs of maintaining the relationship. This is particularly true because the Pradhan and his family have increasingly come to believe that their weight in the alliance is equal to that of Krishna's while the rewards they are receiving are much less.

Neither is there much social intercourse among the family members of the Pradhan's house and those of Raj Kumar. They do not have *kaccha* (boiled food) eating relations with each other. On one occasion, when the Pradhan's younger brother came to eat at a feast in Raj Kumar's house at our insistence, the women did not even know who he was. He said it was the first time he had ever eaten there!

There is competition between Chandra Singh and Jai Singh over who will be known as the real leader of the party and the bigger man. Although Chandra has more wealth and a more logical, clever mind, Jai is more open and better liked. Chandra says of Jai, "He tries to appear as the biggest man outside our village, in the other villages, but is laughed at even in Arunpur. Nobody, not even a fly, will believe and support him." On the other hand, Jai has this to say of his ally:

> It is true that my *pattidar* [Chandra] is dishonest, greedy, and clever and is always after cheating somebody. He is the root of all trouble in our *pura* and the entire village. He is the one who decides all things, but I do not support him in all his dealings for I want no part of another's property, nor would I give mine to anyone.

Thus, when the power of coalition (i.e., faction) members becomes too unequal, or when the advantage that is gained by joining a coalition becomes less than the costs of maintaining it, it appears time for the coalition to disband and realign (see also Mayer 1966:116 and fn. 18). I predict that this is what will happen to the Krishna-Pradhan alliance in the near future. While Jai continues to chafe under his subordinate status, he may eventually ally himself with another big man or attempt to remain neutral.

Despite the existence of such cracks in *partibandi* alliances and ties, an unstated fact seems to be that there is some satisfaction with the way in which this form of conflict has been organizing the political arena and achieving goals. Of course, leaders of both factions often said that the time, energy, and expense involved in pursuing lengthy court cases is a waste and that they truly desire *partibandi* to come to an end. But although time does have a way of healing old wounds, no one has made a real effort to stop this conflict. While in the field, we noted that on several occasions Jai went to Raj Kumar's home and sat with his uncle (Rampat), and that the latter also returned the visit. In addition, Narain has been trying to extend his friendship toward the Brahmans whom he has treated so badly in the past, and they have been responding favorably to his gesture.

But will this put an end to *partibandi?* I think not, even though both the sides may change and the coalitions may be drastically altered, for factionalism has been an integral part of village life. So long as the Indian village remains a focus for changes that are occurring in the nation at large, and until such changes have become integrated into new cultural norms, factions will continue, in the absence of other groups, to be a way of organizing conflicts arising from the introduction of new resources into the political arena. Factionalism is another expression of the competition between men inherent in an Indian village. This point will be discussed more explicitly in the final chapter.

The Organization and Interactions of Partibandi Conflict

Villagers see the major causes for the intensification of village *partibandi* as fights over land, tubewell water, and elections. All of these limited and prized resources in the community are now available for allocation among a greater number of people than ever before. Individuals compete for these goods and, in the process, such competition becomes the raison d'être for factions. At the same time, the competition in home building, acquiring wealth, education, philanthropy, and arranging better marriages becomes both the expression and end result of *partibandi* rivalry.

Although the villagers state that progress is made for the individual families who participate in this sort of competition, *partibandi* on the whole is felt to be destructive to the betterment of the village. No constructive cooperative action, such as building a girls' intercollege, paving the village streets, repairing the broken water taps and meaningfully running a youth club, can be undertaken, because of opposition from one or the other faction (usually Chandra's). Even when two "neutral" people, such as my assistant and I, tried to get the cooperation of Chandra's party to repair the Primary School well and put a roof on the Girls' School, it was with extreme reluctance that they eventually donated some money. Because of *partibandi,* they send their children to the primary school in a neighboring village; hence they felt in this case that there was no sense in giving rupees to a plan from which they would receive no benefit. There was also some suspicion that we might be acting as agents of the Pradhan.

Social intercourse between villagers also suffers from this conflict. In the past there was a single fire to celebrate the festival of Holi. In the morning, all would play Holi, wildly spilling colored water on one another. They would put on new clothes in the evening, walk in the streets, and embrace each other and ask forgiveness for their past errors. Now there are separate fires in each of the two main *pura*s and at the houses of each faction leader; some people refrain from playing Holi at all because of factional feelings. Villagers will not attend special singing or religious performances because the event is sponsored by a rival leader or because such individuals will also be present. If men from the two factions do meet on such occasions, they sit separately. Even the social relations of women, normally not affected by these disputes, can sometimes be severed. Although a girl from the Pradhan's house, who was leaving for her husband's village, did go into the homes of Jai and Chandra to bid the women farewell, she did not enter Narain's home. Visits between women of the two houses have ceased since Case 16 occurred, in which a boy of Narain's family was involved in a fight with one of the Pradhan's *pattidar*s.

Decline in the participation of Holi and other previously panvillage celebrations,[4] as well as those agricultural functions that used to be more communal in the past, cannot, however, be attributed solely to factionalism. They are part of the more general decline of joint community activities that has its roots in changes that are affecting the transformation of a personalistic system of social relations into one based on an impersonal order (see Béteille 1974b:99ff). Thus, while villagers often see factionalism as the dragon behind much of the lack of panvillage cooperation, this is often due to other causes. It can also be seen that factions do organize political conflict in the villagewide arena in the absence of any other political groups capable of so doing.

The people of Arunpur referred to *partibandi* as separate from, for example, conflict within the family or between other kinsmen, and this is important in the attempt to distinguish between political activity occurring at all levels of village society and that of this particular arena. The relevant features of *partibandi* that can be abstracted from the case histories are: (1) concern with competition for the allocation of scarce and valued resources, (2) dependence upon a group's (i.e., others') consent to the decisions made regarding the desired allocation, (3) exploitation or manipulation of a dispute by a big man to further his own interests or advantages or because one of the conflicting parties enlisted his aid and (4) escalation of seemingly nonpolitical events (i.e., children or dogs fighting) to the villagewide political arena when the personnel involved are key faction members.

The focus of factions are the leaders; without leaders, factions would not exist, and without followers, there are no leaders. Interaction among leaders and followers has two main aspects. First, there is the nature of the resources at the command of leaders and second, there is the tie between leader and follower.

Leadership, as Bailey states, is an enterprise (1969:36). Each leader strives to gain access to more resources than his opponents and to employ them to greater advantage. Yet the resources which a leader has to gain his ends are limited and thus he must choose between different strategies of action depending upon the costs involved. Sometimes a leader makes a bad investment and does not receive at least the equal of what was invested. Thus Jai spoke most bitterly against those whom he had helped and who later deserted him. Or if a man loses in a contest in which he has expended much of his resources (such as Chandra's drawn-out fight against the Pradhan and his allies in Case 12), then his cost has again been greater than his gain (if any).

There is a difference in the resources of a leader and his supporters, just as there is between two leaders. It is by the expenditure of these resources or the promise of doing so that a leader attracts others to his side. "What passes between them [leaders and supporters] is not so much an interaction as a transaction" (Bailey 1969:36) in which both individuals must feel that they have gained something or the relationship will not be continued (see also Mayer 1966:112). There are two specific types of transactions between a leader and his supporters: those of patronage and brokerage (Mayer 1966:113-114).

Patronage resources are actual (hence, limited) benefits promised and delivered by the patron in return for services rendered. Most patronage benefits in the village today come from the government through the Community Development and Local Self-Government *(panchayati raj)* programs. There is a great struggle to capture those offices (such as *pradhan*) which provide accessibility to resources that can then be used to forge new links with other individuals. Examples of the Pradhan's patronage in Arunpur are the construction of houses for two Chamars in his party, a well for his Nai follower, paved streets passing by the homes of other supporters and the rent-free use of the *panchayat* house by a teacher in the Intercollege. Krishna Singh, as Secretary of the Intercollege, for example, can provide another form of patronage by agreeing to employ someone as a teacher or clerk, or to provide student scholarships.

In brokerage transactions, the leader becomes a middleman and promises to obtain favors for his supporters from a third party. These are the main transactions in an arena characterized by a "politics of scarcity." It is here that a faction leader's contacts with influentials become an integral part of his resources as compared to those of other leaders. Every time an Arunpur big man intercedes between two parties—the villagers on one hand and the police, courts, Community Development officials, schools, and so on, on the other—he is performing brokerage transactions. The performance of this function also ties the members of a faction to their leader because of their differential access to such influential people. It is more crucial to be able to command brokerage transactions than it is to command the more limited resources of patronage.

The two opposing cultural values that villagers attach to the quality of leader-follower interaction—loyalty or self-interest—hinge on whether or not a faction member will continue to support a leader for reasons other than receipt of benefits. Examples of this are the readiness of the Nai to "lay down his life" for the Pradhan, or the Dharkar who says that he will never waiver in his support of the Little Pura Bhumihars against those of Main Pura. In both cases, a moral tie augments the purely transactional one. Bailey makes a distinction in sociological terms that is similar to this insight of the villagers. He distinguishes between members of a faction according to whether the bond with a leader is moral or purely transactional.[5]

Because factional politics in Arunpur means Bhumihar politics and because the Bhumihars as a group command and control more resources than any other caste group, this form of conflict occupies the major part of the village political arena. Effective competition for new resources that enter the village as well as old ones takes place only within the dominant caste of Bhumihars. The contest between the different factional coalitions is more or less evenly matched and the expenditure of resources is great. This is in stark contrast to the conflict that occurs between Bhumihars and their Untouchable laborers.

NOTES

1. Much has been written about factions in India. Recent articles by Nicholas (1965; 1966; 1968a; 1968b), augmented by the work of Bailey (1968, 1969), have superseded earlier work. Carter (1974:102ff) has a good discussion of various positions.
2. Three years ago, this *pattidar* of Raj Kumar joined the Chandra-Jai faction. His involvement in the case, however, goes back several years before this faction shift. One of the main reasons that many party loyalties remain stable over a long period of time is because of the lengthy process involved in settling disputes, especially through the courts. But, as this case reveals, this is not always so.

THE POLITICAL ARENA: FACTIONS

3. This is one of the worst possible forms of insult.
4. The year I was in Arunpur, an innovation appeared. The Kurmis started their own fire in their separate *pura*. Also unrelated to factionalism is the fact that college-educated men or those who work outside the village (but are home on holidays) do not participate, either.
5. Bailey describes a factional core as consisting, in addition to the leader or coalition of leaders, of those followers whose relationship to the leader is augmented by other moral and multiplex bonds (1969:47). There is some lack of clarity, however, about the presence of cores in factions. At one place he writes, "faction leaders, who by definition have only followers and no core (this will be discussed later), must spend much of their time and energy in keeping the fabric in repair" (43). In the later discussion, he states, "every faction has a leader, whether it be one man or a clique (core) of several men, each with their own followers" (52). He further states that "the faction which is most successful in the competition for new resources develops a core and in time the core expands to the point where a new kind of group, which is no longer a faction, has come into existence" (53).

CHAPTER 8
The Political Arena in Arunpur: Class Conflict

The horizontal cleavage among castes that are competing for power and valued resources in Arunpur has many of the characteristics of class conflict but has thus far not become separate from caste status. The feuding Bhumihars combine on any occasion in which they come into conflict with their laborers, the landless Chamars. Each of these groups is united by the consciousness of a common economic position in relation to the other group, as well as by the knowledge that they either enjoy or are denied the authority to exercise power. The access to property and power which is linked to the caste status of Bhumihar is matched by the complete inaccessibility of these resources to the Chamars. The existence of a separate "caste culture" or lifestyle for each group further widens the gulf between them. Because of the completely dominant positions of the Bhumihars, Arunpur is still a closed society. Status, wealth, and power by and large all accrue to this caste.

The rest of the villagers have associated themselves with the upper castes in this conflict with the Untouchables even though the Kurmis, who own small amounts of land, cultivated almost entirely by themselves, and other castes that do not require agricultural labor play a lesser role in this conflict.[1] Yet the gap in caste status and economic and political power is almost as great between these lower castes and the Bhumihars as it is between them and the Chamars. If economic and political power were the sole measures of class membership in India, it might seem more likely that the low castes (indeed, even the Brahmans) who own little or no land would join their common interests and needs with those of the Chamars. All castes chafe under Bhumihar domination.

THE POLITICAL ARENA: CLASS CONFLICT 161

The phenomenon of caste associations in politics on the wider Indian scene reveals that the inability of many to compete on the open market from a position of equal strength can become a unifier of different groups of people under certain conditions. Caste associations exist to protect the interests of these groups against others (e.g., Srinivas 1962:7; Gough 1960: 44; Mayer 1967a; Rudolph and Rudolph 1960; Kothari 1970). Instead of the fission within a caste that occurs in the vertical cleavage of factions, there is a fusion of different castes in opposition to others.

Two main factors have inhibited the growth of class feelings that cut across caste lines in Arunpur. The traditional sense of a deep status differentiation marking off all castes from the Untouchables still remains. No matter in what situation of misery a man may live, to be above the Untouchables is some consolation in itself. This consolation would be lost if castes low on the hierarchy joined hands with the lowest of the low. Such an identification is inadmissible as long as one believes in the divine ordering of the hierarchy. This also explains why conflicts involving Chamars and non-Bhumihars, described in this chapter, relate not to economic conditions but to questions of status. Where discrimination against Untouchables is joined to purely economic issues, a backlash occurs. Hostility is expressed by others who have otherwise remained neutral on the question of the rights and wages of laborers (see also Juyal 1974).

Second, the closed village society is opening up so that wealth (via education, new jobs, and the availability of some land on the market) and power (through elections) are becoming somewhat more dispersed throughout the population. The people who now have the opportunity, if not always the actual chance, to compete with the Bhumihars for these resources are the lower Touchable castes. Because they now see a way to gain access to valued commodities, these castes have chosen to stand against Chamar aspirations. It is rarely possible for them to prevent the Bhumihars from taking a large share, but it must make no sense to the lower castes to divide things even further by adding the Chamars to the field of competition. This ability to participate in a monetized economy has achieved, for some castes, a greater chance to separate caste from class (or land ownership). Cash transactions have introduced a new flexibility into the system.

The Chamars and other Untouchables, however, have gained no such advantages. If anything, they have become more unequal than ever. Before Independence, they used to till the land; now they have none. Like many others who lost land held on sharecropping arrangements, the Chamars did not gain from zamindari abolition. Rather, they were reduced almost completely to landless laborers and found ready employment with Bhumihars and Brahmans unable to farm their holdings themselves. A surplus of labor combined with the lack of alternatives has reduced Chamars to a condition of what they call *mazburi*—complete dependence.

While others are making new strides, the Chamars have not remained oblivious to or altogether impotent in their backward situation. There has been some increase of education and job opportunities for a few among them. Combined with exposure to outside influences, via Banaras and mass communications, this has been enough to awaken a consciousness of common interests. Much is also heard about Chamar unity at election times. Then, too, Chamars in Arunpur know of the great leaders among their caste: people like Raidas, Ambedkar, and the then Congress Party leader *(neta)* Jagjivan Ram. They are also aware of the achievements of Chamars elsewhere in India.

The catalyst to the deep-rooted dissatisfaction among them was the arrival of myself, my husband, and my assistant in the village. It was the behavior of the latter, especially, that created a potentially explosive situation.

CASTE CULTURE OF THE CHAMARS

At first glance, Arunpur society seems to be a unified whole. People look and dress alike, live in similar types of houses and their customs—for example, arranged early marriages, joint families, position of women, and so on—seem also to be part of a shared culture. An extended stay in the village, however, reveals many areas where this shared culture differs along caste lines. People often speak of the *dharma* (duty or morality) and *rivas* (customs) peculiar to each caste, and these are regarded as inheritable along with rank. For example, certain castes could give rise to the aristocrat style of leadership *(rais),* while others could not. These differences are most clearly revealed when the Chamars are compared to the Touchable castes.

Much of the traditional stigma attached to Untouchability, such as not being able to go through certain parts of the village and polluting others by touch (which still holds true for some ritual occasions), has been discarded. Today a Chamar is no longer barred from wearing clothes that were previously in the domain of other castes if he can afford to do so. Yet they are still forced to live in separate areas and cannot pray in any of the village temples, take water (with the rare idiosyncratic exception) from any village well, or give food to and dine with others.

They have also been caught up in a statewide movement of their caste group to raise their status by abstaining from those activities that had

THE POLITICAL ARENA: CLASS CONFLICT 163

FIGURE 21. Entertainers at a feast honoring a Chamar woman who died at a very old age.

specifically branded them as Untouchable in the past: namely, carting away, eating, and skinning dead animals to make leather goods (see also Lynch 1969). Only two or three old men still work leather into irrigation water bags, but no one would cart away or skin an animal. Chamars from a neighboring village may be called upon when required. Chamar women assist in childbirth by cutting the umbilical cord, burying the afterbirth, and attending to the woman while she is in a polluted state, but there was even mention of abandoning this practice. Some felt that the reward received was not enough to compensate for the disadvantages of performing these polluting functions. Another occupation, peculiar to the Chamars, is that of exorciser of disturbing spirits (an *ohja* who deals with *bhut*s and *pret*s). Being an exorciser is not looked down upon, however, but is regarded as a skill because of the widespread belief in these spirits among all villagers.

Chamar separateness is revealed in other ways as well. Although their ideal is the joint family, the majority live in nuclear households or in joint households of only two generations' depth. Because of the difficulties of remaining together under severe economic pressures, the

Chamars rapidly partition their families while continuing to live under extremely crowded conditions in the same house. In one case, four brothers who are economically independent of one another still share the same small three-room house. It contains a total of thirty-eight people. As Chamars have neither the land nor the money to build new houses, the situation will grow to impossible proportions by the next generation if continued unchecked.

Relations within the family do not have the same formality which governs those of upper-caste homes, particularly those of the Bhumihars. Role expectations are much more fluid. They do not practice the custom of touching the feet of their elders as a sign of respect, which other castes do. Every visit that we made into the Chamar *pura* was accompanied by the screaming exchange that went on between the men and the children. The latter were unmanageable, and no one ever succeeded in getting them to quiet down. Many times Chamars said, referring to the children's behavior, "This is the significance of caste *(jati);* see how low-caste children are born low, and so there must be caste." On other occasions as well, such as talking about the misbehavior of Bhumihars with Chamar women, we were told that Chamars deserve to be Untouchable because they act in such a "low" way.

Marriages that are arranged at an early age can end in divorce or desertion, which are practically unknown among the upper castes and comparatively less frequent among other castes. A common practice among the Chamars is for a widow to live with her husband's younger brother. There was even one instance of a woman living with her deceased husband's elder brother. This is an illicit relationship, not only because a woman must completely avoid males older than her husband, but because the elder brother had a wife and children as well.

A woman is much more independent in a Chamar household and becomes decreasingly so as her caste rank increases. A young Chamar bride may assume the practice of covering her face before elders, but this is quickly disregarded after one or two years. Then she can move freely through the village, and her work as a daily wage laborer for the Bhumihars puts her in the position of being an important provider. Women thus take a more equal part in family decision making. Bhumihar women, on the other hand, generally do not work outside of the home, and although their freedom increases somewhat with advancing age, they practice some form of purdah most of their lives. The Chamars say that their ideal is to have their women in purdah. This should be understood as a desire for greater economic prosperity, which would enable a family to keep a woman's services in the home, and not as a move away from female independence.

FIGURE 22. Enjoying the antics of a performing monkey in Chamar Pura. The woman at the extreme right is of the Teli caste.

I was told that there is a direct relationship between not practicing purdah and their custom of very early marriage:

> We marry off our daughters so young [eight to ten years old] to save our prestige. If they don't work, they don't eat. And if they do work and they are free, not in purdah, anyone can do mischief with them. Therefore, we marry them young to save them from this mischief and gossip. . . . We will only change [this custom] when our caste says to. We will only raise the age of a girl's marriage in our caste if the girls are put in purdah.

The rest of the Chamars' situation can be subsumed under the conditions imposed by poverty. Education is practically nonexistent among them because children are needed to work either in the house, in lieu of their mothers, or in the fields. Many small boys go to a weaving center near Banaras and for eight to twelve rupees a month spend their entire day working as apprentices. "When we do not have enough to eat, who will think of education?" these people say.

Without education, land, or wealth, most Chamars are forced to rely on the work provided by the Bhumihars, and in the process their lives become closely intertwined and dependent upon that of their master's *(malik)*. These positions of labor are not necessarily inheritable from father to son, but indebtedness tends to tie the son to his father's *malik* as well and a bondage much like serfdom is imposed. One Bhumihar revealed to us that when one of his family's agricultural workers attempted to leave their service and support himself by driving a rickshaw, they beat him up and broke the rickshaw one night. After that, he returned to his service as a laborer.

Some Chamars have been able to find other occupations beside that of laborer, but they are few and work mostly in sari weaving. The greatest ambition of those who can foresee any possible changes in their lives is to have some business of their own. Only one Chamar succeeded in opening his own shop for the assembling of scales used in science laboratories. Together with his wife's brother, he borrowed 1,000 rupees and started the business. He told his story as follows:

> I used to work in a factory before, doing the same job which I now do on my own. After working there for five to six years, about seventy people were laid off and I was one of them. There was a dispute about bonuses and salaries. For six months I sat home and did nothing. Then I began to plough the fields of a Brahman for six months. But how can I live on two rupees a month, ten *bise* of land, a little roasted gram, sugar cane juice and half a *ser* [one *ser* = two pounds]of flour which doesn't even fill my stomach?
>
> This is the village of Brahmans and Bhumihars; there is no life for people like us, for Untouchables. They pay you less after lending you some money and then go on multiplying the interest, which you are unable to pay. You can't leave the job or be free of them, for they will ask you to reimburse the loan before you leave. You are forced to work until late at night. Our women also work for small wages; we all get abuses and beatings and our women are violated. So I thought I should utilize my skill and begin to assemble these scales.

But the Chamar was finding it difficult to manage and was constantly short of money. At one time he had fifteen scales ready and had sold only five. His wife was reduced to going from door to door in the village, begging for grain. She said that her children had not eaten for two days. The villagers whom she approached were asking too high a rate of interest for a two months' loan. If she took one *ser* (two pounds) of wheat flour, one and a quarter *sers* would have to be returned. She finally received grain from us. The plight of this Chamar and his family also reveals the conditions under which those who are agricultural workers live.

The Conditions of Mazburi: Agricultural Labor among the Chamars

As agriculture is the predominant mode of production in village India, the basic cleavage within the rural class structure is between owners and nonowners of land. Those who are excluded from the land are also excluded from power. The vast majority of nonowners who are engaged in agricultural labor as their sole means of income in Arunpur come from the Chamar caste. Other low castes that may be nonowners are able to participate more easily in alternative occupations.

While Indian agrarian society might be divided into Marxist categories such as semifeudal landowner, capitalist farmer, independent producer, and landless rural proletariat, the class division that has the most significance for the people of Arunpur is the indigenous one dividing *malik* (master) from *mazdur* (laborer). It is only in this division that a true commonalty of interests is perceived. An Arabic term denoting a "proprietor" in Muslim law, *malik* was the synonym most often used for a zamindar in Mughal times (Habib 1963:140). Today it has the primary meaning of "master."[2] Traditionally a *malik* had mastery not only over the land but also over the men who worked on it, and this control, along with the deference that it implies, is a significant aspect of village life today (see also Béteille 1974a:65ff). *Mazdur* has meant, and still means, a "servant" or "laborer." When the Chamars of Arunpur refer to their condition of life and work, they use the term *mazburi*—a condition of "helplessness," "compulsion," and "constraint." The twin pillars of Chamar dependence lie both in the lack of alternative sources of income available to them and in the large surplus labor pool available to their masters.

Chamars have an interest in the land primarily through the institution of sharecropping *(mafi)*, by which they cultivate a man's land in exchange for exclusive use of a certain portion of the land, plus food, clothing, monthly wages, and a share of the seasonal crops when they participate in harvesting.[3] For the most part, the terms of sharecropping are the same, although there is some variation. There are also discrepancies in the amounts mentioned by the Chamars and their Bhumihar or Brahman *malik*s, the latter being higher.

The major function of the Chamar laborer is to be a ploughman *(halwaha)* of his *malik*'s fields, because a Bhumihar or Brahman will not perform this task. Additional chores include planting, weeding, irrigating, harvesting, caring for animals, and performing other manual work. He receives ten *bise* of land for his own use (or one *bigha* if he works year round), two rupees per month, breakfast (sugar cane juice and roasted grams), lunch (bread and some molasses or lentils) and clothing[4] in return for six months' labor. Additional payments come in the form of food and occasional money at the time of festival celebrations or ceremonies in the *malik*'s house. A few Bhumihars give their ploughman a half *ser* (one pound) of grain daily instead of lunch. One or two gave an extra

FIGURE 23. Ploughman holds two ploughs.

bisa of land or an additional rupee per month. The ploughman receives three to five *sers* per day when the seasonal crops are cut. This period usually lasts about one or two months during the year.

Most high-caste farmers employ only one laborer of this type; those Bhumihars with twenty or more *bigha*s have an extra ploughman. A particular sharecropping arrangement I found, in the case of a Bhumihar who had no interest in agriculture at all, was to give part of the land on half-share to some *pattidar*s and the remaining three *bigha*s to a Chamar who received only one third of the crop. In another case, some Musahars cultivated one *bigha* (twenty *bise*) of Bhumihar land for vegetables, out of which their share was four *bise*. The Bhumihars provided half the seeds and expenses involved in the Musahar's four-*bise* share while the latter provided not only the other half of his expenses but his free labor on the remaining four-fifths of the *bigha* as well.

The tie between a ploughman and his *malik* is very strong, for the Chamar is totally dependent in this situation. The *malik* gives him the only piece of land by which the Chamar can support his family and at times he will also receive seeds. Most important, he can borrow money from his master. It is the fact of almost universal indebtedness that makes it impossible for the *mazdur* even to consider leaving his *malik*'s service. The debts of the father are passed on to the sons, and so high-caste men, who will not touch the plough, are supplied with a constant stream of labor.

Some Chamars work as agricultural laborers (nonploughmen) for a daily wage. If they are employed for the entire year, they receive the same food and clothing as a ploughman, but instead of land are paid thirty rupees per month. Two farmers paid as little as eight and twenty rupees per month for full-time Chamar workers. Others who worked on a daily basis in the village, such as ploughmen in the half of the year they were unemployed, would earn anywhere from one to two rupees per day or one and a half *sers* (three pounds) of grain plus breakfast.[5] Other castes, however, such as the Lohars, Kahars, or Kurmis, received a minimum of three rupees per day for any job they performed.

Men receive anywhere from two to five *sers* per day when labor is contributed on a seasonal basis at the harvest; the average seems to be about three and a half to four *sers*. Other specific types of labor about which we were told are remunerated as follows:[6]

1. Potato worker: One and a half to two *sers* per day plus breakfast and lunch.
2. Potato or sugar cane laborer: One to three rupees per day.
3. Transplanting of padi: Two *sers* plus breakfast.

Women and children who work daily receive half a rupee plus breakfast and lunch. At harvest time they receive one and a half to two *sers* each day they work cutting the crops. Men, women, and children all work approximately twelve hours a day (sunrise to sunset) with about an hour free for lunch. In the hot season, this break is extended another two to three hours during the noon period. Work is often carried on until 10 to 11 P.M. at harvest time.

Chamars must still perform forced labor *(begar)* in addition to the various types of labor for which they are paid. At times of marriages or other ceremonies in the *malik*'s household, or during the six months of the year when a ploughman is not employed by him, Chamars may be called upon to work. They must perform *begar* whether they wish to or not. Usually food, and occasionally some money, is given. Similarly, an independent village rickshaw driver may be pressed into service by some high-caste man. He will have to work for a set fee for the day (e.g., five rupees), which would be less than the amount he could earn if he went to the city or operated in the local open market.

The main complaints of the Chamars about the conditions of their labor are that they do not receive a fair wage or get enough to eat. A Bhumihar (or Brahman) will give them land, they say, but then not let them plough it or give them water and seeds at the right time. While the *mazdur* ploughs his *malik*'s field some eight times, his own ten to twenty *bise* are not overturned even four times. They accuse the Bhumihars of wanting to keep them in dire poverty so that they will remain their dependants. Bhumihars, I was told,

> are afraid that if there is enough food in our stomachs, we will no longer work for them. They keep us in debt by cheating us and charging high interest rates which we can never return. They treat us like shoes and abuse our women. They beat us if we work elsewhere or come late to them. They are so big, they can do as they like. How can we dare to oppose them? Then we cannot even go out of our houses, for all the land around is owned by them.

The Bhumihars are equally antagonistic toward the Chamars, and respected men said on more than one occasion that "Chamars need to be beaten to be brought under control." Unfortunately, this feeling seemed to increase after our arrival in the village. Bhumihars also complained that their laborers were lazy and undependable and alternately said that they do not respect their *malik*s or would not dare to oppose them. While the actual beating of Chamars is not unusual, most Bhumihars seem satisfied with only verbal abuses.

Some Chamars do feel, however, that they have been helped by this system of labor or by the Bhumihars. One worker admitted that he gets more from the traditional system of sharecropping with side payments *(mafi)* than he could make if he drove a rickshaw. Two brothers who worked for a faction leader from Little Pura, Jai Singh, bought three *bise* of land from him to build their house and to plant vegetables on the property that is near their home. These Chamars also received a government grant from the Pradhan, a rival faction leader, to build their house.

For the most part, however, Chamars are bitter about the village *panchayat* and the way in which government resources have been distributed (or not distributed) to them. The two brothers, above, told that of the 500-rupee grant originally allotted by the government, 100 rupees were "eaten up" along the way. The Pradhan also was accused of "eating up" 1,500 rupees given by the government to purchase some land near a well in their *pura* so that needy Chamars could build their houses. Money, they claimed, that was allocated some two or three years ago to repair their two wells and to construct fodder bins for their animals could never be obtained. Finally they accused other villagers of cheating them of the use of public land. They used to tie their animals in the area near the village pond whose ownership is now disputed. The Kahar who is contesting ownership of this property denies them the right to tie their animals there now. The village street that connects their settlement to Main Pura and lies just near a wealthy Kurmi's home has been ploughed by that Kurmi until all that remains is a narrow lane.

These tensions and antagonisms felt by both the Chamars and their Bhumihar and Brahman masters originate from the intimacy of their tie in agricultural production as well as from the great disparity in their relative access to land, other resources and power. Disputes between Chamars and others in the village tend quickly to escalate. A Chamar in trouble will seek help from fellow caste mates who are willing to support him in the conflict, while the upper-caste man never has any trouble in getting others to stand behind him. They come to his aid readily because of the question of prestige involved. At the same time, there is the general fear that if Chamars are not constantly suppressed and kept in their place, they will no longer supply a cheap and satisfactory pool of labor for the village farmers. The disputes in the following section will illustrate the processual form and escalation that occurs in conflict of this type.

Disputes between Malik and Mazdur

Many conflicts in the village occur because a *malik* is not satisfied with the job performance of his Chamar laborer or the way in which he has carried out the terms of their work agreement.

Case 21: Malik and *Mazdur* Dispute   1969

Two men were arguing loudly in a village lane. The Bhumihar was abusing his Chamar ploughman for coming to work late and told him therefore to return the shirt he had just given him, costing twelve rupees. The Chamar replied that he was eating at the time and hence could not come, adding that the shirt he had received was worth no more than four rupees. He also accused his *malik* of giving only one-quarter *ser* of grain daily instead of the regular one-half *ser*.

After a heated exchange in which the Bhumihar threatened to beat his laborer and the latter dared him to do so, they both departed. The laborer went home and got his shirt to show to people and asked them to judge its worth. When the *malik* heard of this, he beat his laborer. The Bhumihar's other *pattidars* looked on but did nothing.

The laborer was advised by another Chamar to report his beating to the Police Sub-Inspector at the Dallia Police Station. His *malik* then threatened that since the Sub-Inspector was also a Bhumihar and unless there is evidence of the beating, he would not believe the Chamar. The latter ultimately did nothing.

Perhaps the most significant point about this dispute is the way in which it reveals Chamar powerlessness *(mazburi)*. Before us and others in the village (non-Bhumihars), the *mazdur* had threatened to leave the employ of his *malik*. He said he had worked and listened to the *malik* for three years, but would now rather starve or jump into a well. He also warned that the population of high castes in India is small when compared to that of the Untouchables and soon the rule of the latter would come. Although most of the bystanders agreed that the Bhumihars were hard masters, they made fun of the Chamar's declaration of independence and his big hopes. The aggrieved worker also knew the validity of the threat of how the Police Sub-Inspector would deal with him and thus saw no point in going there. As Case 25 will show, should a Chamar appeal outside the village, the feuding Bhumihars in Arunpur close ranks and unite against him.

The Bhumihar *malik,* on the other hand, declared that the Chamars had gotten out of control. When he learned of the remarks about the small number of high castes in India, he said to us:

> But remember, one Bhumihar can beat one hundred Chamars. I was trying to show him how a Bhumihar can beat many Chamars. But now that I came to know he has such ideas [i.e., regarding Untouchable rule], we must prepare ourselves in another way and teach them a lesson. . . . It is the Congress Party which has given them so much power and now the Socialist Party wants to do that. . . . And the second man around here who is provoking the Chamars is you [my assistant]! You have made them sit on our heads. But they are fools. They do not understand that you will not remain—that you will not be here for more than two months. After that, who will protect them? We Bhumihars will not say anything now, but after two months . . .

These types of conflicts are bound to increase as Arunpur Chamars become more politically conscious and aware of their rights. If the Untouchables in this area should also have a political party that articulates their own specific interests, then these intravillage and local conflicts could escalate into even wider political issues. Right now, however, there is no group, organization, or party that has either effectively unified all Chamars among themselves or with other Untouchable castes, or has taken up their cause.

Case 22: A *Mazdur* is Denied a Traditional Payment   1968

A Chamar was called to plough the fields of his *malik* but refused to do so. He told us that there is a custom followed in the village whereby after the potato crop is dug out of the soil by the *malik* and his workers, the ploughman is then free to pick up all the potatoes that may have been left in the field as his own. He does not have to return any of these to the *malik*. In this manner, a *mazdur* may sometimes pick as many as two to three maunds (160–240 pounds). This year, when the Chamar's *malik* dug up his field, he did not call his ploughman and instead made sure that all of the crop went to him.

The Chamar further explained, "These are the only attractions that a *mazdur* has to work for more than the agreed upon number of months. That is why I refused to go to the field to plough today. The Bhumihar abused me, threatened to beat me and also said that he would even pick up all the crops produced in the ten *bise* of land he has given to me."

Bhumihars often accuse their laborers of doing mischief when the crop is being collected. Potatoes lend themselves easily to this. A female worker may slip a few in her sari to take home or may give them to her children. It is also easy for potatoes to be dropped in a corner of the field and then collected later in the night. By far the most usual method of ensuring that a laborer will receive his share of the crop is to see that many

FIGURE 24. Chamar and Musahar laborers pick what remains in Chandra Singh's potato fields.

of the potatoes purposely remain in the earth, to be dug up later when the field is in the hands of the laborers. The Bhumihar in the case just mentioned said that the Chamar had told the truth but questioned whether he should be expected to leave all the potatoes to his laborers. In this situation, more than two maunds had been left in the earth after the initial harvesting. The Bhumihar picked up most of this amount and then called upon his ploughman to pick up the rest. The latter refused, saying he had been denied the right to the entire amount. "So," said the *malik*, "do you think that in the name of a custom in the village a farmer will give up all of his property?"

Disputes, as in this case, arise when the laborer claims that he has not received a fair payment. This most often occurs at the harvest time when a certain number of head-loads of the crop cut are allocated to the workers as their share. Sometimes, if the Chamar is to receive a set ratio of the amount harvested, say 2:1 or 3:1, conflict often arises from the simple account keeping of the number of loads. Interestingly enough, however, those conflicts which seem to escalate most quickly from a dispute between the original parties concerned to a much wider network are those involving prestige issues as opposed to purely material interests.

Case 23: Kurmis and Chamars Dispute Access to a Lane   1969

One evening, during the busy harvest season, my assistant and I were standing in the main lane of Chamar Pura and talking with a group of men. All of them were standing at a distance from this main lane. As some Kurmis owned the fields just outside Chamar Pura, there had been constant friction between these men coming from the fields along the Chamar street, carrying heavy loads, and the Chamars who felt that they had a right to congregate in their own *pura* where and when they wanted.

On this particular occasion, a dispute started between a Kurmi and the Chamars with whom we had been speaking. Seeing some people standing in the road [which were us], the Kurmi mistakenly thought them to be Chamars. He abused them; the Chamars answered back. The Kurmi became increasingly angry, dropped his load, and challenged them all. As the words flew back and forth with greater rapidity, I succeeded in taking the Kurmi away from the scene and tried to explain that it was we, and not the Chamars, who had been standing in the road. He acknowledged his mistake and promised the event had ended.

Then the Kurmi returned to Chamar Pura, collected his load and went home. There he gathered his family members and came again to the Chamars, stick in hand. My assistant interceded and finally mediated between the two groups when one of Chamars was about to be beaten.

THE POLITICAL ARENA: CLASS CONFLICT   175

Case 24: A Chamar Touches a Brahman's Cot   1969

One evening, an old Brahman woman put out her cot on the village lane in front of her door. An old Chamar woman came by and, not seeing the cot in the dark, brushed by it with her foot. The Brahman woman abused her. The Chamar version also states the the old Chamar woman was beaten. Then a Chamar man started to abuse the Brahmans for putting their cots in a public lane.

The Brahman woman's son was told by other villagers that the Chamars were abusing him. He ran to the Kurmi's house which is nearest to Chamar Pura, and yelled for the Chamars to come and face him there. Two men came; one was beaten by the Brahman with the aid of the Kurmis.

Other Chamars then came with sticks to beat the Brahman. The Kurmis told them, "What are you doing? You know that he is alone now and you can beat him, but he can kill the whole Chamar Pura in an hour if he wants. So why are you doing this?" The Chamars also understood that the Kurmis would have helped to beat them too, and they returned.

Sometime later, a Bhumihar who heard of the dispute came near Chamar Pura and shouted: "I know that Vijay Misra is of my rival faction; but he is a Brahman and if you are abusing a Brahman it means you are abusing a high caste and I can't tolerate that. So be quiet or I will beat you, too!"

Case 25: Little Pura Bhumihars Fight the Chamars   1969

Most of the village wells had dried up by early March due to an extremely dry winter and hot season. The two wells in Chamar Pura also went dry. One of the Chamars was holding an elaborate double wedding for his two daughters at the end of April. Many relatives and guests from the grooms' sides came to take part in the marriage celebrations.

Because much water was needed to provide for the many guests, two Chamars went to the government tubewell and put their pitchers into the tank where only Touchable castes usually take their water and bathe. A young Bhumihar man yelled at them not to take water from there. The Chamars persisted and then the Bhumihar beat and abused the one with the pitcher, Viren Ram. The latter's brother, Maggu, abused the Bhumihar in return and said, "We must take water and this belongs to the government, not you." The two Chamars then ran to the nearby bazaar of Dallia, fearing retaliation from the other Bhumihars.

They tried to contact the Police Sub-Inspector at Dallia, and stayed away from their home for three days. Finally, they appealed to the Superintendent of Police in Banaras who said that it was up to the Dallia Sub-Inspector to make an investigation. Meanwhile, when the Little Pura Bhumihars learned that the Chamars had fled to Dallia, and suspecting that they were reporting the matter to the police, they tried to destroy the thatched roof of the Chamars' home and did some damage to it.[7]

A week after this event, the Sub-Inspector came to the Pradhan's house in Main Pura. Everybody, including the college-educated teachers in that family, knew what had happened but remained silent. They felt it was a Bhumihar affair and hence they must stand united together against the Chamars. The police investigated the matter in the village, although they did not go into Chamar Pura. Finally, a complaint was signed by the Chamar who was beaten and his brother against nine Little Pura Bhumihars of both factions.

In a letter I received after leaving the field, I was told that the Little Pura Bhumihars, as a whole, subsequently filed some court cases against some Chamars for destruction of crops by animals as well as cheating. The original court case filed by the Chamars was dropped; somehow the "Bhumihars of Little Pura have become successful in dividing Chamars into two groups. They instigated one group to beat the people of the other group."

Whereas the first two cases described in this section involved disputes between individuals over the amount of payment or work to be received, these last three involved access to public resources and quickly escalated until they were regarded as reflecting upon the power and prestige of each group involved. In two instances, the Chamars were denied full access to the village lanes and had to defer to other castes if they wished to use the same area. The Chamars are also systematically denied access to the government tubewell water both for the irrigation of their fields and as drinking and bathing facilities. That this is not so much a caste (i.e., ritual) matter is clear from the preferential treatment the Bhumihars give to the Musahars, who are even lower in the hierarchy than the Chamars. Not only can they take drinking water from the same area that other caste people do, which is forbidden to the Chamars, but they can also bathe in the tubewell tank. The Chamars are forced to bathe in the earthen canal. It seems that the potential disobedience and power of the Chamars because of their greater numbers, combined with the sole reliance upon them as cheap labor, leads the Bhumihars to interpret every dispute as a sign of Chamar "revolution."

Once the original breach occurred in the last three disputes, it quickly widened until it involved all the Chamars ready to support their caste fellows against the upper castes. I doubt, however, that the Untouchables united as a whole in these disputes, although I have no specific information on this point. But certainly, the support the non-Chamar disputants received cut across all other caste and factional cleavages.

In all these cases, the Chamars were verbally abused and someone was beaten. They tried to defend themselves, but most villagers regarded our (and especially my assistant's) presence and encouragement of these people to be the major reason for their outspoken behavior in defying high-caste people. The Chamars received no assistance when they tried to appeal to the Police Sub-Inspector for help. Instead, they found that the officials joined the already closed ranks of the high castes in the village. Even when a court case was filed by a Chamar, it was impossible for them to continue in that fight. They have absolutely no resources and are hopelessly pitted against adversaries who have much more.

The Chamars, however, feel that the biggest obstacle to their achieving any substantial gain, whether it be by raising their caste status, improving their economic situation, or fighting against the Bhumihars, is not the lack of material resources so much as the lack of strength that comes from unity. Unlike the factions among the Bhumihars, which were villagewide, openly spoken about, and easily visible on any of a number of encounters, those among the Chamars were more difficult to learn about. Primarily, this was because proportionately less of our time was spent among them and it was never on the terms of intimacy required for obtaining this type of information. The following discussion of factions or *parti* among them is drawn together from their comments on a number of different occasions.

FACTIONS AMONG THE CHAMARS

Chamars speak of two opposing *parti* within their own *pura* and say that their presence is the major obstacle to unity among them. One of the chief determinants of faction membership is the extent to which a man is economically self-sufficient or is tied to the Bhumihars. The origins of these present factions are said to lie in two events in which certain Chamars opposed the Bhumihars.

Case 26: A Chamar is Beaten by Bhumihars   c. 1962

A Bhumihar once came to Raju Ram, a Chamar, to mate his goat with the Chamar's. Some argument arose at this time; each version of the situation says that the other man was verbally abusive. To take revenge for the Chamar's insolence, the Bhumihar and some of his family members and neighbors caught Raju one night and carried him off to their house. There, they tied him to a tree, put the rope around his mouth as well, and then poured cold water over him in the chilly, winter night. They beat him with sticks until be became unconscious. At this point they untied him and sent word to his mother and wife. (One Bhumihar said that these women were also beaten, but it seems unlikely).

The women, in turn, ran to the *pradhan* who returned with them to see what had happened. Raju filed a suit against the Bhumihar when he recovered. When the Police Sub-Inspector came to investigate, the *pradhan* remained silent, as another Bhumihar was involved. Chandra Singh, the opposing faction leader from Little Pura, helped the Bhumihar fight against Raju in court, as did Jai Singh and Narain Singh. They, as well as other Bhumihars, pressed their Chamar dependents to boycott Raju and one of them even closed his drainage line. Although Mohan Ram, one of the few independent Chamars, never came out openly in support of Raju, he stood by him. They formed one *parti* and the other Chamars formed a second.

Case 27: Some Chamars Oppose the Pradhan   c. 1963

When the village *pradhan* was supervising the paving of some village lanes with bricks provided by the government, he was also to see that some of the bricks were used to repair village wells. One of the two Chamar wells was included in this scheme. The bricks used in paving the streets, however, were quickly used up and the Pradhan then ordered the workers to take the bricks that had been set aside for well repair in order to complete the construction.

Some Chamars, led by Mohan Ram and Raju Ram, opposed this. The Pradhan called them to his house one evening and threatened them. In this way, those who feared him formed one party in opposition to Mohan and Raju, who went against the Bhumihars.

The leader of one party, Mohan Ram, is literate and owns a small amount of land with his brother. His is the largest joint household in this caste and consists of nineteen people. His eldest son has a B.A. and works as a Village Level Worker in the government Community Development Program. Although indebted to one of the Bhumihar faction leaders for possession of his land (Chandra Singh in Case 18, earlier), Mohan is usually referred to as anti-Bhumihar, that is, willing to stand up to them.

Raju Ram also supports Mohan and has left the village and settled on the main road in a small hut since he received his severe beating from the Bhumihars. He has his own rickshaw and goes to the city daily. Another rickshaw driver, Viren Ram (of Case 25, earlier) is also in sympathy with

THE POLITICAL ARENA: CLASS CONFLICT 179

these two men and is the one who is most concerned with the progress and uplift of his caste. Viren is deeply religious and has forsworn meat and drink; he has been trying to get his fellow Chamars in Arunpur also to give these up, especially drink. Viren, together with Mohan Ram and Raju Ram, may be seen as the core of the anti-Bhumihar faction and they are supported by their family members. All of them work independently, and because of this they are less likely to suffer the hardships that a bound Chamar, opposing his *malik,* would face.

The other faction, or "pro-Bhumihar" party, is led by an older man who does not advocate opposing this high caste. The majority of the Chamars who work as ploughmen or as daily laborers for the upper castes follow him. At the same time, from many of our conversations with these people, it seemed that a second line of cleavage was being formed. Age often became a factor in conflict. Older men would become angry when the younger ones started to reveal certain things to us. The latter would become impatient, in turn, and say that times have changed and they no longer have to suffer the indignities their parents did.

Conflict among the Chamars is also bound up with the wider framework of village *partibandi,* and they maintain that the Bhumihars extend their feuds in order to cause dissension among the Untouchables.

Case 28: Bhumihar Involvement in a Dispute Among
    Chamar *Pattidars*   c. 1963–1969

There was a dispute among *pattidars* (two brothers and the sons of a deceased third brother) who had divided their joint property but continued to live in the same house. The question was, who should remain living in the house? One of the *pattidars,* the eldest brother, works for

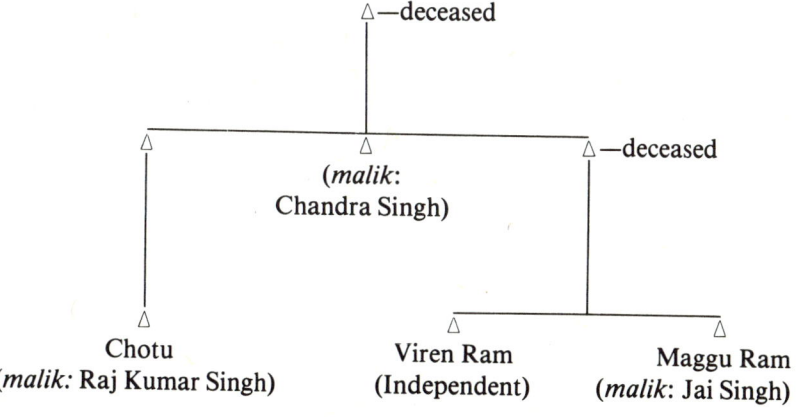

Raj Kumar Singh and is opposed by another, who works for Chandra Singh. In a court case that was filed, each of the *pattidar*s was supported by their *malik*s, who are also leaders of rival Bhumihar factions.

While this dispute was going on, Chotu, the son of the eldest *pattidar*, then tried to evict the sons of the deceased third *pattidar* (Viren and Maggu), one of whom works for Jai Singh. He threatened, abused, and beat them. One day, these two sons went to speak with Chotu and a fight with axes and sticks ensued. This case also went to the court and Chandra Singh and Jai Singh helped the two sons by bailing them out of prison. Chandra and Jai are also eager to lend Viren and Maggu all the money they need, but only to meet their court expenses. The case (or cases) between the *pattidar*s continues.

There seem to be two levels to the strategy of the Bhumihars who involve themselves in Chamar disputes. On the one hand, each *malik* may feel bound by the traditional obligation to help his laborers, while this also presents an opportunity to enter into a court case in which another Chamar is supported by a rival leader. Thus, Bhumihars can extend their own factional rivalry to the field of Chamar interaction. On the other hand, part of the strategy also seems to be that by providing support to the Chamars so they may fight each other, they cannot be unified in their opposition to the Bhumihars. Furthermore, lending money for nonproductive causes such as court cases is another sure way to see that a laborer remains in debt and dependent upon his *malik*.

Six months after leaving the field, I received a letter written by a close friend from Arunpur who is a teacher of English at the Intercollege and whose elder brother is the Pradhan. Though understanding and sympathetic to the plight of the Chamars, he claims he is impotent to act because of his own Bhumihar caste loyalties and fear of his kinsmen's reproaches. He wrote (in English):

> There is a case of beating in the court. This case was started only on the instigation of Bhumihars.[8] There is [also] a burning problem among the Harijans [i.e., Chamars] about spirits and ghosts *[pret* and *bhut]*. Everyday there is a *panchayat* among them. Mohan Ram and Hans [Mohan's son] have spent five hundred rupees on *bhut*. Ballu and other people have spoiled their houses in this. One day some Chamars came to my house for *panchayat* and wanted to beat Kallu who is *ohja* [exorcisor of spirits] because Kallu took money from Ballu and Mohan to control the *bhut*. But Kallu did not do so [control the *bhut*?] and asked more money. Anyhow this dispute was settled in the *panchayat*. In this way Chamars are entangled in their own problems and superstitions, how can they face Bhumihars?

THE POLITICAL ARENA: CLASS CONFLICT 181

CHANGE AND CLASS AMONG ARUNPUR CHAMARS

Amid all their problems of poverty, *mazduri,* relations to the Bhumihars, and the internal conflicts that have divided them, the Chamars still have a desire to change their situation. Their opportunity to do something seemed to come when we arrived in the village and showed them a respect and type of behavior no other people had ever accorded to them. My assistant involved himself most in their affairs, much to the anger of some other villagers, and he gave the Chamars a much higher expectation of what could possibly be achieved.

One of the first things my assistant did, after becoming reconciled to the fact that we had to interact with all castes in the village, was to call a series of rather clandestine nighttime meetings which some ten to twelve Chamars attended at our house. His plan was to have them form a committee which could then decide and act on behalf of the rest of the community, so that something constructive might be done about their working and living conditions. The main topics of discussion at these meetings were certain complaints of Chamars. They also wanted to introduce some reform in their caste and repeatedly asked us to show them the way and tell them how to act.

They wrote a letter to Jagjivan Ram, then the Minister of Food and Agriculture and of their caste, asking his help in these matters. After the Chamars received a reply which advised them to see the Director in Charge of Harijan Welfare, they decided to formulate their complaints in another personal letter to this Congress leader. My assistant helped to draft a letter which drew attention to Chamar needs for (1) drinking wells, (2) a place to throw garbage, (3) a place for the children to play, (4) some land to build a guest house, and (5) change in the treatment of their women.

After the letter was posted, some two weeks passed and still no answer had been received. The Chamars came daily to inquire about the matter from us. Finally, it was learned that Jagjivan Ram was coming to Banaras and my assistant suggested that they go there and meet with him. Another letter was written which was to be given personally to Mr. Ram. On the day of his scheduled talk, some six weeks after the original letter had been sent, three Chamars prepared to meet him in Banaras.

One of them, who had carried the letter, later said that he succeeded in sitting behind the Congress leader on the stage. "But in listening to his views on Christianity, I forgot to notice when he was leaving." The Chamar then managed to push through the crowd and get near the official's car. By shouting loudly, he was noticed by Mr. Ram, who stopped his car and took the letter. When my assistant asked why the villager had become so engrossed in the talk, he replied:

> Because I was thinking that, really speaking, if we leave our religion and go into that religion [Christianity] we will always be considered as newcomers. But, how good it would be if some high-caste Hindus had a place in their hearts for Chamars. Then they [the Chamars] would really be proud of their Hinduism.

The second major plan of the Chamars was an attempt to negotiate with the Bhumihars, through my assistant, for higher wages and better working conditions. After several nighttime meetings, the following demands were agreed upon as being acceptable terms of their labor:

1. A ploughman or full-time agricultural worker should receive sixty rupees per month[9] + one half *paua* (one quarter pound) roasted grain and one half *paua* molasses.
2. Ten hours of work a day with a two-hour break in the middle.

or,

1. One *bigha* of land plus eight rupees per month for six months' labor.
2. Ten hours a day of work.

and

3. Women should receive food once a day or one half *ser* (one pound) flour + one half *paua* roasted grain and a jug of sugared water.
4. Women should work ten hours a day.
5. One day in a month free for all workers.
6. At harvest time: (a) women should receive three *sers* (six pounds) daily.
    (b) men should receive one head-load out of sixteen cut.

My assistant started to speak with some of the Bhumihars with whom he was on more friendly terms, notably faction leaders Jai Singh and Chandra Singh, after these demands were agreed upon. Their reaction was one of dismay; when the Chamars don't even work honestly for their present wages, what was the sense of increasing them? In the context of a discussion about the need for a leader *(neta)* who can help both the poor and the rich, Chandra said,

> But how will the man whose leg is not hurt feel the pain of others? Somebody comes from outside, initiates a "strike," and then goes away. Then the strikers as well as the other party suffers. In the same way, people

come from somewhere, plead for change in the village, such as *mazduri*, and then go from here, leaving the villagers to remain and suffer.

The position and seeming arrogance of my assistant not only angered most of the Bhumihars, but was even regarded as being anomalous by some Chamars. One of them was led to comment:

> The man who thinks of helping this *pura* is a fool. He loses his prestige because everyone knows that if he comes to help the Chamars, whom nobody likes, he becomes a stone in the eyes of high-caste people. And the Chamars, who are lazy, are not going to start the work [of repairing their wells]—and so this man gets a bad name. . . . You [my assistant] just said that you will give the people bricks to fix their wells, but still they didn't start. Yet everyone in the village who knows this thing [the offer of bricks] is saying, "Look, look, they are helping the Chamars." So neither do you get something [i.e., prestige], nor do we [repair of the wells]. So that is why the man who thinks of helping these people is a fool.

Thus, the only result of a rather abortive attempt to help the Chamars was, unfortunately, to heighten the already existing conflict between them and the Bhumihars. It also added to the Untouchables' consciousness of the inequity of their position as well as to the growing desire, especially among the younger and sometimes more educated ones, to do something to remedy the situation. Although before we came to the village, there had been some expression of class conflict between those with and those without land, between landlords and laborers, by all accounts it now became more open. Not only did the Chamars feel that they had an ally in us, but our intercession in physical fights on several occasions assured them that Bhumihar wrath would be held in check so long as we would remain in the village.

We were not to remain for long, of course, and as Chandra Singh so incisively noted, it is the ones whom we left behind, not we the interlopers, who suffered most. Although the Chamars seem back in the same position as before our arrival, that is, totally on their own and with no outside resources on which to depend in their struggle, the form of the conflict is bound to have changed somewhat. They dared to oppose the Bhumihars on several occasions and, perhaps with the lessening of the ill feeling between the pro- and anti-Bhumihar factions, they may be in a position of more strength in the future. For the Chamars, who have so far been effectively barred from any meaningful participation in the "new" India, it seems that the only way they can change their class position is by a conscious working toward that goal. It will take a concentrated and united effort on their part to arrest the stagnating conditions of their lives as changes, which are affecting others, bypass the Chamars.

NOTES

1. Their small number and situation of total dependence upon the Bhumihars have prevented the Musahars and Dharkars from joining with the Chamars. In addition, Chamar belief in values sustaining hierarchy (that these castes are below them; thus, they will not accept food or water from them), plus their physical separation from other Untouchables, has prevented action based on the recognition of their common interests (see also Juyal 1974).
2. Other meanings are "owner," "lord," and "husband."
3. Although it may be literally true that Chamars are "sharecroppers" insofar as they cultivate the land and share in the harvest, in reality the land and share received is so small that it may be better understood as part of a wage *(mazduri)*.
4. The usual items given are two towels, two shirts, and two *dhotis* (long pieces of cloth).
5. Cohn, reporting on fieldwork conducted in neighboring Jaunpur District in 1952 to 1953, writes that the daily wage for agricultural labor was two *sers* of grain plus breakfast (1955:64). Fifteen years later, the wage had decreased!
6. These figures were given by Kurmi informants. Telis are known to pay two rupees per day plus lunch and breakfast and Kahars will pay three rupees for Chamar labor. This is higher than Bhumihars and Brahmans are willing to pay, although four Bhumihars are said to pay two rupees per day to laborers.
7. In Kilavenmani village (Tanjore District, Tamilnadu), forty-two children and women—including three old men—were burnt alive in a hut in the Untouchable quarter on December 25, 1968. Ostensibly due to a dispute over wages, the tragedy was closely linked to an effort of local landlords to root out "troublesome" farm laborers. As far as I know, no one was prosecuted in the case.
8. It is not clear, however, whether or not this case has to do with the information that follows.
9. They originally wanted to ask for a minimum of three rupees per day.

CHAPTER 9
The Politics of Water

Classes as well as factions are both ultimately concerned with the same phenomenon—conflict—and represent two different ways of organizing the villagewide political arena in India. This conflict is over the distribution of prizes a society has to offer its members, and these prizes are its scarce and valued resources. The political arena has widened because local authority is no longer vested in any specific position. There is no counterpart to the formal power that the British-appointed headman wielded, nor do the present-day big men and traditional *panchayats* command the same respect as they had previously. The resulting competition for leadership takes place in an arena containing expanded resources. In addition to the old conflicts over land, prestige and display, power, followers, and women, there is now competition for water, government aid, education, elective offices, and contact with influential outsiders.

Although there have always been disputes over land, particularly among kinsmen, those over elective offices and government tubewell water are post-Independence phenomena. Competition for water is the cause of most disputes; elections are held only every few years and available land is in short supply, but water is almost always available for distribution. At the same time, because of the great demand for irrigation in agriculture, water is perennially scarce. Hence, constant and fierce political activity revolves around this resource. The competition for water also reveals the range of activity in the Arunpur political arena, for it figures in conflict among factions, classes, and individuals.

DISTRIBUTION OF WATER IN ARUNPUR

The competition for resources is a complex matter in Arunpur, and the lack of any definite and widely accepted rules according to which certain things of value are distributed accounts for much of the conflict. The distribution of water is a case in point. This section will describe how one of the major factors influencing conflict is the lack of agreement regarding who has the authority to make decisions about the allocation of water from the government tubewell.

Case 29: Main Pura versus Little Pura for Mismanagement
of Water Distribution 1966–1967

A record book on water distribution kept by the Pradhan reveals that the government tubewell, built near Little Pura in 1953, was to serve Arunpur and five other neighboring villages. The village official in charge of water distribution *(thokdar)* was the elected village head *(pradhan)*. Arunpur, however, had two such officials—one was the Pradhan from Main Pura and the other was Jai Singh, appointed to protect the interest of the Bhumihars of Little Pura. Because the latter managed to keep the Tubewell Operator (who implemented decisions regarding allocation) on their side, they received the lion's share.

A new Tubewell Operator was appointed in 1966. He discovered this monopoly and lodged a complaint with the Irrigation Department, District Magistrate, and Police Inspector (dated November 9, 1966). The *thokdar*s of the five other villages also made complaints, as did several farmers. The Police Inspector was ordered to look into the matter; subsequently a lawsuit was filed against the Little Pura Bhumihars. After a number of court appearances by both sides, a compromise was reached and the case was dropped on May 24, 1967.

At the time of the inauguration of the government tubewell, and indeed at the present time as well, it was in the best interests of the Bhumihars of Little Pura to unite together against the rest of the village (specifically, Main Pura). The twelve households of Bhumihars and Kurmis in that *pura* hold 106 and 26 *bigha*s of land, respectively. This is a proportionately greater amount of land than the Bhumihars and other castes of Main Pura own (see Tables 1 and 2). In addition, their land is nearer to the tubewell and a larger area can be irrigated in a shorter time compared with land that is at a greater distance.

Most of the other five villages depend less upon this tubewell for water today, as they have their own government tubewells or private pumping sets. Only a negligible amount of land, lying near Arunpur borders, need be irrigated by its tubewell. The two exceptions are the villages of Saranpur and Ramapur. Saranpur, lying nearest to Arunpur and with a population of about seventy-five people, has no other source of irrigation. Krishna Singh of Ramapur is supposed to receive twelve hours of water per week as a result of a confrontation between his younger brother and Jai Singh (along with other Little Pura Bhumihars) in 1967. Krishna's brother was denied water for his fields when he requested it on one occasion. Then "one hundred" of Krishna's men returned to the tubewell, armed with sticks, spears, and hatchets, and received the water that was demanded.

The Little Pura-Main Pura dichotomy over water has remained because it coincides with their land interests and is reinforced by the actions of the Tubewell Operator. He is a government appointee who looks after the running of the tubewell, decides allocation priorities, implements the decisions of the *thokdars*, keeps the records, and collects the fees for water consumed. Since 1967, the Operator has been a Brahman who comes from a nearby village. Although he is always supposed to remain at the tubewell (even to sleep), he was scarcely ever there. He seems to have informally delegated some responsibilities to two men from an Untouchable family of Dharkars that live near the tubewell. In return, they were able to bathe in the tubewell tank and could take water from there.

The Operator had a close relationship with the Little Pura Bhumihars, especially with the younger brothers of Chandra Singh and Raj Kumar Singh who are in charge of their families' farming. The Operator readily admitted to taking bribes from them, and, since they have the most land, they gave the most. The people in Main Pura were reluctant to give such gifts. When they did so, it was usually in small amounts. The Operator also said that taking bribes presented no special risk because he shared his "black" money with other officials. Nor was he adverse to falsifying his records. An agriculturalist may receive more water than he should and the excess amount will not be listed or, worse yet, will be charged against another.

The Tubewell Operator was not only dependent upon the big men of Little Pura and their families for bribery but also, as an outsider, for hospitality as well. He would often eat at their houses and was most often in their company on the days that he was in the village. Toward the end of my stay, however, a dispute occurred between him and a Little Pura Bhumihar. It created much ill feeling and the operator was transferred to another area.

It is hard to assess where the actual authority lies in making decisions regarding the distribution of tubewell water. There is supposed to be an agreed upon allocation of hours to Little Pura and Main Pura (including the other *puras*). The *thokdars*, in consultation with the villagers, are then to draw up a schedule for the allocation of water under their control and present this to the Operator. Actually, the situation is complex because of a number of factors: the power of the Little Pura Bhumihars to claim more hours, the monopoly of the remaining time for the rest of the village by the Pradhan's family, his *pattidars* and another *patti* of allied Bhumihars (the Choudhuris),[1] and the inability of the Operator to make any decisions independently of the Bhumihars, especially those of Little Pura. In addition, decisions must also take into account the nature of the crops to be irrigated.

The roles of Jai Singh and the Pradhan are equally hard to assess. When Jai became the *thokdar* in 1953 to safeguard the interests of his *pura,* factional conflict within his *khandan* had not crystallized to the current extent. Although he officially resigned from this position a few years ago, he is still influential in decision making (see Case 32). The duties of the *thokdar* of Little Pura are now carried out by Chandra Singh and Raj Kumar Singh's uncle, Rampat, as well. The Pradhan has delegated his authority to a young (age twenty-six) Bhumihar of the allied *patti* of Choudhuri Bhumihars, Kallu Singh. Complaints and the threat and use of force became so divisive in his *pura* by March, 1969, that the Pradhan established a committee of three villagers (a man from his family, Kallu Singh and a Brahman—Vijay Misra) to supervise water distribution.

A farmer, especially from one of the other villages, does not know whom to approach with his request for water. The result is a situation of uncertainty in which each dispute seems to be settled on the spot with reference to the people involved, the force or threat of force they use, and their whims regarding compromise. This uncertainty means that every actual case of allocation is potentially a conflict situation. The result has been not only to increase disputes in the village, but to cause ill will and anger among people who would otherwise be friends.

COMPETITION FOR WATER ORGANIZED BY FACTIONS

One way in which the competition for government tubewell water is organized is by the two village factions. These delineate different channels of support which a farmer may call upon and which can prove crucial in settling a dispute.

Case 30: Bhumihars of Three Villages Fight over Water   c. 1957

Chandra Singh of Arunpur wanted his close friend from Saranpur,

Nandalal Singh, to be in charge of water distribution *(thokdar)* for that village. Saranpur shares water from Arunpur's tubewell. Chandra approached an influential Bhumihar of that village, Kumar Singh, who agreed to back Nandalal, even though he knew that the latter was a staunch follower of Chandra. After signing the *thokdar* nomination papers, the Bhumihar (Kumar) told his friend Krishna Singh of Ramapur what he had done. As Krishna was a rival of Chandra Singh, he had the nomination paper legally canceled.

The next time tubewell water was flowing into Kumar Singh's fields, Chandra retaliated by diverting the water. Then he locked the tubewell engine room and removed various machinery parts to his house. Kumar went to see the Tubewell Operator in Arunpur. There he met a member of Chandra's *khandan,* Ram Singh, who belonged to the rival faction. Ram helped Kumar enter the engine room and start the motor. The two men then remained all night guarding the tubewell.

Chandra Singh then filed a suit against Ram Singh and some other rival kinsmen of his *khandan* for having started the tubewell in the absence of the Operator and for stealing part of the machinery, which Chandra himself had done. Krishna Singh helped Ram Singh and the other rivals of Chandra named in the court case. Krishna also succeeded in bribing the Tubewell Operator who testified in court that the man who appeared there as Ram Singh was not the true Ram Singh (though in fact he was). As the "true" Ram Singh could not be found, the Judge dismissed the case.

Case 31: The Beating of Jai Singh's *Mazdur*   1969

The Musahar servant boy of Jai Singh refused to divert water from his *malik*'s field into that of a rival's, Raj Kumar Singh. Moti, Raj Kumar's younger brother, beat the Musahar and diverted the water into his own field.

Jai's son heard the noise in the fields and went to see what had happened. He then went to Chandra Singh's house, where some other Bhumihars and ourselves had gathered. Some spoke of going to beat Moti Singh, but Chandra only dispatched someone to summon up Jai Singh who was visiting in a nearby village.

When Jai returned, the matter was talked out with an elder of Raj Kumar's family (Rampat Singh), and water flowed once again to Jai's fields. Jai said, several days later, that he had really been angry and would have beaten Moti but for the restraining influence of the men gathered at Chandra's door. He was, however, ready to file a lawsuit against the next man who might try to divert his water.

These two cases illustrate how factions organize competition for water. They consist of networks of support between faction leaders and their followers which are utilized in the struggle for water. Case 30 reveals the crosscutting ties and links between several villages which are activated by competition for a single resource. The original issue involved Chandra Singh of Arunpur, his man Nandalal Singh of Saranpur, and a third Bhumihar of that village, Kumar Singh. Krishna Singh of Ramapur became involved because of his friendship with the latter and his enmity with Chandra. The aid of Chandra's own *khandan* rivals was also enlisted. It is not unusual for factions in two or more villages to be linked together in such a way that the friend of any man's rival is his enemy, and the rival's enemies are his friends. When this case is connected to the factions that exist in Ramapur, where Krishna's foremost rival is his own *pattidar,* then we can see a series of alliances across three villages; these can extend outward to encompass even larger areas.

ARUNPUR	RAMAPUR	SARANPUR
Chandra Singh et al.	allied with Jangi Singh	allied with Nandalal Singh
versus	versus	versus
Pradhan and Raj Kumar Singh	allied with Krishna Singh	allied with Kumar Singh

Case 31, although remaining a purely Arunpur affair, goes through the typical developmental cycle characteristic of factional conflict (see Chapter 7). The initial break of relations began with the demand that the *mazdur* of Jai Singh divert water into a rival's field and was followed by the beating of the boy. The crisis then spread to extend to the members of the two factions in Little Pura. Raj Kumar Singh's uncle, Chandra Singh's younger brother, and another follower became involved, the latter two demanding that Moti be beaten. Jai and Raj Kumar's uncle attempted to settle the dispute peaceably, and it was mainly through the restraining presence of Chandra Singh, ourselves, and other men that Jai's temper was "cooled." This crisis also underlines the fact that conflict between factions always reinforces the schism between them; conflict reinforces the need for factions.

Allocation of water is also used by one faction to create divisions within the other. I was told by members of the Pradhan's party that the Tubewell Operator, induced by Chandra Singh, would refuse to give extra hours to the Kurmis in Main Pura. In this way, the Kurmis turn against the Pradhan and other Bhumihars, for the latter would already have irrigated their own fields and used up most of the time allotted to Main Pura. In addition, the allocation of water is also used to force men who attempt to remain independent of factions to recognize their folly.

Such a man will be unsuccessful in obtaining water from the leaders of either faction. Each side he approaches will taunt him to request help from the other side with which he is also friendly.

COMPETITION BETWEEN CLASSES

The allocation of water to the Chamars is perhaps the best example of the way that Bhumihars use the distribution of resources to further their own political ends. With water being such a scarce and valued resource, it is understandable why the low and powerless Chamars suffer most. The stronger villagers (Brahman, Bhumihar, and Kurmi) divert water that goes into Chamar fields to their own. The latter, rightly, also see this denial of water as reflecting the desire of high castes to keep them in poverty and subjugation. Over and over again, Bhumihars would say (and Chamars affirm) that, "If they get too much in their stomachs, they will not work for us." Or, "They have filled their stomachs too well and that is why they dare to act this way."

No Bhumihar cared to see that water was given properly to Chamars. In each case that they did receive some, it was only because some upper-caste men saw an advantage in manipulating the situation in that way. The information presented in the following case histories, relating to two separate occasions on which the Chamars received water, is not exhaustive. Chamars and others had been talking for days, indeed months, about their problem. Even in these situations, there were many differences of opinion regarding what actually took place (especially from the two factions), but the main points remain clear.

Case 32: Jai Singh "Gives" Water to the Chamars 1968

The Pradhan told some Chamars to take water early in the morning. When they went to divert the water into their fields, they were then told that two Kurmis and a Brahman were taking (and going to take) water. A Chamar boy tried to divert water from the tubewell canal, but one of the Kurmis and the Brahman[2] threatened to beat him. Mohan Ram, a Chamar leader, went to the tubewell and said that he was going to take water into his fields. Some Bhumihars came and threatened to beat him as well. Other Chamars restrained Mohan and they all returned home without receiving any water.

In the evening, the Chamars said that they still had not received water, although Jai Singh had promised my assistant and myself that he would give them water on this day. The Chamars blamed the Pradhan, who is supposed to have jurisdiction over water allocation to their *pura*.

Jai Singh came the next morning to tell us that all who needed water, save one Chamar, had received it. He said that the previous day, when he had gone to the tubewell to divert water for the Chamars, the Pradhan and some other Bhumihars (of Main Pura) came there to take water for themselves. After an exchange of verbal abuse, it was decided when and whom among the Chamars would receive water. The latter agreed that it was really Jai who had helped them.

Case 33: The Brahman *Thokdar* and Chandra Singh
Support the Chamars   1969

Beginning March 5, water was to flow into Main Pura's (including Chamar Pura) fields for four days. The next day, Mohan Ram Chamar went to the Pradhan to request water and was told: "First let those with onions in their fields take water, and then you will get some for your wheat." A Bhumihar of the Choudhuri *patti,* allied to the Pradhan, took water for his onions and then for his wheat. The Chamars were bypassed but they planned to get water somehow.

On March 7, a Chamar follower of Chandra Singh complained to the latter that, "We have elected one man as *pradhan,* but if you go to his house you will find eight people who act as *pradhan.*" The Chamar threatened to divert the water, even if it was flowing into Chandra's own fields. Chandra at first retaliated with a clenched fist and then said that he was a friend of Chamars. He berated the Pradhan and told the Chamar to take water the next time it went into the Pradhan's fields. Chandra also promised to help in this matter.

When only eight hours remained of Main Pura's allotment of water, on March 8, a Bhumihar of the Choudhuri *patti* took water for his fields. It was going to be taken by one of his *pattidars* after him.

The Brahman *thokdar,* Vijay Misra, and some other Bhumihars (one of the Kolha *patti* and one belonging to that of Narain Singh) and Chamars were discussing how to get water for themselves. The Tubewell Operator came by and told them of a big fight at the tubewell. Mohan Ram and some other Chamars had diverted water from the fields of the two Choudhuri Bhumihars. Vijay Misra went to the tubewell and, along with Chandra Singh's younger brother and an ally, supported the Chamars' claim for water. Chandra's brother and the two Choudhuri Bhumihars abused each other and accused each other of being dishonest. Finally, it was agreed that the Chamars could take the water.

Several hours later, in the evening, a third Choudhuri *pattidar* came and rediverted the water into his fields. Vijay Misra then advised the Chamars to divert the water back into their fields. They went to do this some time after 9 p.m. The Choudhuri Bhumihar and some other Bhumihars from Main Pura started pushing and abusing the Chamars. While this altercation was going on, one Bhumihar in the group (a Kolha) took water into his fields.

When it was finally decided that the Chamars could take the water, again by the support of Vijay Misra, Chandra Singh's brother and his ally, they received it for only a short time. At midnight, Little Pura Bhumihars said, "It is the next day and so now we are taking the water." And they began their five days (see also Case 36).

The significant points that result from an analysis of these (and other) disputes between Chamars and village landowners relate to the lack of authority in water allocation, the role of the disaffected farmers in Main Pura, the threat or use of force, and the role of factions.

The lack of authority of any one person or position to make decisions about the allocation of water that are obeyed by all has been discussed in the first section of this chapter. The Pradhan may direct or "suggest" that the Chamars take water, but he does not enforce this decision and instead departs to his business outside the village. Although the Pradhan has delegated certain people to look after his own interests and those of other Bhumihars and villagers (i.e., his new committee of three *thokdars*), no one is concerned with implementing decisions relating to the Chamars. Each person they approach tells them to see someone else and they shuffle back and forth in a futile gesture. Those who do intervene have other motives for doing so and regard the Chamars as pawns in their own power struggle.

Landowners with more power than the Chamars do not hesitate to deprive them of this resource. When water is allotted to Main Pura (and includes the rest of the village except for Little Pura), it is the Pradhan, his *pattidars*, and the closely allied Bhumihar *patti* of Choudhuris who receive the first share. Those who are not members of these two groups must then fight among themselves to receive what little time remains. These disaffected others are primarily from the *patti* of the Brahman who was appointed a *thokdar*, Vijay Misra, the *patti* of Kolha Bhumihars, and the two major Kurmi farmers. It is these people who most often divert the water from the Chamars by threats or the use of force. There is no way, at present, for the Chamars to react against this. The one Chamar leader most willing to fight back, Mohan Ram, owns 1.25 *bighas* of land and is independent of the Bhumihars. But others, who are dependent laborers and fear the repercussions of their actions, most often restrain Mohan.

The information I have allows me only to guess at the reasons that Vijay Misra chose to support the Chamars in Case 32 (unlike his position in

Case 31). Four months before this incident, Vijay had a big dispute over water with Kallu Singh of the Bhumihar Choudhuri *patti,* who at that time was the only *thokdar* in Main Pura (Case 36, following). Vijay may have backed the Chamars because he was still smarting from that humiliation and wanted to take the opportunity to get back at Kallu Singh's *pattidars.* Clearly, he was still ill disposed toward these Bhumihars at the time.

Village factionalism is also an important factor in the Chamars' quest for water. A Nai, who is a "hardcore" follower of the Pradhan, recommended that the Chamars fight against the Little Pura Bhumihars; Chandra Singh similarly told them to fight against the Pradhan. Each one blamed the other side for not giving water to Chamars and each one promised support if they did take a stand. The Nai is known himself to have a number of Chamar supporters, and his purpose in promising to be their *agua* (leader) is clearly to strengthen the Pradhan's position. Chandra's own thinking was disclosed when he reacted violently each time a Chamar threatened to divert water going into his fields.

Water distribution among the Chamars represents another area of village life which is used as a means to promote factional interests and to gain supporters (this time among the Chamars). Jai Singh and other Bhumihars in his party did back the Chamars in their conflict with Main Pura Bhumihars. The role that Jai played in allocating (or in being attributed with the allocation of) water to the Chamars further points to the diffuse nature of decision making in the village mentioned earlier. Although he is no longer *thokdar* and thus has no official power to make such decisions, Jai does have informal power and authority in these matters. This is not only because of his past position, but also because of his friendly nature and easy accessibility to villagers.

COMPETITION AMONG INDIVIDUALS

Besides the conflict over water, in which people compete as members of factions or classes, a third type of conflict characterizes competition in the political arena of Arunpur that is not encompassed by these two forms. This takes place among people who are in the same faction or class and who are otherwise on good terms with one another. Although I have information about this type of competition only for one resource, water, an examination of the disputes in question reveals that a pattern emerges that even makes it possible to predict the actions of people in other specific situations. This is because there is a relatively stable distribution of power in Arunpur at present and water is allocated according to the structure of this hierarchy.

The pattern of conflict in this third field of the political arena involves

THE POLITICS OF WATER 195

the disputes over allocation to Little Pura and to Main Pura (including the rest of the village). Then there is the conflict between the Pradhan and his allies, who receive water first, and the other farmers. The position of three other Bhumihars who have much land but have no *pattidars* is also discussed.

Cases 34 and 35: Disputes between Main Pura and Little
Pura over Water Allocation   1968, 1969

34. Water was running for ten days and nights into Little Pura's fields. It was decided that water would then go into Main Pura for the same amount of time. On November 19, water started going into Main Pura, but on the third day (November 22), Jai Singh ordered that the water be returned to Little Pura. The potato fields of his ally, Chandra Singh, were drying up. A Bhumihar from the Pradhan's family and one from the Choudhuri *patti* went to speak with Jai and the Tubewell Operator. It was then agreed that water would not be diverted from Main Pura for another two days—long enough to irrigate the Pradhan's fields. It was also decided that water would start coming again to Main Pura during the day. However, word was later sent that water would not be available until the night of the 22nd. Some men in the Pradhan's family wanted to beat the Bhumihars of Little Pura (meaning their rivals, of course) for their behavior, but were restrained by a family elder.

35. Water was to go into Main Pura from Little Pura one morning, but it did not. About fifteen to twenty men from the Pradhan's *patti* and that of the Choudhuri Bhumihars went to the Tubewell Operator to find out what had happened. Chandra Singh was there and said that the water was going into Raj Kumar Singh's fields for an extra six hours. Since Raj Kumar is allied to the Pradhan's family, the latter kept quiet and returned without taking water at that time.

It is generally acknowledged that decisions about which *pura* or village should receive water are made by the people in Little Pura (especially Chandra Singh and Jai Singh), who have influence and control over the Tubewell Operator. Raj Kumar Singh and his family serve to benefit from this because a greater number of hours are allotted to Little Pura. This causes stress on alliances and friendships that run between the two *puras* and people often talk disparagingly of the behavior of "so-called friends." On one occasion, old Amar Singh of the Pradhan's household went to see Raj Kumar's uncle to request help in getting water for his fields. Amar related that his family had not taken any water during the previous period allotted to Main Pura because others needed it more. The two old men exchanged hot words and ended up cursing each other.

The Pradhan's *pattidars* and supporters say that the Little Pura people use water allocation to create divisions within Main Pura by cutting back in the amount of time that is allotted for the latter. This leads the Main Pura farmers to fight among themselves; it also makes certain people more dependent upon the Little Pura Bhumihars. For example, the *pattidar* of Narain Singh who attempts to be friendly with both sides will go and beg for water from Jai Singh. The shortage of time allowed for Main Pura creates conflict between men in the same *pura* as well. The following dispute was between the *thokdar* Kallu Singh and the Brahman Vijay Misra (before he became *thokdar,* four months later).

Case 36: Water Dispute between the *Thokdar* and a Brahman   1968

Water had been going into the fields of Kallu Singh, the *thokdar* for Main Pura. Vijay Misra was to receive water next. Instead, a Bhumihar of the Kolha *patti* asked Kallu if he could have the water, and the *thokdar* agreed. When Vijay went to take the water, he found the Kolha Bhumihar had already taken it and waited for him to finish irrigating his fields. However, the Bhumihar then said that the water would go next into the fields of a *pattidar* of Kallu Singh, Lakkhan Singh.

Vijay became angry with this and diverted the water into the canal leading to his field. Some of the water ran out of the dirt canal and into the potato field of Lakkhan Singh because of a difference in the levels of the fields. When the latter heard that his potatoes were being "flooded," he, Kallu Singh, and some other *pattidars* ran to the tubewell with sticks. Kallu cursed Vijay. The latter said that at the time he "wanted to beat Kallu and his *pattidars* because they were proud of their education, wealth and power."

One of the Kolha Bhumihars and Chandra Singh settled the dispute. Kallu was later ashamed of his behavior and apologized to Vijay Misra.

In this case, the two Bhumihar *patti*s of the Kolhas and the Choudhuris stood together against the Brahman, Vijay Misra. On other occasions the Kurmis vent their anger at the Bhumihars, especially Kallu Singh, the *thokdar,* and say that they are "low" men who seek to deprive the Kurmis of those things they have a right to—such as, tubewell water, student subsidies, and teaching positions at the Intercollege. The Kurmis, Brahmans, and Kolha Bhumihars (who alternate in siding with Kallu Singh's *patti* or with Vijay Misra and other farmers, as well as with the two village factions) turn against one another in the process of struggling and manipulating to gain water.

The most luckless people in Main Pura are those Bhumihars who are not in the Pradhan's faction and are known to be friendly with Chandra and Jai. They are often denied water by the Pradhan and others who control the distribution in that *pura,* as well as by their "friends" in Little Pura. There is also conflict for water within a single *patti.* On several occasions I noted one of the Pradhan's *pattidars* abusing and arguing with him for denying a sufficient amount of water to his relatives.

I know of only one real attempt made to settle these disputes and fights raging daily within Main Pura while we were there. It seems that matters had come to a head and many were threatening to use force to take water for themselves. The original decisions about allocation were disregarded, and as soon as one man began to irrigate his fields, someone else would divert the water to his own field. One of the Pradhan's family members and the *thokdar* (Kallu Singh) called a meeting of the people from Main Pura and from the Chamar *pura.* Several men were chosen to decide the order of water allocation and all present agreed to the new schedule. Soon after this water *"panchayat"* had taken place, however, one of the Pradhan's *pattidars* demanded that he receive water earlier. He tried to divert water which was then irrigating Vijay Misra's fields, and the two came to blows.

THE STRUCTURE OF CONFLICT

Political conflict in the villagewide arena has been approached from another perspective than the one that characterized the two previous chapters, which focus on the different cleavages present in society and how these are articulated on a wide range of issues. By contrast, this chapter contains information on a single resource to show how the different forms of conflict organization operate with respect to it. More specifically, it reveals the complexity of even so small an arena as a village and identifies a third field of political activity in addition to factional and class conflict.

The people involved in this third sphere of political action do not engage in competition as members of different factions or classes (although individual caste differences may be a part of the situation). A man may be simultaneously acting in different roles when competing for a resource. He may compete as a member of a specific *pura* for the right to have water, only to find that this also draws him into disputes with his allies in another *pura.* He may also come into conflict with men of his own *pura* with whom he is usually friendly. A noticeable difference,

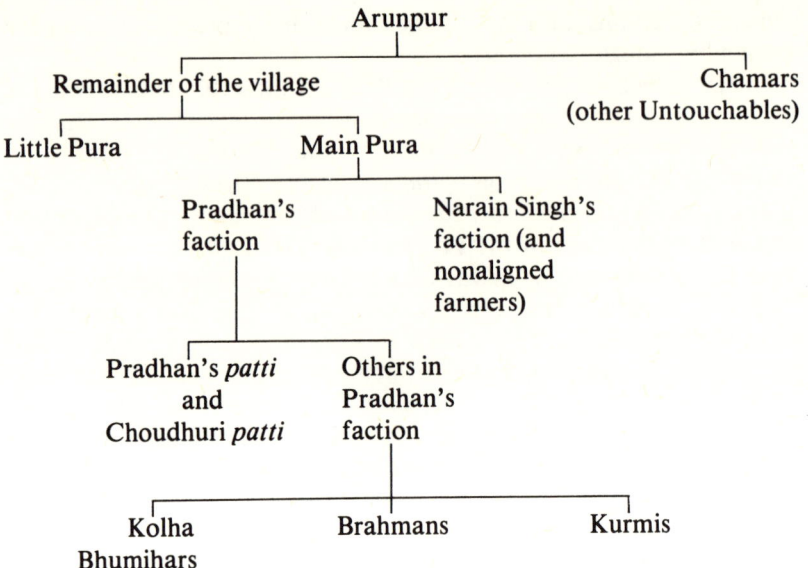

CHART 3. Conflict over resources: water from the government tubewell.

however, between conflict among individuals as opposed to that involving groups or quasigroups is that the breach does not widen as greatly in most cases and there is a tendency for these disputes to be settled more quickly.

By integrating the different fields of the villagewide political arena identified through the study of a single resource, a certain predictable pattern of conflict emerges which coincides with the distribution of power. Chart 3 indicates that the conflict over resources is of a segmentary nature.[3] Although the specification of who will compete at each level will differ according to the resource in question and the people for whom it has relevance, it can be expected that the general pattern will remain the same.

The diagram in Chart 3 reads from top to bottom; the groups on the left are successful in competition at each level. In other words, water from the government tubewell is a resource which has come to the village and is theoretically available to all who have land. At the highest level of conflict, the Chamars are denied water and it is allocated to the rest of the village (i.e., Main Pura and Little Pura). Little Pura gets water first and a certain amount of time remains for Main Pura. The lion's share is then taken by the Pradhan's faction—the Pradhan, his *pattidar*s, and subsequently the closely allied *patti* of Choudhuri Bhumihars. This faction attempts to prevent the nonaligned farmers and those of Narain Singh's faction from obtaining a share in the distribution of water. If sufficient time is allocated to Main Pura, other supporters of the Pradhan's faction will compete with one another.

An element affecting factional alignments is this competition between allies over the distribution of water (or other resources). It would seem that as available resources increase in abundance so that they can percolate downward among the population, there will be more conflict between the village big man and those who join his faction. The latter will no longer be satisfied with simply basking in the light of the prestige gained by their leader, but will demand a larger share of the rewards that accrue to their coalition. The necessary condition for the extension of conflict seems to be that the specific resource in question is present in sufficient quantity so that, after the big men have received their share, enough still remains for which others can compete. The converse of this is that a scarcity of resources makes the power of the leaders more secure.

The introduction of new resources into the rural area has had a definite effect on village conflict. These resources are introduced from the outside (i.e., from the government) and are theoretically available to all villagers. This results in conflict which filters downward along the power hierarchy of the village. The greater the amount of a resource, the more competition will be generated at the lower levels and it seems correct to conclude that the introduction of resources into a "politics of scarcity" will generate more, not less, conflict. While the distribution of many new resources thus tends to follow a pattern congruent with the distribution of power, the picture becomes more complex when the village is incorporated into a larger political arena. In such a situation, lines of cleavage often submerged in village politics may come to the fore in the politics of the region.

NOTES

1. There are four different *pattis* of Bhumihars in Main Pura, that is, groups of patrilineally related kinsmen. In the following caste histories of water disputes, I shall refer to the different *pattis* as follows: (1) the Pradhan's family and their *pattidars*, (2) the Choudhuris (a Bhumihar *gotra* name), neighbors and close allies of the Pradhan (including the recently appointed *thokdar* Kallu Singh), (3) the Kolhas (another *gotra* name), a *patti* of Bhumihars who are reputed to switch their loyalties easily, and (4) Narain Singh and his *pattidars*. This does not include those Bhumihars who have no *pattidars*.

2. Vijay Misra, who was to become one of the three *thokdars* (see Case 33).
3. It will be noticed that, unlike that conflict in which the segments are equal at each level, conflict at the highest level is between decided unequals. In fact, except for water, labor, and elections, Untouchables are rarely contestants in the distribution of resources.

CHAPTER 10
Electoral Politics in Arunpur: The 1969 Midterm Poll

A village is not an isolated system; the links between Arunpur and the outside environment are manifold and expressed in varied ways (see Chapter 3). In this connection, Béteille has remarked that "political alignments and cleavages in the village have to be understood not only in relation to other features of its social structure, but also in terms of the divisions and tensions in the regional society" (1965:142). In the more recent past, the villagers have had a history of involvement in outside political activities stemming from the links of the zamindar and *mukhiya* with the British Raj and participation of some villagers in Gandhi's Non-Cooperation Movement. Subsequently, big men of opposing factions aligned themselves with different political parties and carried their supporters' votes with them.

The 1969 midterm election highlights the processes of interaction between two arenas. By concentrating on the political participation and perceptions of villagers rather than on the activities of the candidates themselves, I found several points of departure from previous elections and from the dominant mode of Arunpur politics. Membership in village factions had little impact on voter decision making in this election, whereas horizontal ties of caste and kinship, overlaid by class interests, were used effectively to recruit votes. This discontinuity between village politics and regional elections serves to underscore the lines of divergent interests within the village arena that, failing to find any suitable outlet there because of continuing Bhumihar dominance, seek expression within the wider arena.

Village Participation in State Politics

During the period 1967 to early 1969, villagers participated in several important political events that affected the state and regional arenas. A statewide agitation to replace English completely by Hindi in the government and the schools was led by the Samyukta Socialist Party (SSP) and involved students and teachers from Arunpur. Both the Principal of the Intercollege and Krishna Singh of Ramapur (the Intercollege Secretary) opposed them on this issue and were supporters of the Congress party position. Some village men who teach at the Intercollege also took part, and were later imprisoned, in the strike of the Uttar Pradesh secondary school teachers that started at the end of 1968. In the last quarter of that year, the campus of Banaras Hindu University was racked with conflict and violence, ostensibly due to student factions associated with different political affiliations (the right-wing Jan Sangh against a limited left coalition). Boys from Arunpur who attend the university expressed loyalty to the SSP-left coalition.

These events, however, did not truly affect most of the villagers. Instead, the major point of articulation between the village political system and that of the wider arena lies in the elections for state and national representatives. Four national and local elections have taken place since Independence,[1] and these were open to all villagers. The most important element of the political environment at the time of the present midterm poll was that the SSP candidate, who won in the 1967 general election from the constituency to which Arunpur belongs, is a Kurmi. Many Bhumihars and Brahmans harbored ill feelings from that time, and the element of caste loyalties (or casteism) figured significantly in the subsequent poll.

A detailed discussion of the factors leading up to the need to call another election only two years after the last one was held is outside the scope of this work (see, e.g., Baxter 1975; Brass 1968; Burger 1969; Graham 1968). It may be said, however, that the crisis was precipitated by the severe setback of the dominant Congress Party in the 1967 elections when its majorities were either lost or greatly reduced in almost all states. The Congress failed to win a majority in the U. P. State Legislative Assembly, and internal bargaining and a fragile alliance with the Independents did not sustain them in power for long. Factionalism within this dominant party and the new device of rampant defection ("floor crossing") was marked by the startling defection of a charismatic Congress Party leader in U.P., Charan Singh. He organized a new party—the Bharatiya Kranti Dal (BKD)—that was to be "spokesmen for the middle farmer and individual ownership." It was particularly to represent the interests of the Jat caste of peasant proprietors, living mainly in western U.P., to which Charan Singh belonged (Baxter 1975:113ff).[2] His chief lieutenant was a Kurmi leader from Faizabad District, bordering on the eastern region of the state.

Charan Singh assumed the office of Chief Minister of the state as the head of the Samyukta Vidhayak Dal (SVD), a united front consisting of non-Congress Party members of the State Assembly. They struggled along for some ten months, when large-scale defections led to his resignation and the imposition of President's Rule. New state elections were set for February 9, 1969 and a prominent new party on the scene was Charan Singh's BKD.

Out of the large array of candidates presented to the voters, only four were serious contenders belonging to major parties.[3] Bhaggu Ram (Brighunath), the Kurmi SSP incumbent, had won the election in 1967 with 55 percent of the constituency vote. In the midterm poll, he placed third, with only 17.4 percent of the popular votes. The "flash" BKD also put forward a Kurmi named Bal Dev. The Congress and Jan Sangh candidates were both Bhumihars who had many kinsmen and personal contacts with leading Bhumihar families in the area. Raj Bihari Singh was the eventual winner in the election. Jan Sangh's Vishwanath Singh, however, was a most respected candidate. An independently wealthy ex-magistrate with no immediate family members, he had failed twice before to win an election as a Member of Parliament. Much was made of his wealth and lack of relatives to claim favors from him, and he was put forward as the selfless politician; this was in contrast to what was believed about the incumbent. Villagers said that Bhaggu Ram had been a poor man with only two *bighas* of land before winning in 1967, but that less than two years later he had twenty-six *bighas* and had constructed a three-story brick house. Of the other candidates, only the Independent Chamar held appeal for Arunpur voters of that caste.

PERCEPTIONS OF VOTING AND POLITICAL IDEOLOGIES

Few people replied in the negative to a question asked of all household heads in the village: "Is it a good thing to vote?" Although the majority think that the idea of voting is a good one, they do not feel that they have derived much personal benefit from elections; it is the politician, they believe, who gains the most. This is particularly true among Chamars. One of them declared, "They run after us at election time, but afterwards we are forgotten and we don't have enough food and water." Others, perhaps more radical in their outlook, believe that democracy with one man and one vote is not really suited to their country. Corruption, selfishness, and casteism interferes with its workings in a population that is mostly illiterate. A few men went so far as to speak of a revolution to overthrow the Congress Party and the need for a dictatorship that could deal effectively with the country's problems.

While it is said that elections have served to increase factional conflicts within the village by extending them to yet another area of political competition, it is the relation between voting and caste that is most decried and decried most of all by the upper castes of Bhumihars and Brahmans. There was unanimity in the view that since elections depend upon numbers, the caste with the largest population (in this case, the Kurmis) has a decisive advantage. One of the primary school teachers commented:

> In my village, people are going to vote for four different parties. BKD is a new party—whoever is a Yadiv [Ahir surname] will vote for it and talks only about Charan Singh. A candidate may have no substance, no qualifications, but people of his caste will vote for him.

Similarly, a tubewell operator from a nearby village perceptively noted that caste feeling influences the vote

> because who knows the ideology of a political party? Voting is always a game which is played with a familiar trick. That trick can be introduced either by winning the vote of a man by party ideology, or by showing his affinity with a certain caste. As soon as the candidate and his followers say, "Such and such is a man of your caste," the listener feels an identification and some psychological satisfaction.

Casteism was regarded as being a particularly important issue upon which this election would hinge. It is interesting to note that there is only talk of casteism when high castes speak of politics and the vote. Other forms of casteism (e.g., discrimination on the basis of caste in determining access to valued resources such as land, water, jobs, or status) seem to be accepted as something natural and are certainly not lamented by the upper castes. It is likely that only because they are outnumbered and because numbers win elections that the latter spoke of and decried casteism at election time.

A major reason given for the increase in exploiting caste loyalties during elections is that lower castes no longer listen to high-caste men, voting as the latter dictate, but rather vote for their own caste man. It was widely recognized by the upper castes that although the Chamars (and others) would say yes to whichever candidate they were urged to vote for, they would actually vote for whomever they themselves decided upon. This increasing independence of the lower-caste vote and the decreasing effectiveness of pressure tactics was evident in the 1969 election and clearly demonstrated by the Chamar vote (see later).

Many Bhumihars and Brahmans also felt that the Kurmis had "become too big" since winning the 1967 election and had begun to regard the area as a sort of "Kunbistan." It was thought necessary to "teach them a lesson" in the midterm poll. A Bhumihar Socialist, for example, said that he would not vote for Bhaggu Ram again. It rankled him that after the last election, when he and his other Bhumihar relatives had worked so hard for the Kurmi SSP candidate, the latter discounted their contribution. Instead, Bhaggu Ram said that it was really the Kurmi vote which enabled him to win.

There were some in the village who did express a commitment to the ideology of certain political parties and voted along these lines.[4] This was most true of the upper castes. In addition to the faction leaders who have a history of association with, if not commitment to, different parties (see later), there is also a small core of four young, college-educated teachers (three are kinsmen of the Pradhan and all belong to his faction) who had supported and campaigned for the SSP in previous elections. They had voted for that party's candidate in 1967 despite considerable pressure from faction comembers and Bhumihars who switched to support the Congress candidate from their own caste. One of these teachers said that he wanted politics in India to be as "Marx philosophized it" and spoke of achieving absolute equality. Another Bhumihar, related to one of these Intercollege teachers and working as a truck driver in Banaras, is also a staunch supporter of the SSP. Although he has little free time to spend in the village, he tries to coordinate the young boys into a youth club. He assembled about sixty boys from Arunpur and a neighboring village before the election and explained the party platforms and symbols to them. The boys and a few adults sympathetic to the SSP led a procession through their village and several others nearby. Many Bhumihars and Brahmans were reportedly angered that a Bhumihar was openly canvassing votes for a Kurmi. He persisted in his support of the Kurmi candidate and was instrumental in arranging the SSP rally held at nearby Dallia bazaar just before the election, which featured a major student leader from the university.

SSP supporters decried anti-Muslim feelings as well as caste inequalities; those who voted for the Jan Sangh candidate said that he stood for the preservation of Hindu values and protection from the Muslims. A religious Bhumihar explained why he would vote for Vishwanath Singh, standing from the Jan Sangh: this candidate was a fellow caste man and a relative. Furthermore, the party believed in traditional Hindu ways, was against Muslims, and for caste and Untouchability.

While there were villagers who continued or decided to support the Congress candidate in this election, many said that the party, so long in

FIGURE 25. Raj Narain, member of Parliament (now Minister of Health and Family Welfare in the central government), gives a campaign speech during an SSP rally in Dallia bazaar.

power, had "done nothing for twenty years and it was time for a change." An old Brahman, who claimed to be able to deliver fifty votes from among his own relatives and the neighboring Lohars, stated:

> We could see Congress and SSP for the last twenty years, who did nothing for us. So we are thinking to vote for the *dipak* [Jan Sangh symbol]. Congress did all kinds of bad things. It never cared for our thoughts of caste *(jati vichar)* and now everything has become a hodgepodge *(khichari)*. We should not vote for Congress. We voted for the SSP and found it was worthless. We voted for Bhaggu Ram who built his own house and doesn't care about us.
> Now we are thinking of voting for Vishwanath Singh, for he is from our area, the most educated candidate, and has no selfish ideas. We have all decided to vote for Jan Sangh. I will canvass for them if they promise to get my well repaired.

Caste affiliation was a dominant consideration in voting, especially for the Kurmis and the Chamars, but there were additional important factors. A tie of kinship or friendship with a candidate or his supporters could determine the way a vote was cast. If a villager was known to be able to influence others, candidates would approach such a potential supporter through the latter's relatives. This was a particularly compelling issue for those Bhumihars who were related to the Jan Sangh or Congress candidates. Most of the Bhumihars who were considered to be big men had ties of friendship and obligation to both candidates as well. Ironically, they too (like the Chamars) often had to avoid expressing an open preference for one or the other candidate at the risk of invoking the displeasure of the person not supported.

VILLAGE FACTIONALISM AND THE ELECTION

Village factionalism was an important factor in previous elections, for opposing village leaders aligned themselves with different parties and carried their supporters with them. After the first election in 1952, the elders of the Pradhan's house, many of whom had taken some part in the freedom struggle, switched from supporting the Congress Party to the SSP. They were joined in this move by members of Raj Kumar's family and by a younger brother of Krishna Singh. Jai Singh and Chandra Singh, of Little Pura Bhumihar families that had been allied with the British, became Congress members, as did the third person in their coalition, Narain Singh. Leader-follower ties were highly important, although faction membership and voting choice did not always present a one-to-one relationship. Even those castes that are economically independent of the Bhumihars, such as the Kurmi, Kahar, Lohar, and others, as well as the Brahmans and some other Bhumihars, said that they had looked to the big men for advice because they were more knowledgeable and "advanced" in these matters. In this election, however, factions and family members split their vote according to personal reasons, while other villagers decided their votes independently, consulting only with their kinsmen or caste fellows.

The Pradhan was inactive during the campaign and would not even reveal his choice. He did not speak openly for any candidate, although he had been an SSP supporter in the past. One major difficulty was that in this election both the Congress and Jan Sangh candidates were Bhumihars well known to him. At the same time, the opposing faction came out in support of the Jan Sangh, a party that he might have preferred. His family's vote was also dispersed. Most of them were SSP supporters (as were the majority of their kinsmen) except for Amar Singh, backing the Jan Sangh, and his "grandson" Chandra, who voted Congress. The former's decision was based on two factors. First, the Jan Sangh candidate, Vishwanath Singh, was the first to come personally to him and request his vote. Both he and his father are well known to Amar. They have a long family connection and are also related. Second, Amar has become more religious in his advanced age and expressed a belief in the values and ideology of Hinduism, for which he believed the Jan Sangh stood, and a hope that this newer party might accomplish more than Congress or the SSP did.

Chandra Singh,[5] a teacher at Arunpur Intercollege, was extremely angered at the ingratitude he said Bhaggu Ram had expressed to him and other Bhumihars who took part in his 1967 campaign. He vowed never to vote for him again. He supported the Congress candidate in this election because he was indebted to him for certain past favors and because he hoped it might reap him some monetary benefits at the Intercollege. Both the Principal and the Secretary are Congress supporters. Chandra originally said that he would not openly canvass for that party, though later he did, and that he is still an admirer of the late Ram Manohar Lohia and Raj Narain.[6]

The coleader of the Pradhan's faction in Little Pura, Raj Kumar Singh, and his family supported the Jan Sangh but were not active campaigners in the village and local area, either. The major difficulty here was that the opposing faction, composed of his kinsmen, had declared themselves as Jan Sangh canvassers first, and hostile kin would not sit together in the same jeep while visiting other villages. While neither Raj Kumar nor the Pradhan adopted a public stance, those *bare admi* who were members of the opposition faction campaigned openly. A schism developed within their initial united stand for the Jan Sangh, and details of this incident vividly portray some of the pressures that served to diffuse the upper-caste vote along nonfactional lines.

Sometime in December, an influential relative came to Narain Singh's house and convinced them to support the Jan Sangh candidate in the forthcoming election. As Narain lives and votes in Calcutta, his older brother's son, Lalji, was chosen to campaign for the *dipak* and to bring the weight of his family connections with him. Lalji was a "life-member" of Congress but now succumbed to pressure and took his relative to Little Pura, where his allies Chandra Singh and Jai Singh live. Because they all felt united as faction coleaders, these two men, also staunch Congresswallas in the past, agreed to support the Jan Sangh. Chandra might possibly have been promised that the office of *pramukh*, now held by his rival Krishna Singh, could be his if the Jan Sangh candidate won. Jai Singh, however, was particularly annoyed and reluctant at having to switch his party and assured them that his ideology was still that of the Congress. All three then began to campaign in the villages of the constituency.

In mid-January, Lalji was called to the home of a highly regarded and influential *rais* from a nearby village. This man was also a relation of Lalji's and requested the latter to campaign for the Congress Party. "As my family respects him," said Lalji, "it was hard to say no," although he declared that he would still cast his personal vote for the Jan Sangh. The next day, a Congress *neta* and the Intercollege Principal came to the village and asked Chandra and Jai also to return to the Congress fold and join them in canvassing. Chandra refused, saying that he had already promised to vote for Vishwanath Singh, but could "advise how to win back people I have turned to Jan Sangh." My assistant, a staunch Jan Sanghi, was appalled at this about-face. Chandra answered him: "I should please by [my] talk the man who is pleasing me by [his] talk."

On January 20, several important Congress Party members, including Kamalapati Tripati (President of the U.P. Congress Party), went to Lalji's house as well as to see Chandra, Jai, and the Pradhan. They prevailed upon Lalji as a "life member" of Congress not to vote for the Jan Sangh and not to refuse their request, since he was their relation. They further said that they would send around a jeep so that he could canvass for the party. Lalji was faced with a terrible conflict; he cursed the Pradhan, who had kept his voting preference to himself and managed to avoid such a clash of loyalties. Jai Singh was also persuaded to return to Congress, and he and Lalji went campaigning for that party in the last two weeks before the election. The deserted Chandra tried to weave a middle course, although he was angered by Jai's open switch and said that as they had given their word to the Jan Sangh candidate, it was a matter of *izzat* (honor) not to change. He also added that he would not let the Intercollege Principal, whom he opposes, think that he could influence all their faction's leaders.

Vishwanath Singh came again to Arunpur soon after all this occurred. He went through the village and, at my assistant's urging, to all the *puras* (including those of the Kurmis, other low castes, and Chamars). When he came to where Chandra and Jai lived, he was admonished by the latter for not campaigning hard enough, while Chandra said that Vishwanath was wasting his time and energy in contesting an election that could not be won. Nevertheless, Chandra agreed to go canvassing with a now deeply discouraged contender. The Congress candidate, Raj Bihari Singh, also came to Arunpur at least twice in the last few days before the election, and it was said that even Chandra was seen riding in the Congress jeep.

With Arunpur big men voting along lines other than that of factional considerations, the attempt to mobilize support along these lines was negligible. Members of the Kurmi, Kahar, Kalwar, and other castes said that while they may verbally accede to any voting request a *thakur* might make, ultimately they will decide among themselves for whom to vote. The elderly Brahman who claimed he could deliver some fifty votes had made the decision to vote for the Jan Sangh, however, on the basis of his allegiance to, and advice from, Raj Kumar. When Jai Singh came to his house with some Congress people, he stayed inside "because if I went out they would take my promise [of support] and I had already promised my vote to Jan Sangh."

While this decision to follow a big man was a voluntary one, the Untouchable Musahars and Dharkars had no such choice. They are in an extremely dependent position, and unlike the Chamars, followed the bidding of their employers and patrons when voting. These castes are few in number and live near Little Pura, where opposing faction leaders abide. Their predicament is great because they cannot afford to incur the displeasure of either side. One Dharkar, after expressing his own opinions of and preferences for candidates and parties, stated:

> But I will vote for the man who is the choice of Little Pura. . . . Even if those people tell us to stand in the sun for twenty-four hours, I will do so. Our voting depends on them. . . . But if one *thakur* advises us to vote for someone and another *thakur* [who opposes him] advises me to vote for someone else, I will leave the village on election day as I did last time. For me both men are equal and I cannot obey only one.

In contrast to this situation of the Musahars and Dharkars, where economic dependence led to compliance in voting according to the will of their *malik*s, the Chamars' vote was strikingly independent. Their normally weak corporate links within the village, hindered by economic dependency and vertical ties of patronage with the upper castes, were strengthened in this election.

CLASS TENSIONS AND THE CHAMAR VOTE

The horizontal cleavage within the village political arena between the dependent, landless Chamar *mazdur*s and their upper-caste *malik*s reveals a growing classlike struggle. This conflict cuts across factions within the dominant caste of Bhumihars and serves increasingly to unite rival leaders against their laborers. Despite such conflict, there appears to be no change in the position of the Chamars in the village or in their subservient economic and political condition. By taking an independent stand in the wider arena, however, they expressed their solidarity with caste fellows in other villages and their desire to be free men within Arunpur.

Chamars had voted Congress for the most part in past elections. At the time of the midterm poll, they were initially undecided about which candidate they should support. A number consulted with my assistant and he advised them to vote for the *dipak,* as did many of the leading Bhumihars and Brahmans in the village who had influence over and employed Chamars. My assistant also tried to arrange several meetings between those Untouchables who expressed an interest in that party and a *neta* in Banaras or the candidate himself. In the beginning of January, one of the more religious men said that he was willing to meet with the Jan Sangh leader, even though many of his caste men warned that the party stood for a return of zamindari and Untouchability. Taking a letter of introduction from my assistant, as well as a notice regarding the deployment of government funds to construct wells for Untouchables, Viren Ram (see Chapter 8) went to Banaras. He was also prepared to canvass for the party if they could pay him just two rupees a day to feed his family. This offer was never accepted. When the leader met Viren Ram, he said that he had to go to court that morning and was too busy to talk further.

In the third week of January, another meeting was arranged between a Chamar, from the only family which owns a little land and could boast of a college-educated son (see Chapter 8), and the Jan Sangh candidate. Sometime earlier, this Chamar had declared the Jan Singh to be the party of casteism, communalism, and Untouchability. Now, after speaking with my assistant, he was willing to sound out the candidate and determine whether anything could possibly be gained from giving him the vote. His family was particularly interested in getting the well near their house repaired so that it could be usable.[7] The results of the meeting were disappointing, if not unexpected. The candidate promised to help them only after the elections were over. Other Chamars declared that they would vote for the party which gave them money to fix their houses and wells and to buy some land where they could tether and feed their animals. "Unless a party is doing this much," a Chamar said, "we aren't going to vote for them. Who counts the price of our votes?" Even Viren Ram, who had declared his support for the Jan Sangh through the urgings of my assistant, became angry with the latter when he did not personally speak to the candidate on their behalf and extract a concrete promise of help.

The Chamars had a meeting in their *pura* at the end of January and decided to support the Independent Chamar candidate, a physician from

Mirzapur District. They said that he had come to them one night and asked for their vote. He told them, "After high-caste people win the election, they will not let those of low caste even touch the chair they are sitting on," and promised to help all. The Chamars also felt that a vote for this man might raise their status in the eyes of others. News of the meeting and their decision soon reached the Bhumihars. Although Chamars generally denied any such decision when confronted with it by Bhumihars, and reaffirmed their allegiance to follow their *maliks*' advice, occasionally a younger man would be more outspoken in his views: "It is a question of principle *[siddhant]*. I am voting for the *hathi* [elephant symbol of the Chamar Independent]. What is wrong with that? I am voting as I like."

Men from practically all Arunpur Chamar households subsequently participated in the inauguration of a temple in Banaras dedicated to their hero, Raidas. The meeting was said to have attracted some twenty thousand Chamars and was marked by the appearance of the Independent candidate on an elephant. He appealed for unity among the caste and a vote for their caste man. It is also reported that he advised them not to tell high-caste people that they would vote for him but to agree verbally to whomever they suggested. For, he continued, if he loses, then Chamars will be the enemy of the high-caste men in office. Arunpur Chamars were impressed by the candidate's call for unity and most of their votes went for him. Those few who had promised my assistant to vote for the Jan Sangh persisted in telling him that they did so.

The inability of the Bhumihars to control the Chamar vote, as opposed to that of the Musahars and Dharkars, lay largely with the former's greater numbers, which allowed them to act with a measure of unity, and with the secret balloting. This angered many, who abused Chamars for their ungratefulness in not voting for Congress, or ridiculed them for believing that their candidate could win. Even the group of college-educated men who believed in the SSP ideology of caste equality spoke of trying to keep Chamars from reaching the voting booth on election day. "But I also feel this way," said one young man, "that they have to come on my roads, in my streets, through my fields, and have to eat food from my house. So they should stop doing all this if they don't like to listen to us."

The voting decisions of the Chamars, as well as those of faction members and other castes, were clearly influenced by many factors and events external to village affairs. Contact with different parties and their candidates, through village canvassing or campaign speeches at political rallies, combined with other election activities. Toward the end of January, there was an increased amount of election bustle: cars, jeeps, and rickshaws with signs, slogans, and speeches traveled the Grand Truck Road day and night. The Intercollege was also enmeshed in electoral politics, and this involved the village directly through its several teachers and students.

ARUNPUR INTERCOLLEGE AND THE MIDTERM POLL

Two men who are in a strong position to affect the voting of others are the Intercollege Principal and the Secretary. The Secretary is Krishna Singh, Block *pramukh* and close ally of the Pradhan. He too, however, was forced to adopt a low profile in this election. He had joined the Congress Party after Independence but openly helped his brother contest for the District Board as a Socialist. This brother had worked with famed freedom fighter Subash Chandra Bose in the Forward Bloc and later supported the Socialist Lohia. Backing his brother led to Krishna's expulsion from Congress. For some fifteen years, as he explains it, he supported the SSP and appreciated their views without ever becoming a formal party worker; at the same time, he remained close to many Congress Party notables. In the language question he favored the Congress position and in this election, although he would not openly canvass, he supported the Congress candidate.

When the Jan Sangh aspirant requested Krishna's support, he said that he could personally vote for him but could not speak openly; rather, he had already pledged to support Raj Bihari Singh and to win over other big men as the Congress candidate had requested. At the same time, one of the teachers at the Intercollege is a nephew of Raj Bihari and Krishna feared possible repercussions if it was learned that he was for the Jan Sangh. It is also unlikely that the Secretary, known for his great dislike of Kurmis stemming from the time they opposed him in his village, voted for other than the Bhumihar Congress candidate in the 1967 election.

The Intercollege Principal, also a Bhumihar, was an active Congress campaigner. He had been in the SSP but, failing to get on the party ticket, stood as an Independent candidate for the State Assembly in the last election. Bhumihars feared that his candidacy would serve only to split their caste vote and pressured him into withdrawing his name. Subsequently, the school was investigated for certain financial irregularities; the head of the investigating committee was a high officer in the state Congress Party. The Principal incurred a debt to this official when he was exonerated of any wrongdoing. He also wanted the school to become a Degree College and the decision whether to approve such a request lay with the state government and was often a political one.

Therefore, the Principal had convincing reasons for supporting the Congress as the most powerful party in the state and compelled many teachers to do likewise.

He gave teachers free time from their classes to canvass votes, reportedly harassed those who were SSP or other supporters, urged the students to back Congress (if they have "faith in him"), and spoke in the same manner to the teachers. He also asked the latter to give a donation to the party and even included those whom he knew to support other candidates. Most of the political parties had established some kind of office in the constituency from which they could distribute material, have meetings of party workers, make out voter cards, and so on. This kind of work was done for Congress at the Intercollege. Teachers, clerks, and students worked in the office there. Students were also canvassers and might have influenced their more uneducated parents or the women in their households. That village boys did become involved intimately in the election is evident from a fight that continued for several days in the school between Arunpur SSP supporters and Congress supporters from another village. The school remained a hum of election activities right up to election day, when the people from Arunpur and a neighboring village came to cast their votes at the Intercollege polling station.

ELECTION DAY IN ARUNPUR: REGIONAL POLITICS AND THE VILLAGE ARENA

Voting was carried out smoothly, with a sixty-six percent turnout of Arunpur's voters (397 out of 602). The vote was split primarily between the Congress candidate (victorious in the constituency) and the Jan Sangh, SSP, and Chamar Independent candidates—with some Kurmis voting for the BKD. Each of these political parties had set aside a small area on the road outside the Intercollege with their party flag. Agents of the respective political parties handed out prepared slips containing a voter's name and his registration number, which was required in the polling station. The agent from which a voter took his slip (unless he had one already) would be one indicator of how he would vote. There were strange bedfellows under different party flags; members of opposing factions stood together, while members of the same faction or family were with different parties.

The only incidents which marred the otherwise peaceful day were a number of hot disputes between Jai Singh, Chandra Singh, and some other kinsmen and friends who, though members of the same faction, were divided between the Jan Sangh and Congress candidates. I had been told of incidents in the previous election where lower-caste people were prevented from voting by threats or physical violence, but observed no

FIGURE 26. Women wait to cast their votes at the Arunpur Intercollege polling station.

overt intimidation at the polling station. Admittedly, this might have been accomplished beforehand, and my findings are partly contrary to those of one writer in a reputed national political weekly. He says:

> The fact is that never before in U.P. have terrorism and casteism been practised on such a scale. Even leftist parties set up candidates on the criterion of caste origins. . . . It is clear that not national politics but regional politics is getting the upper hand in U.P. Casteism and fear are becoming significant factors *(Economic and Political Weekly* 1969:384*)*.[8]

This election was instead marked by a lessening of voting along dependency ties that is characteristic of the patron-client bond in village politics. Factions did not act as units, and the Bhumihar vote was dispersed. This was most pronounced among the big men, to whom candidates personally appealed for support, and their families. The Pradhan, his family, and allies all voted independently of one another, but this was not seen as a mark of weakness in their alliance. There was tacit recognition of the fact that as village links with the outside increase, there is bound to be a diffusion of interests among the different allies. As one Bhumihar observed:

> The Pradhan may not vote for the Jan Sangh. Because we are both educated, he understands that friendship is something other than the right to vote. He and his family will never tell us which party to vote for because he has his own individuality and thoughts [and we ours]. He will vote for whom he likes—and I'll vote for whom I like. So there is nothing like a conflict. I will vote Jan Sangh and they for SSP. It makes no difference.

Only Jai, Chandra, and their allies fought over their divided votes and took it as a sign of lessening prestige that they were not united. Yet while Chandra refused to switch back to the Congress and to support a candidate which his enemies did, Jai was less hesitant about associating with those he formerly despised (and perhaps still does).

The cleavage among castes came out much more strongly in this election and votes were decided along horizontal lines of caste. This was particularly true of the Chamars, who were almost unanimous in their support for the Independent contestant. This autonomy in voting is closely connected to their growing struggle for independence from the Bhumihars in their working conditions and agrarian relations within the village. In purely village politics, however, they still remain bound to the upper castes and have further antagonized their superiors by this show of independence. The old Brahman who was influential in organizing his family's and possibly neighboring Lohars' votes for the Jan Sangh declared after the election:

> Yesterday I decided that I can't let any Chamar go on cycle past my door. Now I can't tolerate this. [Abuses] . . . Everyone is out of his mind. These people never listen to us and didn't vote for Jan Sangh, so what right do they have to come by my door sitting high upon their cycles while we may be squatting on the ground. It is impossible. If they don't listen to us, I will break their legs. I have started shouting abuses to our worker [a female Chamar] and now they will understand the cost of not listening to us. How will I remain a Brahman if I will not "beat" the Chamars?

After the election was over, many Bhumihars also commented that it was good that the Kurmis had lost. They were berated for never having canvassed for Bhumihar votes (as indeed, the latter were not seen to canvass among the Kurmis) and for thinking that numbers alone would win them the office. Others declared that if the Kurmis had won again they would have "cut our noses in the village."

This election reveals the extent to which the model of a political arena encompassing a number of villages has been shifting from a fragmented one to one in which the relationship between a specific village and the wider arena is marked by certain discontinuities. In the model of a fragmented arena, the voting outcome within individual villages would be primarily determined by vertical clientelist bonds and there would be no necessary connection between the way that different villages voted. Each would be determined by its own particular configuration of factional ties and patron-client bonds. Politics at the village level would then be continuous with constituency politics; voting would ideally be determined by vertical ties in both arenas.

The shift to a model of a regional arena, which is characterized by discontinuities with the village arena, exhibits, on the contrary, connections among villages for certain castes whose collective interests express themselves in a unified voting pattern. Arunpur voting disclosed three discontinuities. The comparatively weak corporate links among the Chamars and the vertical ties with upper castes within the village, which in the past would have determined their voting, were juxtaposed with a united position in the present election. The Kurmis, who take no active role in village politics remained, however, an important force in the supravillage arena. Finally, the weak corporate links of the Bhumihars, which are expressed in competitive village factionalism, continued as such but gave way to a division of interests along other lines of cleavage. The question for future elections remains whether there will be an increasing proliferation of upper-caste political loyalties, due to greater education, awareness of political ideologies, and extensive participation in the world outside, or whether they will unite behind a major party as the cleavage among castes comes to predominate over vertical ties for the lower castes.

NOTES

1. They were held in 1952, 1957, 1962, and 1967.
2. The translation of BKD as "Indian Revolutionary Party" is, as Baxter points out, somewhat misleading for a party dominated by landowners of medium-sized holdings belonging primarily to Jat and Ahir castes (1975:121).
3. See Brass (1968) for a discussion of party ideologies.
4. It does not seem completely correct to conclude, as Brass does, that "in the rural areas, ideology is hardly a factor. Neither in urban nor in rural areas are there many people who vote Congress because of habit or family tradition" (1968:76).
5. Amar's "grandson," not to be confused with the big man, Chandra Singh.
6. Lohia was a major Socialist leader and, with others, formed a new Socialist Party after differences with some leaders in the Praja Socialist Party. In 1964, these two combined into the SSP, only to find former PSP leaders opposed to

Lohia leave the Party and revive their own party a year later. Raj Narain is the SSP Member of Parliament from the Constituency who later came into national prominence by opposing Mrs. Gandhi.

7. Failure to get this well repaired was later the cause of a severe conflict between the Bhumihars and Chamars (see Case 26 earlier).

8. A similar conclusion is expressed in a government report on the midterm polls held in several states, although it does reveal that a "comparatively large number of complaints regarding coercion and intimidation were received from Bihar and U.P.—especially the western region" (Election Commission of India 1970:26, 28).

CHAPTER 11
Conclusions

Every society has some way in which it organizes the competition for scarce and valued resources among its members. It also has some way of designating who makes decisions about the allocation of resources and how these decisions are made. Taken together, these may be regarded as the cultural rules pertaining to political activity. Such rules interact with the actual situation regarding the distribution of power and resources in a community. The divergence between the rules of political activity and their applicability to the situation within which members of society find themselves is greater in times of change, when new lines of cleavage emerge. The need to find new cultural solutions for coping with the problems raised by such changes can ultimately lead to a change in the rules themselves. It seems that what is happening in rural India today can be understood in this light.

THE POLITICAL ARENA IN ARUNPUR

An analysis of the organization of political activity in Arunpur reveals an arena in flux. New ideas reach the village from nearby Banaras city, and its social life has been affected to some extent by the increasing mobility characteristic of the wider Indian scene. Significant areas of conflict lie in the changes in land tenure, the introduction of government tubewells and other resources, and the system of agricultural labor. The decline in the traditional form of conflict resolution, the *panchayat,* the failure of the new statutory *panchayat*s, and the increasing appeal to institutions that lie outside the village have provided people with the opportunity to choose between alternative structures. To settle a dispute, for example, a person might appeal to either the traditional or new *panchayats*, or to the courts. The distribution of wealth, status, and power, however, still tends to coalesce within the dominant caste of Bhumihars. Although other castes have made some advances, notably the agricultural Kurmis, power (and most land) in the village belongs to the Bhumihars.

The separation of the political activity which is a part of all human interaction from that which involved most villagers was the first step in an attempt to circumscribe a villagewide arena (see Chapter 5). This involved trying to classify different case histories of disputes according to the way in which villagers spoke about them. The key factors seem to be how wide a breach becomes and the way in which conflict is resolved. Four propositions were stated which denote the characteristics of political activity that did not escalate to the villagewide arena.

In contrast to this, conflict in the wider arena was found to have different characteristics. The keys to village political activity are the big men who figure as leaders of factions and main participants in the disputes between the landed and landless. These men control whatever resources enter the village and make decisions about their distribution. Arunpur villagers hold two cultural models of leadership styles—that of the aristocrat *(rais)*, who is generous and helps others selflessly, and that of the big man *(bara admi)*. The latter is best recognized as the village politician who takes an active role in village affairs by virtue of his wealth and power and who is concerned only with the pursuit of self-interest.

A big man becomes a leader when he can claim to have a core of followers and attempts to increase his network of supporters by offers of mutual gain. The present village big men are all wealthy Bhumihars who desire to advance their own families' wealth and position and whose involvement in the political arena is regulated by belonging to one or the other faction. This situation is somewhat different from what prevailed in the past when, it is said, the zamindar and the appointed village headman, acting in counsel with a village and local *panchayat* of selected villagers, were able to control conflict more effectively.

The traditional and predominant form of rural conflict—factionalism—seems clearly related to the diffuse nature of authority inherent in the caste system. This condition is intensified today by the fact that leadership or big man status no longer adheres to any position but is a commodity on the open market for which many are competing. The big men who have emerged are organized into two competing parties in the absence of any single authority to which all will accede. Effective power lies with wealthy Bhumihars who belong to families that had a recognized status in the past. They engage in entrepreneurial activity by ac-

CONCLUSIONS

cepting innovations to increase material wealth and by acting as mediators between villagers and outsiders.

Factional strife in Arunpur exemplifies a vertical cleavage that is surprisingly stable in terms of its coalitions and followers. Each encounter between the factions reveals a patterned sequence of phases approximating Turner's developmental cycle (1957). Any dispute has the potentiality of escalating to the political arena via factions if it concerns faction leaders and their family members initially or if they become involved as third parties when it is to their advantage.

Factional politics in Arunpur means Bhumihar politics and, because they command and control more resources than any other caste group, this form of conflict occupies the major part of the village political arena. The contest between different factional coalitions is evenly matched and there is a great expenditure of resources in each conflict encounter. This situation contrasts markedly with the horizontal cleavage that takes the form of class conflict between the subordinate (and landless) Chamars and their Bhumihar masters. The present class alignments in Arunpur which oppose these Untouchables to the rest of the villagers are based not only upon ideological opposition but also upon the fact that the Chamars have hardly benefited from recent changes. The numerous Chamars are kept separate from the few and even poorer Musahars and Dharkars by an isolation rooted in the ideology of hierarchy and separate living quarters. This, combined with Bhumihar actions that politically enforce such separation, prevents any feeling of unity among all Untouchables in the village.

The way in which factions and classes organize the political arena was seen more clearly by focusing upon the allocation of a single resource, water from the government tubewell. This focus also served to isolate another field of the arena which consisted, negatively, of conflict not organized by factions or classes. A relatively stable distribution of power exists in the village, though authority is diffuse, and the conflict over the allocation of water follows a segmentary pattern. It would seem that the same general pattern would be reflected in the distribution of other things of value within the village—land, education, elective office, the distribution of public services, the allocation of government development resources or those which accrue to the village *panchayat,* and, to some extent, the allocation of prestige.

This study has also shown that the boundaries of the political arena of a single village are markedly fluid and can extend outward to become involved in a wider network of relations. This was seen in a number of ways. A big man from the neighboring village of Ramapur has been intimately involved in Arunpur politics; he is credited with having created its factions and is considered the main leader of one coalition. Political activity in the Intercollege also spills over to the village arena, and the relationships which Arunpur big men have with others in the area are strategically formed so that factions in this village are connected with those existing in other villages. Certain resources, such as water from the government tubewell, are intended for distribution among two or more villages. Other resources lie outside the village arena, and access to them necessitates interaction with external institutions, groups, and individuals.

That the boundaries of the village political arena are in flux, due to changes in a wider arena, is reflected in the increasing demand for village big men to act as entrepreneurial middlemen who can transform and exploit resources from one arena to another. This was highlighted by the part that the big men took in the 1969 midterm poll to elect a new member of the State Legislative Assembly from their district. Big men were induced to support one or another candidate on the basis of preexisting ties of friendship or kinship and the promise of political perquisites. Villagers attempted, on the other hand, to bargain with their votes in exchange for declarations of future help. The discontinuities between the village and regional areas reveal that there are competing ways of organizing political activity that lie outside the vertical patron-client bonds.

Rules of the political arena relating to who the decision makers are, how decisions are made, and how conflict is resolved are are also in flux in Arunpur due to changes in the wider arenas. The political activity of a single village is intimately related to changes that have been occurring at the local, state, and national levels. The greater part of the changes which have taken place in Independent India have come about through government initiatives and legislation. The abolition of zamindari and subsequent land reform measures, in conjunction with the rise of new occupations, a monetized economy, and market relations, have created new economic opportunities. Government resources are reaching areas previously untouched by them. The vote, Local Self-Government institutions, legal provisions for scheduled castes, and the legal protection (ideally) available for all villagers have brought about an increased political consciousness and awareness of the identity of interests. Economic and political gains have been consolidated by the increasing importance and accessibility of education.

Such changes have had three major effects in Arunpur which, in turn, have altered the rules and organization of its political arena. These are: the introduction of new resources, new alternatives for action, and the breakup of the old authority system backed by the British Raj. It is perhaps the last of these which has had the most crucial effect.

From British Raj to Entrepreneurial Big Man

With the removal of the only real basis for a panvillage authority such as the zamindar and the British-appointed headman—that is, backing by an external power—the inherent diffuseness of rural authority was clearly revealed. The principle of caste hierarchy, combined with that of dominance, results in a situation of "fragmented" authority within the village. There is no single head or uncontested leader within each caste of a given status, but more or less rival leaders coexist (especially in the dominant caste). Thus, each caste has its own men of power and influence within the village as a whole, and authority over a given caste is concentrated in the hands of castes which are superior to it either directly, by the principle of hierarchy, or indirectly, because they are dominant (see Dumont 1972:209, 228–229). This was true of British India as it is true of India today.

The people of Arunpur, however, are commenting on the state of flux existing in the current village political situation when they say that all men think themselves equal today and no one man is obeyed by all. The abolition of zamindari secured previously favored Bhumihars in their control of the land, while the old positions of panvillage leadership supported by the British have been eliminated. In its place, the elected *pradhan* has no special power to enforce his decisions. Second, the elective system of Local Self-Government (as well as the state and national elections) has led to a weakening of the power of the dominant caste over all others in the village within certain spheres of action. Finally, leadership within the dominant caste of Bhumihars has become more open to competition and control from entrepreneurial village big men and it is they who have emerged as the new leaders and decision makers. The fact that these men all belong to families that were influential in the past provides the link of continuity.

The interaction between the struggle for power and the authority structure reveals political process. Authority ensures the routinization of political decisions and associates decision making with various roles (see Cohen 1970:492–495). But each decision in Arunpur causes a crisis which is mediated only by the competition for power. Most villagers seem to regard the decisions of big men as backed solely by their personal power and oppose such decisions to the more authoritative ones that the British-appointed headman made (i.e., he had the *right* to decide for others). It is in this sense that I said that big men are self-appointed and do not fulfill any role in the authority structure; it is only when they act in a *panchayat* or in some official capacity that they can be said to have authority. Some big men are attempting to consolidate and legitimize their positions and control over certain processes. Krishna Singh, *pramukh* of the Community Development Block, *pradhan* of his village, and Secretary of the Intercollege, is one who is most concerned with legitimizing the newfound wealth and consequent power that has come to him.

Krishna and other big men have responded to the situation by becoming entrepreneurs who may well succeed in bringing about a new authority structure. Changes in the functions of village leaders as traditional patrons have transformed them into "brokers" with connections outside the village.[1] The key to entrepreneurial activity is innovativeness, specifically in the ability to convert and exploit resources of one kind into another where no such connection existed (e.g., turn money or kin ties into votes). The entrepreneur also becomes an essential broker in situations of culture contact or change by establishing linkages between spheres of exchange formerly kept separate (see Bailey on "bridge-actions" 1960: 248, 252).

Entrepreneurs act out of self-interest and seek to maximize their profit (material goods, power, prestige, and so on) in all transactional relations. The potential for profit exists when the disparity between the two kinds of resources involved in a transaction, the different spheres of exchange, is greatest, and this state of affairs is maintained by the lack of any such previous transactions or "bridge-actions." Another characteristic of entrepreneurial activity is the willingness to be experimental and speculative. This is accompanied by risk taking in an enterprise and by a trust in one's own judgment of success rather than common opinion (Barth 1963:7–9; 1966:17–20; 1967:64; Bailey 1960:256–257).

The entrepreneurial activity of big men takes several forms. They seek the way by which they can best obtain, control, and allocate new resources entering the political arena so as to gain the most profit, and keenly compete for the position of *pradhan* because the patronage that adheres to this office can be translated into personal loyalties. They also establish network ties which link the village to the wider society and transmit exchanges from one sphere to another. When a big man, for example, campaigns for a particular candidate, he converts his own local ties into votes for a man from whom he will, in turn, receive a subsequent payoff. This payoff is later utilized in the village arena, and so the cycle of transactions continues. A big man is therefore greatly concerned with backing the winning candidate in state and national elections because the latter is in a position to honor his debts. At the same time, this enables the big man to improve his position in the village by maintaining access to power outside it (Weiner 1965b:202).

An important function of the big man is to act as a middleman who mediates extravillage relations, and the strength and importance of outside contacts reflects his power and the extent to which he can obtain brokerage transactions. The increasing importance of such transactions over that of patronage further emphasizes the entrepreneurial aspect of being "big" in village politics. Big men have become more crucial to villagers as their dependence upon the outside (especially government) for necessary services continues to expand.

As the opportunistic seeker of power and the promoter of his own interests, the big man is also willing to act experimentally. It was the village big men (some attribute it first to Jai Singh) who saw the economic advantage of employing Chamar labor to walk behind the bullocks when the sugar cane is being crushed, cook the sugar cane juice, and then even make the molasses formed into large cakes. Today they justify this behavior by saying that molasses cooked in this manner (i.e., polluted by the Chamars' touch) is sold in the market and not retained for home consumption. Chandra Singh, however, accepted and ate the molasses offered by a Chamar in another village when he was campaigning for a Jan Sangh candidate in the midterm election. Arunpur big men have also adopted innovations in agriculture, business pursuits, and material betterment.

New Alternatives for Action

The removal of positions of authority within the village that had the strong backing of an external power, and the need for leaders to respond to a situation of change, has promoted the rise of big men as political entrepreneurs and influenced the nature of village politics. At the same time, the creation of alternative structures has widened the arena of conflict. When an individual has an option regarding the choice of structures he can employ in decision making, the power which any single alternative exercised in the past is subsequently weakened. The presence of new and alternative modes for action and conflict resolution, which are often based on rules of behavior that are contradictory, will lead to structural change in Arunpur society and the society at large (see Bailey 1960:7).

Choice can now be made, for example, among decision-making bodies which settle disputes: among the traditional *panchayat*s, the statutory ones, or the courts. Each of these operates on a different basis, that is, on caste or dominance, on personal or factional loyalties, and on supposed "impartiality." Political competition on the basis of "one man, one vote" results in different types of cleavages from that of the old consensus, which was based on a concentration of power in the hands of a dominant caste. A Chamar can alternately view himself as an Untouchable or an equal citizen of free India; he may choose to renounce his ascribed status by becoming a Christian or a Buddhist. Participation in "caste-free" occupations and a monetized economy present alternatives to *jajmani* relationships.

COMPETITION FOR NEW RESOURCES

The third major way in which changes in the wider society have affected the village political arena is through the introduction of new resources for which no widely accepted rules exist regarding their allocation. The range of contestants who can compete for a scarce resource has also increased, and this has had a decided effect on the way in which politics are organized in Arunpur. The case of the village *panchayat* elections may make this clearer (see Case 15, earlier). Elective office represents a new resource. As such, there is an absence of rules to determine who should *automatically* fill these positions and who can compete for them. In contrast to this, for example, rules did (do) exist which specify who could hold the office of village headman under the British and who can compete for the division of family property. The lack of rules in determining elected officers, however, means that the range of possible contestants has also increased. To be elected to the *panchayat,* one must only fulfill a minimum age and residence requirement. In this way, elections are like the resources of government tubewell water, land on the open market, and education.

The competition for power among leaders and factions is quite different from the competition for tangible resources, such as those mentioned earlier, or money. The latter can presumably be made more available if its amount is increased, and the money that one has gained does not necessarily affect the amount of value in the hands of others. However, competition for intangible social resources, such as prestige, success, recognition, and power, cannot be ameliorated by increasing the resource pool. There can be only one winner if winning is to have a value. Therefore, to become powerful one necessarily weakens others (Swingle 1970:ix; Riker 1962:190). In this manner the competition for power resembles a zero-sum game.

The big men of Arunpur who enter the political arena may be seen as engaging in a zero-sum game of conflict insofar as they are engaged in a struggle for power to acquire distribution prerogatives over scarce resources (see Southwold 1969:29; Swingle 1970:ix; Nicholas 1966:57; Dahrendorf 1959:196). The villagers also perceive the situation as one in which the total quantity of available power is limited in amount. A big man's sphere becomes smaller by the presence of other competitors, and any increase in the power of one of them results in a corresponding change in the weight of at least one other.

CONCLUSIONS

EFFECT OF A CHANGED POLITICAL ARENA ON FACTIONAL CONFLICT

The creation of new resources, the increase of choice among alternatives for action, and the emergence of the big man as an entrepreneur have changed the nature of the political arena in which the village politician operates and the strategies which he employs. A major change in the organization of the arena, which its inhabitants as well as observers of the rural scene note, has been the increase of factional conflict.

Factions are most certainly not recent phenomena in Indian villages and are related to the fragmentation of authority discussed earlier. The resulting diffusion of power and authority has been a stimulus for the formation of factions both in the past and at present. Because no one man has (or had) complete power to obtain a decision, he must constantly ally himself with others against a common opponent. In Arunpur, the present-day factions are essentially composed of coalitions of village big men, that is, temporary, means-oriented alliances among individuals who differ in goals (see Gamson 1961:374; Boissevain 1971:470-471).[2] We may hypothesize that the more diffuse the power base in a village is, the greater will be the scope for factions based on coalitions of leaders as opposed to single-leader factions.

Although factional conflict is not peculiar to groups undergoing rapid transformations and was present in traditional India as well (cf. Beals 1962:247-248; Siegel and Beals 1960b:399), this does not explain the increase in frequency of this type of conflict. It is important to realize that the big men who are faction leaders act as opportunistic entrepreneurs engaged in political competition to gain power, if we are to understand why they participate in conflict which to some appears to be solely "disruptive" to public enterprise, unregulated, and interfering with the achievement of group goals (e.g., Beals 1962; Beals and Siegel 1966; Siegel and Beals 1960a; 1960b; Dhillon 1955; Singh 1961).

The increase of this type of conflict is intimately related to the three changes just outlined that affect the village and is "likely to be the most efficient way that is available to the competitors for taking part in politics" (Nicholas 1966:58). More explicitly, factions organize the arena when there is increasing competition for resources and an absence of any other effective decision-making bodies or widely accepted rules to determine their allocation. It seems logical to assume that in times of change, these conditions will be exaggerated and will provide factions with more conflict occasions on which to operate.[3]

Several writers have noted the adaptive functions performed by factions and advocate a more positive approach to them (e.g., Weiner

1965a; 1965b; Firth 1957; Chance 1962; Gallin 1968; Boissevain 1964; 1968; Brass 1965; Bailey 1969; Miller 1965; Schwartz 1969; Nicholas 1965; 1966; 1968a; 1968b). While Boissevain states that factions are the basic units of conflict in any society and are not disruptive (1968:551; 1964:1286), Gould sees them as manifestations of a basic *jati* model governing group formation (1969:292-294). Nor is factional conflict necessarily detrimental to the implementation of group goals; consensus politics may be another name for the effective suppression of dissent (see Weiner 1965a; Gallin 1968; Schwartz 1969; Bailey 1965:19). The conclusions of Schwartz and Nicholas come closest to my own.

Schwartz related factionalism in Guatemala to: (1) the absence of other structures to organize and channel political activity, (2) the fragmentation of the power base, and (3) a weakening of traditional authority before new forms of authority could be effectively instituted (1969). Nicholas also found that

> factions constitute a form of political organization that is particularly well adapted to certain kinds of arenas. In an Indian peasant village, where resources are fixed, or nearly so, the only gain one can make is at the expense of his opponent, and any loss by one's opponent is a relative gain in resources. (1966:58)

In addition, he sees the changes taking place outside the village as bringing about structural changes in the village system. These changes relate to the scope of resources and the different sets of rules which govern their use. In situations of uncertainty, pragmatic rules, ad hoc decisions made by politicians, seem to come to the fore and political activity crosses the boundaries of the community itself (Nicholas 1968b).

The actual relationship of rules, resources, and decision making to factionalism may be made clearer by referring again to the example of *panchayat* elections. The competition for elective office in the village must be organized in some way. There is neither a group of elders with recognized panvillage power, nor are there politically active corporate lineages or political parties that could settle the issue. In the absence of any other decision-making body, factions serve to fill the vacuum by canalizing and promoting specific interests, articulating demands, and recruiting members. They organize political conflict despite the increase of factionalism in the absence of traditional forms of conflict resolution. Factions achieve goals for their members, and villagers have an awareness of the progress that accompanies this form of competition. The VLW reports that factionalism in no way inhibits agricultural advances or innovation; rather, the antagonisms between the two sides act as a spur to competition for material gain. Competition of this sort also extends to acts of generosity and giving. We may assume that the same was true in the past.

The relationship between factions, disruptiveness, and change is also a critical one and appears to have confused some writers. Siegel and Beals, for example, view factions as "divisive," "disruptive," "nonadaptive," and "one of the more common maladaptive reactions to stress" (Beals 1962:247; Siegel and Beals 1960a:107, 108, 115). They may be drawn to the disruptive features of factionalism because of the fact that an increase in this form of conflict is often associated with "rapidly changed or changing societies and institutions" (Nicholas 1965:57). It is important, however, to distinguish between the disorganization caused by rapid change and the organization brought about by factionalism, which often increases and intensifies during such periods.[4] Factions themselves are an old and universal political phenomenon appearing even beneath bureaucratic infrastructures. Rather than being the cause of division, they are a result of, and reflect, preexisting cleavages (Gould 1969:292; Cohn 1955:65–66; 1965:96–97). Factionalism has been and still remains the most efficient way to organize political activity and effect decisions despite the fact that the escalation of disputes may regrettably often prove an obstacle to certain cooperative ventures in Arunpur.

DEVELOPMENT OF CLASS CONFLICT

Factional conflict cuts across classes.[5] Factions do not reflect the cleavage between the dominant landed Bhumihars and their landless laborers, nor do they represent the interests of those dominated (most villagers) against the dominant (the Bhumihars). A focus on factionalism alone emphasizes the stability of the village political situation and the competition that has been traditional in Indian society. Because factions are still preeminent, the importance of class conflict and its possibilities for providing the basis of future political action, as well as the indications of contradiction and change that lie outside the village arena, have often been minimized. The changes that are occurring in India and affecting its multitude of villagers are, moreover, placing a strain on the ability of caste rules to encompass the political activity emerging in response to these transformations.

A major effect of recent change in India is that the distribution of status, wealth, and power has become more dispersed throughout the population. Economic opportunities, educational facilities, and the increase of other resources have introduced a greater mobility among the middle castes, while adult franchise gives an advantage to the more populous ones. Hand in hand with this process has been another by which economic disparities have increased between certain caste groups. As greater disparities in wealth arise in the population, those groups which have least succeeded in disassociating caste from wealth and power will mark new lines of cleavage—horizontal in nature (cf. Dahrendorf 1959).

Earlier ethnographies have reported incidents of conflict between castes acting as classes (listed in Nicholas 1968a:277). This has been corroborated by a recent and growing body of literature which indicates or predicts the increase of class conflict in rural India. Although many of these studies specifically relate to the "Green Revolution," they have a more general significance and are akin to the findings of others on village society and politics (e.g., Byres 1972; Jannuzi 1974; Mamdani 1972; Parthasarathy 1971; Frankel 1971; Frankel and von Vorys 1972; Sivertson 1963; Pohekar 1970; Sharma 1973; Zagoria 1971; Breman 1974; Epstein 1973; Gough 1960; 1970; 1973; Juyal 1974; Wood 1973; *Economic and Political Weekly* 1974) These writers all note that major changes in the technology and economic organization of agriculture have had far-reaching effects on other aspects of social life, especially the political. This position may best be summarized by Frankel and von Vorys:

> In the agro-economic setting of the Asian countryside, the introduction of capital-intensive technologies simultaneously (1) increases economic disparities between the dominant landowning groups on the one hand and the majority of subsistence cultivators, sharecroppers and landless laborers on the other; and (2) intensifies the predisposition of large landowners to adopt profit-maximizing criteria in their relations with the landless. This combination of growing disparities and the increasing commercialization of agriculture accelerates the erosion of traditional norms of agrarian relationships based on the exchange of mutual, albeit non-symmetrical, benefits and services that have historically provided a justification for inequalities between the propertied upper and middle status groups and the landless low castes and classes. The immediate political consequences are a decline in the moral claim of landed elites to positions of authority and the breakdown of vertical patterns of peasant mobilization. Over the long term, large numbers of the landless become available for participation in new political commitments and groups based on egalitarian values and class-struggle doctrines. (1972:2)[6]

Although the overall decline of patron-client ties in *jajmani* relationships was a gradual process in India (Wiser 1936; Kessinger 1974:60ff, 123ff), the landlord-laborer bond has been more drastically affected by the increasing capitalization of agriculture, mechanization of farming, and conversion to contractual labor which the Green Revolution and agricultural advances of the 1950s and 1960s intensified.[7] The decline of these traditional ties has affected caste groups differentially, and the situation in Arunpur generally mirrors that of India as a whole. Mason has commented that Harijans (Untouchables), whom he includes in toto in *jajmani*, have been adversely affected by societal change. He points out that "the old structure was rigidly stratified—and therefore abhorrent to the modern West—but it was a way of existence" (1967:18). Despite their serflike existence, which entailed a hereditary bond to the landowner of the dominant class, their *jajman* or patron, Harijans were at least assured of a minimum subsistence. "If the patron exploited, he also protected" (Mason 1967:18). Mason goes on to say:

> ... The Chamars were unprepared for freedom. They were not trained in its ways. As *jajmani*—hereditary patronage—gives way to a cash nexus, to competition and contract, insecurity grows more rapidly than social esteem, and real advance is for a very few. ... Legal emancipation does not bring a job. (1967:18; also see Béteille 1969b:143, 200; Epstein 1967; 1973:46)[8]

The Untouchables, with few alternative sources of livelihood, are effectively barred from new opportunities by other castes who came first and are handicapped by their lack of education and capital and by social discrimination. Some students of the Indian scene have concluded that their problem is essentially an economic one, that of landlessness, poverty, and unemployment (e.g., Béteille 1969b:142; Epstein 1973). The frequently quoted study on poverty in India by Dandekar and Rath reveals that the poor are getting poorer and that inequities in the distribution of resources are widening (1971; also Etienne 1968:319; Byres 1972:109; Frankel 1971:8, 198). Whether or not the prediction that agrarian tensions will be exacerbated and that conflict will increasingly occur along class lines is fulfilled (Frankel 1971:8; Béteille 1969b:136; Jannuzi 1974: chap. 8; Gough 1960:59; cf. Mencher 1974b:317; Aggarwal 1973:131; Jannuzi 1974:160–161), there can be little doubt that those sections of the population left behind will not remain satisfied with their lot. The disenchantment of these poorer people with the lack of any significant structural changes that affect their lives is leading to a greater involvement in politics (Béteille 1969b:110, 142; Sharma 1973:95).

The microcosm of Arunpur substantiates many of the points made earlier which apply to various parts of the country. I have described the rise of entrepreneurial big men whose maximization of profit through capital investments in agriculture and related businesses increasingly conflicts with the traditional pattern of their ties with laborers and with their clients in *jajmani*. To some extent, they have succeeded in transforming the moral bond between patron and client into an instrumental tie between the big man and his followers that is utilized in the political arena. But, except possibly for Jai Singh, they have become alienated from their fellow villagers and are no longer interested in the well-being of the community as a whole, rather seeking prestige outside the village. Their involvement in entrepreneurial business activities, and their role as aspiring capitalist farmers seeking maximum profits, leaves them little time to be engaged in village affairs. People say that they have no real interest in helping the lower castes and now even charge for their services as brokers.

The Chamars accuse them (as well as their other Bhumihar and Brahman masters) of not providing a minimum subsistence, while on occasion customary perquisites have been discontinued (see chapters 6 and 8). The Bhumihars also manipulate and, in many ways, incite factionalism among their *mazdur*s so that by being divided they will be easier to control. They are also willing to lend Chamars money for nonproductive court cases that engage them in conflict and keep them in debt and, hence, in continual bondage. Chamars have described a worsening of their economic condition: before Independence they used to lease land, but now they have none. Most men now subsist as casual day laborers earning two rupees, and it is not unlikely that even the ploughman, who is still paid in land and in kind (that is, in grain), may soon be reduced to a purely monetized form of contractual labor. With the disappearance of the traditional economic bond between patron and client, it can be expected that the ritual aspect will become dissipated (Epstein 1973:47). Already some Chamar women spoke about discontinuing their services at childbirth, which are considered polluting but not profitable.

As the Chamars of Arunpur have not achieved the dispersion of inequalities in wealth, status, and power that has characterized other castes, they are in the process of forming themselves into a class. It seems that the more conscious they become of their own situation and what is happening to their caste brothers elsewhere, the stronger they will emerge as a class. This, in turn, is bound to affect the vertical cleavage among the dominant Bhumihars when the two factions find that they must increasingly fuse to oppose their subordinates as the Chamars press forward their own interests. The Chamars have also found scope for their political aspirations within the wider political arena of the region. While their Independent candidate could not possibly win because of a narrow caste appeal, there is no reason to doubt that a Chamar (or other Untouchable) leader of greater repute could command a wider base of support among the dispossessed.

CASTE AND CLASS IN INDIAN POLITICS

I have described the ill feelings between Bhumihars and Chamars, especially among the younger generation of Untouchables (see also Béteille 1969b:111, 135–136). The latter feel that they are exploited, while their *maliks* believe that the workers have become impertinent and lazy. During the year I was in Arunpur, for reasons already noted (see chapters 1 and 8), these tensions and hostilities led to several incidents of open conflict. On each occasion, without fail, the two factions united against the Chamar threat.[9] Until the time I left, however, there was no clear indication of the cumulative effect upon factions of this type of conflict within the village, although it may become increasingly important in regional and national politics.

Several writers foresee the demise of clientelist politics under the pressures which are affecting traditional vertical bonds. Frankel has been the most explicit. She writes that

> the multicaste political faction led by traditional landowning patrons and constructed with support from families of low-status client groups, especially tenants and farm workers, will become more and more difficult to sustain as a viable political unit at the local level. The question is not whether the old pattern of clientelist politics can be put back together again, but how to fill the political vacuum in the rural areas as a result of its collapse. (1971:208; also Frankel and von Vorys 1972:9, 38; Sharma 1973:80).[10]

Prophecies aside, there is also no clear indication of the transformation of a caste into a class society. Both factionalism (and clientelist politics) and intercaste conflict in the form of classes seem certain to coexist in rural India into the foreseeable future, as each succeeds in articulating the demands and interests of various elements of society (see Singer on "adaptive strategies" 1972:285; 357ff; also Alavi 1973:59; Nicholas 1968b:275; Mayer 1967a:124).[11] Furthermore, contrary to some interpretations, it is not the caste system per se that has inhibited the growth of class feeling but the presence of factionalism based on vertical patron-client bonds as the characteristic mode of politics (Alavi 1965:273-274; 1973:46; Powell 1970:420; Mencher 1974a; see also note 9 to this chapter). Nor does factionalism necessarily exclude class solidarity or class conflict (Alavi 1973:46ff; see also note 5 to this chapter). The importance of these two forces on the political scene in India must be viewed at their point of contact within the wider regional arena. The extent to which political parties consciously foster and manipulate class interests, as well as taking a lead in defining them, will also determine the direction of political activity. The "traditional idiom" of politics, expressed through caste and factionalism at the village level, has been considered a major force in determining such a direction in the past. Today we may witness, in turn, that the village arena will become more and more a reflection of those conflicts and interests expressed in the wider political arena.

NOTES

1. Mayer has noticed a similar transformation in the leadership of four overseas Indian communities. Conditions that previously favored the emergence of patrons—since leaders were appointed—have changed and become more favorable to the rise of brokers (1967b).
2. My approach is different from that of those writers who have been mistaken about the nature of factions as I understand them, either confining them to kin groups or confusing them with classes (e.g., Singh 1961; Lewis 1958; Shepperdson 1969).
3. Boissevain's work, which came to my notice after the final draft was prepared, contains a similar conclusion in a succinctly written page (1974:199).
4. Indeed, Miller is led to conclude that the highly disruptive form of "pervasive" factionalism which Beals describes for Namhalli (1952-1953) illustrates an uncommon form of conflict, "significantly different from types of behavior and social organization normally treated as factionalism in Indian villages" (1965:23, 24). He, like Nicholas, also criticizes the assumption that the village constitutes a corporate entity as a group with defined common aims. It is misleading "to idealize the autonomy and integrity of Indian villages" (Nicholas 1968b:295; also Miller 1965:18).
5. There is a need to reexamine the relationship between factionalism, regarded as relating to conflicts of personal interests, and ideological issues. Brass raises the question of whether it is not that the "personalization of conflict is merely a stylistic cultural form that covers more deep-seated ideological, social or institutional conflicts" (n.d.:2). A closer analysis of data regarding the diversity of factional recruitment for a *panchayat* election in a West Bengal village (from Nicholas 1965) leads Alavi to conclude: "The principle of diversity of factional recruitment, looked at from the point of view of the faction leader, may well justify indifference about who votes for him, so long as he gets support. But, looked at from the point of view of the followers, the basis of support is by no means a matter of indifference" (1973:49). The data show that whereas the Congress candidate drew most support from vertical ties, the Communist one relied mostly on the factor of kinship and, secondarily, caste. "There is, therefore," Alavi believes, "a strong suggestion of an underlying structural pattern" (1973:49).
6. A closely related model for the growth of peasant unrest and rebellion linked to the erosion of patron-client bonds has been developed for Southeast Asia (Kerkvliet 1972; Scott 1972; Scott and Kerkvliet 1973).
7. The debate concerning the extent, success, and effects of the Green Revolution is far from settled. The situation of Indian agriculture has also been drastically affected by recent international economic and political events.
8. Cohn had written much earlier that the "movements for social and economic uplift of the low castes have destroyed the moral base of the relationships of super-ordination—subordination among the Thakurs and their low caste dependents" (1959:89). He seemingly invites contradiction when he then states, "Indian peasant society is still largely dominated by values surrounding the concept of 'status' [as opposed to contractual relations]" (1959:91).
9. This fact casts strong doubt on the validity of Dube's position that factionalism within a dominant caste inhibits its power and will threaten its position of dominance (1968). The situation in Arunpur reveals, as it must elsewhere, that

what is crucial is not that such castes are divided as that they are secure enough in their dominance to tolerate division because of the lack of any serious threat to their power. Dube appears to be speaking more of a class than dominance when he refers to a strong feeling of group unity, leadership, and sense of direction combined with an internal parity of wealth and a use of economic power to further the interests of the caste. It is only at the crucial test of a conflict of interests between the dominant caste and a group opposed to them that the weakness of factionalism in threatening their true dominance can be ascertained. The Bhumihars have closed their ranks when faced with such a threat. Chamars perceive that their masters succeed in dividing others by flattery and fear because they themselves are united against others. Cohn also confuses the situation when he writes that a threat to their position of dominance from the lower caste (or castes) can prevent the factionalization of the dominant caste (1965:94). However, he goes on to recognize that these are situational responses that may reflect a developmental cycle of conflict (1965:97).

10. Unlike Siegel and Beals who find it highly probable that pervasive factionalism will lead to a "developing anomie which would result from a loss of interest in the traditional integration of values" (1960b:413), Frankel and von Vorys see the *decline* of clientelist politics as a step in that direction (1972:38).

11. Philippine society contains a definite two-class horizontal cleavage that is crosscut by a network of patron-client relationships tying the poor to the rich. The line of cleavage between the rich and the poor is thus turned into a bridge uniting them (Lande 1965:6–10).

Glossary of Commonly Used Terms

agua	leader or foremost among equals
amin panchayat	the British local council
bara admi	big man
bare admi	big men
bare admi panchayat	council of big men
bigha	0.67 of an acre; approximately one-fourth hectare
biradari	subcaste
biradari panchayat	subcaste council
bisa	one twentieth of a *bigha*
bise	plural of *bisa*
brahman	priest and intellectual; one of the four *varna*s
dipak	oil lamp, symbol of Jan Sangh party
gauna	second marriage ceremony
jajman	patron
jajmani	ritualized economic interaction of the caste system
jati	caste
khandan	male descendants of a common-named ancestor, their wives, and unmarried daughters; might be equated with a lineage

kshatriya	ruler and warrior; one of the four *varna*s
malik	master
maund	forty *ser*s or eighty pounds
mazburi	condition of helplessness
mazdur	laborer
mazduri	wages
mukhiya	headman, appointed by the British
neta	political party leader
nyaya panchayat	justice council in the Local Self-Government system
panchayat	council
panchayati raj	Local Self-Government program
purdah	seclusion of women
parti	party or faction
partibandi	factionalism
patti	place where *pattidar*s live
pattidar	kinsmen who have rights to property that is divided; might be equated with a minimal lineage
paua	one quarter *ser* or one half pound
pradhan	elected head of the village
praja	client or dependent
pura	main village settlement or associated hamlets
rais	aristocrat
rupee	thirteen cents
ser	two pounds
shudra	servant; one of the four *varna*s
thokdar	official in charge of water distribution from the government tubewell
vaishya	artisan, merchant, or farmer; one of the four *varna*s
varna	class division of ancient India
zamindar	landlord
zamindari	landlordship

Bibliography

AGGARWAL, P. C.
1973　*The Green Revolution and Rural Labor.* New Delhi: Shri Ram Centre for Industrial Relations and Human Resources.

AJ
1968　August 25. Special issue on the expansion of Banaras city municipal limits. Banaras.

ALAVI, HAMZA
1965　Peasants and Revolution. In Ralph Miliband and John Saville, eds., *Socialist Register 1965.* New York: Monthly Review Press, pp. 241-227.

1973　Peasant Classes and Primordial Loyalties. *Journal of Peasant Studies* 1:23-62.

BAILEY, F. G.
1957　*Caste and the Economic Frontier.* Manchester: Manchester University Press.

1960　*Tribe, Caste and Nation.* Manchester: Manchester University Press.

1963a　Closed Social Stratification in India. *Archives Européenes de Sociologie* 4:107-124.

1963b　*Politics and Social Change.* Manchester: Manchester University Press.

1968　Parapolitical Systems. In Marc J. Swartz, ed., *Local-Level Politics.* Chicago: Aldine Publishing Company, pp. 281-294.

1969　*Stratagems and Spoils.* Oxford: Blackwell.

BARTH, FREDRIK
1963   *The Role of the Entrepreneur in Social Change in Northern Norway.* Bergen-Oslo: Norwegian Universities Press.
1966   *Notes on Models of Social Organization.* Royal Anthropological Institute Occasional Paper no. 23.
1967   On the Study of Social Change. *American Anthropologist* 69:661-669.

BAXTER, CRAIG
1975   The Rise and Fall of the Bharatiya Kranti Dal in Uttar Pradesh. In Marguerite Ross Barnett et al., *Electoral Politics in the Indian States.* Delhi: Manohar Book Service, pp. 113-142.

BEALS, ALAN R.
1962   Pervasive Factionalism in a South Indian Village. In M. Sherif, ed., *Intergroup Relations and Leadership.* New York: John Wiley & Sons, Inc., pp. 247-266.

BEALS, ALAN R. AND BERNARD J. SIEGEL
1966   *Divisiveness and Social Conflict.* Stanford, California: Stanford University Press (Indian edition).

BEIDELMAN, T. O.
1959   *A Comparative Analysis of the Jajmani System.* Monograph of the Association for Asian Studies no. 8. Locust Valley, New York: J. J. Augustin, Inc.-Publisher.

BENDIX, R. AND S. M. LIPSET
1966   Karl Marx's Theory of Social Classes. In R. Bendix and S. M. Lipset, eds., *Class, Status and Power.* 2d ed. New York: The Free Press, pp. 6-11.

BÉTEILLE, ANDRÉ
1965   *Caste, Class and Power.* Berkeley, California: University of California Press.
1969a The Politics of "Non-Antagonistic" Strata. *Contributions to Indian Sociology* n.s. 3:17-31.
1969b *Castes: Old and New.* Bombay: Asia Publishing House.
1972   *Inequality and Social Change.* Delhi: Oxford University Press.
1974a *Studies In Agrarian Social Structure.* Delhi: Oxford University Press.
1974b *Six Essays in Comparative Sociology.* Delhi: Oxford University Press.

BHARGAVA'S STANDARD ILLUSTRATED DICTIONARY OF THE HINDI LANGUAGE
1964   Hindi-English Edition. R. C. Pathak, compiler and ed. Banaras: Bhargava Book Depot.

BOISSEVAIN, JEREMY
1964   Factions, Parties and Politics in Malta. *American Anthropologist* 66:1275-1287.
1968   The Place of Non-Groups in the Social Sciences. *Man* 3:542-556.
1971   Second Thoughts on Quasi-groups, Categories and Coalitions. *Man* 6:468-472.
1974   *Friends of Friends*. Oxford: Blackwell.

BRASS, PAUL R.
1965   *Factional Politics in an Indian State*. Berkeley, California: University of California Press.
1968   Uttar Pradesh. In Myron Weiner, ed., *State Politics in India*. Princeton, New Jersey: Princeton University Press, pp. 61-126.
n. d.   Leadership Conflict and the Disintegration of the Indian Socialist Movement: Personal Ambition, Power, and Policy. [Unpublished paper, mimeograph.]

BREMAN, JAN
1974   *Patronage and Exploitation*. Berkeley, California: University of California Press.

BURGER, ANGELA SUTHERLAND
1969   *Opposition in a Dominant Party System*. Berkeley, California: University of California Press.

BYRES, T. J.
1972   The Dialectic of India's Green Revolution. *South Asian Review* 5:99-116.

CAPLAN, A. PATRICIA
1972   *Priests and Cobblers*. San Francisco: Chandler Publishing Company.

CARTER, ANTHONY
1974   *Elite Politics in Rural India*. Cambridge: Cambridge University Press.

CHAKRAVARTI, ANAND
1975   *Contradiction and Change*. Delhi: Oxford University Press.

CHANCE, NORMAN A.
1962   Factionalism as a Process of Social and Cultural Change. In M. Sherif, ed., *Intergroup Relations and Leadership*. New York: John Wiley & Sons, Inc., pp. 267-273.

COHEN, RONALD
1970   The Political System. In Raoul Naroll and Ronald Cohen, eds., *A Handbook of Methodology in Cultural Anthropology*. Garden City, N.Y.: The Natural History Press.

COHN, BARNEY S.
1955 The Changing Status of a Depressed Caste. In McKim Marriott, ed., *Village India*. Chicago: Chicago University Press, pp. 53-77.
1959 Some Notes on Law and Change in North India. *Economic Development and Cultural Change* 8:79-93.
1965 Anthropological Notes on Disputes and Law in India. *American Anthropologist* 67:82-122.

DAHRENDORF, RALF
1959 *Class and Class Conflict in Industrial Society*. Stanford, California: Stanford University Press.

DANDEKAR, V. M. AND N. RATH
1971 Poverty—1: Dimensions and Trends. *Economic and Political Weekly* 6:25-48.

DHILLON, H.
1955 *Leadership and Groups in a South Indian Village*. New Delhi: Planning Commission, Government of India Press.

DUBE, S. C.
1968 Caste Dominance and Factionalism. *Contributions to Indian Sociology* n.s. 2:58-81.

DUMONT, LOUIS
1962 Kingship in Ancient India. *Contributions to Indian Sociology* 6: 48-77.
1972 *Homo Hierarchicus*. London: Granada Publishing, Ltd.

EASTON, DAVID
1959 Political Anthropology. In Bernard J. Siegel, ed., *Biennial Review of Anthropology 1959*. Stanford, California: Stanford University Press, pp. 210-262.

ECONOMIC AND POLITICAL WEEKLY [Bombay: Sameeksha Trust.]
1969 Illusion of Stability. 4:383-384.
1974 Landed and Landless in Surat District. 9:974-977.

ELECTION COMMISSION OF INDIA
1970 *Report on the Mid-Term General Election in India*. New Delhi.

ELLIOTT, CAROLYN M.
1970 Caste and Faction among the Dominant Caste: The Reddis and Kammas of Andhra. In Rajni Kothari, ed., *Caste in Indian Politics*. New Delhi: Orient Longmans, pp. 129-171.

EPSTEIN, T. SCARLETT
1967 Productive Efficiency and Customary Systems of Rewards in Rural South India. In Raymond Firth, ed., *Themes in Economic Anthropology*. ASA Monograph no. 6. London: Tavistock Publications, pp. 229-252.

1973   *South India: Yesterday, Today and Tomorrow.* New York: Holmes and Meier Publishers, Inc.

ETIENNE, GILBERT
1968   *Studies in Indian Agriculture: The Art of the Possible.* Berkeley, California: University of California Press.

FIRTH, RAYMOND
1957   Factions in India and Overseas Indian Communities. *British Journal of Sociology* 8:391-395.

FOSTER, GEORGE
1963   The Dyadic Contract in Tzintzuntzan. II: Patron-Client Relationship. *American Anthropologist* 65:1280-1294.

FRANKEL, FRANCINE R.
1971   *India's Green Revolution.* Princeton, New Jersey: Princeton University Press.

FRANKEL, FRANCINE R. AND KARL VON VORYS
1972   *The Political Challenge of the Green Revolution: Shifting Patterns of Peasant Participation in India and Pakistan.* Policy Memorandum no. 38. Princeton, New Jersey: Center of International Studies, Woodrow Wilson School of Public and International Affairs, Princeton University.

GALLIN, BERNARD
1968   Political Factionalism and its Impact on Chinese Village Social Organization in Taiwan. In Marc J. Swartz, ed., *Local-Level Politics.* Chicago: Aldine Publishing Company, pp. 377-400.

GAMSON, WILLIAM A.
1961   A Theory of Coalition Formation. *American Sociological Review* 26:373-382.

GARDNER, PETER M.
1968   Dominance in India: A Reappraisal. *Contributions to Indian Sociology* n.s. 2:82-97.

GHURYE, G. S.
1950   *Caste and Class in India.* Bombay: Asia Publishing House.

GOUGH, KATHLEEN
1960   Caste in a Tanjore Village. In E. R. Leach, ed., *Aspects of Caste in South India, Ceylon and North-West Pakistan.* Cambridge: Cambridge University Press, pp. 11-60.

1970   Social Structure of a Tanjore Village. In K. Ishwaran, ed., *Change and Continuity in India's Villages.* New York: Columbia University Press.

1973   Harijans in Thanjavur. In Kathleen Gough and Hari P. Sharma, eds., *Imperialism and Revolution in South Asia.* New York: Monthly Review Press, pp. 222-245.

GOULD, HAROLD
1967   Priest and Contrapriest: A Structural Analysis of Jajmani Relationships in the Hindu Plains and the Nilgiri Hills. *Contributions to Indian Sociology* n.s. 1:26-55.
1969   Toward a "Jati" Model for Indian Politics. *Economic and Political Weekly* 4:291-297.

GOVERNMENT OF INDIA
1965   Census of 1961—Uttar Pradesh. Vol. 53, *District Census Handbook: Varanasi District*. Lucknow: Superintendent, Printing and Stationers.

GRAHAM, B. D.
1968   The Succession of Factional Systems in the Uttar Pradesh Congress Party, 1937-66. In Marc J. Swartz, ed., *Local-Level Politics*. Chicago: Aldine Publishing Company, pp. 323-360.

HABIB, IRFAN
1963   *Agrarian System of Mughal India, 1556-1707*. Bombay: Asia Publishing House.

HARPER, EDWARD
1968   Social Consequences of an "Unsuccessful" Low Caste Movement. In James Silverberg, ed., *Social Mobility in the Caste System in India. Comparative Studies in Society and History* Supplement 3:36-65.

HOCART, A. M.
1950   *Caste: A Comparative Study*. London: Methuen & Company.

ISHWARAN, K.
1966   *Tradition and Economy in Village India*. Delhi: Allied Publishers.

ISLAM, A. K. M. AMINUL
1974   *A Bangladesh Village: Conflict and Cohesion*. Cambridge, Massachusetts: Schenkman Publishing Co., Inc.

JANNUZI, F. TOMASSON
1974   *Agrarian Crisis in India*. Austin, Texas: University of Texas Press.

JUYAL, B. N.
1974   India. In Friedrich-Ebert-Stiftring, *Organization of Peasants in Asia*. Regional Experts Workshop organized by Friedrich-Ebert-Stiftring in cooperation with the FAO of the U.N. and the I.L.O., 28.10-2.11.74. Bangkok: F.E.S. and the Federal Republic of Germany.

KERKVLIET, BENEDICT JOHN
1972   *Peasant Rebellion in the Philippines*. Unpublished Ph.D. dissertation in political science, University of Wisconsin.

KESSINGER, Tom G.
1974   *Vilyatpur 1848-1968*. Berkeley, California: University of California Press.

KOLENDA, PAULINE M.
1966 Toward a Model of the Hindu Jajmani System. In William L. Rowe, *Contours of Culture Change in South Asia. Human Organization* Monograph no. 9, pp. 11–31.

KOTHARI, RAJNI, Ed.
1970 Introduction. In *Caste in Indian Politics*. New Delhi: Orient Longmans, pp. 3–25.

LANDE, CARL H.
1965 *Leaders, Factions, and Parties*. Southeast Asia Studies, Monograph Series no. 6. New Haven, Connecticut: Yale University Press.

LEACH, EDMUND R., Ed.
1960 Introduction: What Should We Mean by Caste. In *Aspects of Caste in South India, Ceylon and North-West Pakistan*. Cambridge: Cambridge University Press, pp. 1–10.

LENIN, V. I.
1971 A Great Beginning. In *Selected Works*, vol. 3. Moscow: Progress Publishers, pp. 219–242.

LENSKI, GERHARD E.
1966 *Power and Privilege*. New York: McGraw Hill Book Company.

LEWIS, OSCAR
1958 *Village Life in Northern India*. Urbana, Illinois: University of Illinois Press.

LIPSET, SEYMOUR M.
1968 Social Class. In David L. Sills, ed., *International Encyclopedia of the Social Sciences*, vol. 15. New York, Macmillan, Inc. and The Free Press, pp. 296–316.

LYNCH, OWEN
1969 *Politics of Untouchability*. New York: Columbia University Press.

MAMDANI, MAHMOOD
1972 *The Myth of Population Control*. New York: Monthly Review Press.

MARK, RAYMOND W. AND RICHARD C. SNYDER
1957 The Analysis of Social Conflict—toward an Overview and Synthesis. *Journal of Conflict Resolution* 1:212–248.

MASON, PHILIP, Ed.
1967 Unity and Diversity: An Introductory Review. In *India and Ceylon: Unity and Diversity*. Oxford: Oxford University Press, pp. 1–29.

MARX, KARL
1963 *The Eighteenth Brumaire of Louis Bonaparte*. New York: International Publishers Co., Inc.

MAYER, ADRIAN
1958 The Dominant Caste in a Region of Central India. *Southwest Journal of Anthropology* 14:407–427.

1960 *Caste and Kinship in Central India*. Berkeley, California: University of California Press.

1966 Significance of Quasi-groups in the Study of Complex Societies. In M. Banton, ed., *Anthropological Approaches to the Study of Complex Societies*. ASA Monograph no. 4. London: Tavistock Publications, pp. 97-122.

1967a Caste and Local Politics in India. In Philip Mason, ed., *India and Ceylon: Unity and Diversity*. Oxford: Oxford University Press, pp. 121-141.

1967b Patrons and Brokers: Rural Leadership in Four Overseas Indian Communities. In Maurice Freedman, ed., *Social Organization: Essays Presented to Raymond Firth*. London: Frank Cass & Co. Ltd., pp. 167-188.

MEILLASSOUX, CLAUDE
1973 Are There Castes in India? *Economy and Society* 2:89-111.

MENCHER, JOAN P.
1974a The Caste System Upside Down, or The Not-So-Mysterious East. *Current Anthropology* 15:469-493.

1974b Conflict and Contradiction in the 'Green Revolution': The Case of Tamil Nadu. *Economic and Political Weekly* 9:309-323.

MILLER, D. B.
1975 *From Hierarchy to Stratification*. Delhi: Oxford University Press.

MILLER, D. F.
1965 Factions in Indian Village Politics. *Pacific Affairs* 38:17-31.

MOFFATT, MICHAEL
1975 Untouchables and the Caste System: A Tamil Case Study. *Contributions to Indian Sociology* 9:111-112.

MORRIS-JONES, W. H.
1963 India's Political Idioms. In C. H. Philips, ed., *Politics and Society in India*. London: George Allen & Unwin, Ltd., pp. 133-154.

1964 Politics and Society. In *The Government and Politics of India*. London: Hutchinson University Library, pp. 48-72.

MUKHERJEE, S. N.
1970 Class, Caste and Politics in Calcutta, 1815-38. In Edmund Leach and S. N. Mukherjee, eds., *Elites in South Asia*. Cambridge: Cambridge University Press, pp. 33-78.

NARAIN, IQBAL
1969 The Emerging Concept. In M. V. Mathur and I. Narain, eds., *Panchayati Raj, Planning and Democracy*. Bombay: Asia Publishing House, pp. 19-34.

NICHOLAS, RALPH W.
- 1965 Factions: A Comparative Analysis. In M. Banton, ed., *Political Systems and the Distribution of Power.* ASA Monograph no. 2. London: Tavistock Publications, pp. 21-62.
- 1966 Segmentary Factional Political Systems. In Marc Swartz, et al., *Political Anthropology.* Chicago, Aldine Publishing Company, pp. 44-60.
- 1968a Structures of Politics in the Villages of South Asia. In Milton Singer and Bernard S. Cohn, eds., *Structure and Change in Indian Society.* Chicago, Aldine Publishing Company, pp. 243-284.
- 1968b Rules, Resources, and Political Activity. In Marc J. Swartz, ed., *Local-Level Politics.* Chicago, Aldine Publishing Company, pp. 295-321.
- 1973 Elites, Class and Factions in Indian Politics. Review Article. *South Asian Review* 6:145-153.

OOMMEN, T. K.
- 1969 Political Leadership in Rural India: Image and Reality. Unpublished manuscript.

OPLER, MORRIS AND RUDRA DUTT SINGH
- 1948 The Division of Labor in an Indian Village. In Carleton S. Coon, ed., *A Reader in General Anthropology.* New York: Holt, Rinehart and Winston, pp. 464-496.

ORANS, MARTIN
- 1968 Maximizing in Jajmaniland: A Model of Caste Relations. *American Anthropologist* 70:875-897.

ORENSTEIN, HENRY
- 1965 *Gaon: Conflict and Cohesion in an Indian Village.* Princeton, New Jersey: Princeton University Press.

PARTHASARATHY, G.
- 1971 *Green Revolution and the Weaker Sections.* Bombay: Thacker & Co., Ltd.

POCOCK, DAVID
- 1962 Notes on *Jajmani* Relationships. *Contributions to Indian Sociology* 6:78-95.

POHEKAR, G. S.
- 1970 *Studies in Green Revolution.* Bombay: United Asia Publications Pvt., Ltd.

POWELL, JOHN DUNCAN
- 1970 Peasant Society and Clientelist Politics. *American Political Science Review* 64:411-425.

RANGNATH
1967   Rural Leadership Old and New. In L. P. Vidyarthi, ed., *Leadership in India*. Bombay: Asia Publishing House, pp. 267-276.

RETZLAFF, RALPH H.
1962   *Village Government in India*. Bombay: Asia Publishing House.

RIKER, WILLIAM H.
1962   *The Theory of Political Coalitions*. New Haven, Connecticut: Yale University Press.

ROWE, WILLIAM L.
1968   The New Cauhans: A Caste Mobility Movement in North India. In James Silverberg, ed., *Social Mobility in the Caste System in India. Comparative Studies in Society and History* Supplement 3:66-77.

RUDOLPH, LLOYD I. AND SUSANNE H. RUDOLPH
1960   The Political Role of India's Caste Associations. *Pacific Affairs* 33:5-22.

RUDOLPH, SUSANNE H.
1961   Consensus and Conflict in Indian Politics. *World Politics* 13:385-399.

SCHWARTZ, NORMAN
1969   Goal Attainment through Factionalism: A Guatemala Case. *American Anthropologist* 71:1088-1108.

SCHWARTZBERG, JOSEPH E.
1968   Caste Regions of the North Indian Plains. In Milton Singer and Bernard S. Cohn, eds., *Structure and Change in Indian Society*. Chicago: Aldine Publishing Company, pp. 81-113.

SCOTT, JAMES
1972   The Erosion of Patron-Client Bonds and Social Change in Rural Southeast Asia. *Journal of Asian Studies* 32:2-38.

SCOTT, JAMES AND BENEDICT J. KERKVLIET
1973   The Politics of Survival: Peasant Response to "Progress" in Southeast Asia. *Journal of Southeast Asian History* 4:241-268.

SHARMA, HARI P.
1973   The Green Revolution in India: Prelude to a Red One? In Kathleen Gough and Hari P. Sharma, eds., *Imperialism and Revolution in South Asia*. New York: Monthly Review Press, pp. 77-102.

SHEPPERDSON, M. J.
1969   Political Conflict in Ten Villages in India, Pakistan and Ceylon. *Contributions to Indian Sociology* n.s. 3:45-75.

SIEGEL, BERNARD J. AND ALAN R. BEALS
1960a   Conflict and Factionalist Dispute. *Journal of the Royal Anthropological Institute* 90:107-117.
1960b   Pervasive Factionalism. *American Anthropologist* 62:394-417.

SINGER, MILTON
1972   *When a Great Tradition Modernizes.* New York: Praeger Publishers, Inc.

SINHA, SURJIT AND RANJIT BHATTACHARYA
1969   Bhadralok and Chhotolok in a Rural Area of West Bengal. *Sociological Bulletin* 18:50-66.

SINGH, BALJIT
1961   *Next Step in Village India.* Bombay: Asia Publishing House.

SIVERTSEN, DAGFINN
1963   *When Caste Barriers Fall.* Oslo, Norway: Universitets forlaget; London: George Allen & Unwin Ltd.

SOMJEE, A. H.
1964   *Politics of a Periurban Community in India.* Bombay: Asia Publishing House.

SOUTHWOLD, MARTIN
1969   A Game Model of African Tribal Politics. In Ira Buchler and Hugh Nutini, eds., *Game Theory in the Social Sciences.* Pittsburgh, Pennsylvania: University of Pittsburgh Press, pp. 23-43.

SRINIVAS, M. N.
1955   The Social System of a Mysore Village. In McKim Marriott, ed., *Village India.* Chicago: Chicago University Press, pp. 1-35.

1959   The Dominant Caste in Rampura. *American Anthropologist* 61:1-16.

1962   *Caste in Modern India and Other Essays.* Bombay: Asia Publishing House.

SWARTZ, MARC J., Ed.
1968   Introduction. In *Local-Level Politics.* Chicago: Aldine Publishing Company, pp. 1-46.

SWARTZ, MARC, VICTOR TURNER, AND ARTHUR TUDEN, Eds.
1966   Introduction. In *Political Anthropology.* Chicago: Aldine Publishing Company, pp. 1-41.

SWINGLE, PAUL, Ed.
1970   Preface. In *The Structure of Conflict.* New York: Academic Press, Inc., pp. ix-x.

TERRAY, EMMANUEL
1975   Classes and Class Consciousness in the Abron Kingdom of Gyaman. In Maurice Bloch, ed., *Marxist Analyses and Social Anthropology.* New York: John Wiley & Sons, Inc. pp. 85-135.

THORNER, DANIEL
1956   *The Agrarian Prospect in India.* Delhi: University Press.

TURNER, VICTOR
1957   *Schism and Continuity in an African Society.* Manchester: Manchester University Press.

WEBER, MAX
1966   Class, Status and Party. In R. Bendix and S. M. Lipset, eds., *Class, Status and Power,* 2nd ed. New York: The Free Press, pp. 21-28.

WEINER, MYRON
1965a Party Politics and Panchayati Raj. In S. P. Aiyar and R. Srinivasan, eds., *Studies in Indian Democracy.* Bombay: Allied Publishers, pp. 405-411.

1965b Village and Party Factionalism in Andhra: Pannur Constituency. In M. Weiner and Rajni Kothari, eds., *Indian Voting Behavior.* Calcutta: Firma K. L. Mukhopadhyay, pp. 177-202.

WISER, W. H.
1936   *The Hindu Jajmani System.* Lucknow: Lucknow Publishing House.

WOOD, GEOF
1973   From Raiyat to Rich Peasant. *South Asian Review* 7:1-16.

YADAVA, J. S.
1968   Factionalism in a Haryana Village. *American Anthropologist* 70:898-910.

YALMAN, NUR
1960   The Flexibility of Caste Principles in a Kandyan Community. In Edmund Leach, ed., *Aspects of Caste in South India, Ceylon and North-West Pakistan.* Cambridge: Cambridge University Press, pp. 78-112.

ZAGORIA, DONALD S.
1971   The Ecology of Peasant Communism in India. *American Political Science Review* 55:144-160.

Index

Agrarian society, 167
Agrawals, 25
Agricultural cycle, 28-30
Agriculture, 34 (Fig. 3), 36 (Fig. 4), 40-41, 55-57, 73-74, 113-114, 117, 123, 166-171; commercialization of, 41, 117, 131, 230-231; crops, 25, 29, 41
Agua, 110, 131
Allahabad High Court. *See* Court, high
ALAVI, HAMZA, 12, 234n
Ambedkar, 162
Amin Panchayat. See Panchayat, amin
Arena, 201, 210; fragmented, 217; political, 5, 19, 21, 114, 117, 119, 134-165, 194, 216, 221, 227, 233; regional, 217; villagewide, 4, 185, 198-199
Aristocrat. *See Rais*
Arunpur, 5, 21, 22 (Map 3)
Arunpur Intercollege. *See* Intercollege
Assistant, research project: and the Chamars, 181-183; in disputes, 172; and the Jan Sangh, 211; role of, in fieldwork, xvi, 15-16
Authority structure, 132n, 223-224; and *bare admi,* 224-225; and caste system, 220-221, 223, 227-228; decrease of, 118-119, 225; lack of, 193; under British, 117, 132-133n, 222

BAILEY, F. G., 134, 157-158, 159n
Banaras, 5, 20, 181; effects on Arunpur life, 21, 24, 54, 74, 162, 165; location, 211-212
Banaras Hindu University, 90, 98, 127, 202
Banaras Lower court. *See* Court, lower
Banaras Rajas, 63
Bans, 81, 91
Bara admi (big man). *See Bare admi*
Bare admi, 54, 109-132, 149, 156, 185, 223-232; conflicts involving, 5-6, 153-154, 158, 199; defined, 110-112; entrepreneurial activity of, 57, 220-222; as entrepreneurs, 224-225, 227, 231-232; political involvement of, 201, 207-210, 213, 215, 220; preferential treatment of, 57-59, 64
Bare admi panchayat. See Panchayat, bare admi
BDO. *See* Block Development Officer

This index was compiled as a joint effort by students of the Graduate School of Library Studies, University of Hawaii, LS664 [Abstracting and Indexing], under the direction of Dr. Sarah K. Vann. Class members were as follows: Dee Ann Allison, Zulkifli Amsyah, Loretta Andress, Joseph Benson, Pauline Edelstein, Dona Lyn Foster, and Audrey H. Graham. Also, Karen A. Hatakenaka, Suzanne Madigan Irvin, Sandy Mow, Dana Neff, Michael D. Reed, and Marilyn Reese.
The final coordination was the responsibility of Audrey H. Graham and Michael D. Reed.

BKD. *See* Bharatiya Kranti Dal
BEALS, ALAN R., 229, 234n, 235n
Begar, 35, 169
Bengal, 29, 127
BÉTEILLE, ANDRÉ, 10-11, 17n, 201
Bharatiya Kranti Dal (BKD), 202-203, 218n
Bhojpuri, 19, 123
Bhumidar, 31, 33
Bhumihars, 38, 119n, 170-171, 220; as *bare admi,* 92-93, 102-103, 114, 116-120, 131; in Choudhuri *gotras,* 188, 192-196, 198, 199n; and class conflict, 160-161, 170-180; dignity and prestige of, 35, 112, 167-168; as dominant caste, 5, 17n, 46, 63-64, 79, 119, 220, 229; economic and political control of, 3, 58-59, 120; factional conflicts of, 5-6, 8, 135-137, 144, 150-152, 161, 197, 232; family relationships of, 78-81, 84-86, 96, 164-165; *jajmani* relationships of, 62-64, 66-69, 71, 75-76; and Kolha *gotra,* 192-193, 196, 198, 200n; and ownership of resources, 40-41, 44 (Table 6), 46, 158, 223; political involvement of, 201-205, 207-208, 210-213, 215-217; in water disputes, 189-192. *See also* Little Pura Bhumihars; Main Pura Bhumihars
Bhumihar settlements, 24-25
Big men. *See Bare admi*
Big men *panchayat. See Panchayat, bare admi*
Bihar, 19, 29, 139
Biradari, 63, 66, 86
Biradari panchayat. See Panchayat, biradari
Black money. *See* Bribery
Block Development Officer (BDO), 14, 50, 56-57
BOISSEVAIN, JEREMY, 234n
Bose, Subash Chandra, 213
Brahmans, 38, 64, 66, 119, 132n; agricultural involvement of, 41, 46, 155, 171, 198; involvement in conflicts, 149, 175, 191-193, 196; personal relationships of, 68, 75-78, 86, 90-92, 96-97, 139; political involvement of, 202, 204-207, 211, 216
BRASS, PAUL R., 217n, 234n
Bribery, 58, 60n, 113-115, 121, 149, 187, 189
Brides, 84, 101
British-appointed headman. *See Mukhiya*
British military depot, 28
British *panchayat. See Panchayat, amin*
British Raj, 49, 110, 115, 222-223; administration of, 49, 55, 59; and power to appoint, 117, 119, 132n; and introduction of *neta,* 110. *See also Mukhiya; Zamindar*
Brokerage transactions, 157-158, 225
Brokers, 113, 132, 221-222, 224, 234n
Business, 41, 117, 166

Calcutta, 127
Canal network, 29
Case history method, 14
Cash income, 41, 44, 46 (Table 8)
Cash transactions, 161
Caste, 9, 11-12, 112, 117, 119, 126, 202; hierarchy, 6, 76, 87n, 184n, 223; relations, 62-70, 76-79, 142, 150, 161, 204; rules, 38, 61-62, 76-79, 80 (Fig. 11), 150; values, 72. *See also Biradiri; Jati; Varna*
Caste associations, 161
Caste conflict. *See* Factional conflict
"Caste culture," 160
Caste, dominant. *See* Dominant caste
Caste *panchayat. See Panchayat, biradari*
Casteism. *See Jatpat*
Castes, 5, 40-41, 44-45 (Tables 5, 6, 7), 46, 52, 216. *See also* individual caste names
CHAKRAVARTI, ANAND, 133n
Chamar Independent Party, 214
Chamar Pura, 174-175
Chamars, 8, 15, 44, 46, 54, 57-58, 78-79, 92-93, 148, 150, 171-180, 184n, 191-194, 198, 210, 231-233; in Arunpur, 17n; change among, 181-183, 231-232; economic conditions of, 44, 163-164, 232; factionalism among, 177-180, 232; family relationships of, 81, 163-165; in politics, 137, 144, 203-204, 207, 211-212, 217; land ownership among, 33, 35, 40-41, 168; occupations of, 35, 67, 71, 73, 75-76, 134, 163, 165-171, 225; restrictions on, 25, 161-162; unity among, 5, 160, 162, 176-177. *See also Mazdura; Mazduri*
Children, 92, 169
Chaudhuri, 38
Clan. *See Gotra*
Class, 10-12, 18n, 166-167, 181-183, 210-211, 234n
Client. *See Jajmani*
Class conflict, 4, 6, 8-11, 17-18n, 20, 86n, 160-183, 221, 229-231
Closed society, 160
Coalitions. *See Parti; Partibandi*
COHN, BARNEY S., 38-39, 184n, 234n, 235n
Community development, 50, 52, 55-56, 59, 113, 120

INDEX

Community Development Block, 50, 57, 99, 130, 132, 224
Community Development program, 76, 157-158
Competition, 64, 88, 97, 107, 137-138; for land, 103-105; for a pond, 104-105; for power, 226. See also *Partibandi*
Conflict, xv, 81, 185, 197-198; family, 82-86, 89-107; *jajman-praja*, 88, 105-107; resolution of, 50, 53-55, 58-59; village-wide, 8, 88, 199. See also Class conflict; Disputes; Factional conflict; *Panchayat*; Political conflict
Conflict, caste. See Factional conflict
Conflict, class. See Class conflict
Congress Party, 28, 202-214; Uttar Pradesh, 130
Constitution (of Independent India), 49-50
Council. See *Panchayat*
Court, 18n, 53-55, 58, 93, 105, 107; lower, 136; high, 136-137, 149
Cultural categories, native terminology for, 11, 17-18n, 109-114
Customs. See *Rivas*

Dallia bazaar, 21, 205
DANDEKAR, V. M., 231
Data: analysis, 89; collection, 13-16; evaluation, 12
Daughter, branded, 102-103
Daya, 96-97, 107
Debt. See Indebtedness
Decision-making, 193, 223, 225. See also Conflict, resolution of
Democracy, 203
Dharkars, 40, 73, 151, 158, 184n, 187, 210, 212, 221
Dharma, 93, 119, 162
Dhobis, 68-69
Disputes, 31; escalation of, 107, 145, 147, 171; labor, 171-174, 176-177; land, 28, 37, 136-137, 139-141, 148; settlement of, 37-40, 114, 119; water, 141, 149, 175-176, 186, 188-189, 195-196. See also Conflict
Dogs, 145-146
Dominance, 9-10, 62-63, 78, 223, 235n; decisive, 63
Dominant caste, 8-10, 17n, 39, 79, 107, 112, 225, 234-235n
DUBE, S. C., 234n
Dust storms. See *Loo*

Economic interaction. See *Jajmani*
Economic mobility, 44

Economy, monetized. See Monetized economy
Education, 41, 46, 47 (Table 9), 78, 82-83, 113, 119, 131, 165. See also Literacy
Elections, 50, 53-54, 185, 222-223; and campaigning, 212-213; 1967 general, 202, 208, 217n; 1969 midterm, 201, 203, 207, 209-212, 214-215, 218n, 222; of village *panchayat*, 141-144, 228
ELLIOTT, CAROLYN M., 107
Entrepreneurs, 224-225. See also *Bare admi*, as entrepreneurs
EPSTEIN, T. SCARLETT, 73
ETIENNE, GILBERT, 37

Factional conflict, 8-10, 20, 79, 188-191, 193, 197, 199; and change, 155, 227-229; organization of, 155-158; scholars on, 17n, 158n, 235n. See also *Partibandi*
Faction leaders, 5, 137, 153, 157, 205, 210; relationships of, 149-153, 157-158, 159n
Factionalism. See *Partibandi*
Factions. See *Parti*
Faizabad District, 203
Family, 21, 117, 164. See also *Khandan; Pattidar; Parivar*
Family planning, 56, 60n
Family Size, 44, 81
Farming, 33, 35, 37, 41, 123
Fieldwork. See Data, collection
First Five Year Plan (1951), 50
Food, 73, 76
Forced labor. See *Begar*
Ford Foundation, 50
FRANKEL, FRANCINE R., 230, 233, 235n
Friendship, 21, 76

Ganges River, 21, 29
Ganjha, 66, 77, 123
Gauna, 90-91, 99-102, 129
Gaya, 139
Genealogy, 26-27 (Charts 1, 2)
Gram panchayat. See *Panchayati raj*
Gotra, 86
Government administration, 49-53, 55, 57, 59-60, 135, 141-142. See also Politics
Government aid. See Resources, government
Grand Trunk Road, 21, 213
Green Revolution, 230, 234n

Harijans, 55, 73, 77, 150-151, 179, 187, 200n, 205, 225; in disputes, 176-177, 198; as laborers, 73, 158; in politics, 210-211; status of, 40-41, 61, 63, 67, 161-163,

183; women, 83. *See also* Chamars; Dharkars; Musahars
Helplessness. See *Mazburi*
Hierarchy, caste. See Caste, hierarchy
High Court (in Allahabad). *See* Court, high
Hindi, 123
Hinduism, 205, 208
Holi, 156, 159n
Horizontal cleavage. See Class conflict
Households. See *Khandan*
Hypergamy, 98, 101, 108n

Illicit relationships, 64, 76, 78, 145, 164
Income. *See* Cash income
Indebtedness, 37, 44, 67, 135, 165; of Krishna Singh to Chandra Singh, 137–139; in recruiting faction personnel, 149
Independence, 49, 213
Independence Movement, 28, 116, 135, 139
Independents, 202
Intercaste conflict. *See* Class conflict
Intercollege, 21, 24, 28, 116, 119, 129–130, 135, 208, 213; during midterm elections, 213–214; Principal of, 202, 208–209, 213–214; Secretary of, 99, 208, 213
Interviews. *See* Data, collection
Intracaste conflict. *See* Factional conflict
Irrigation, 29, 44–45, 187, 190, 195, 197; old method, 31. *See also* Tubewell; Pumping set
Irrigation ditch, 32 (Fig. 2)

Jajman. See *Jajmani*
Jajmani, 11, 62, 66–69, 86n, 134, 226; disputes in, 105–106; lessening of, 74–76, 134, 230–231; nature of, 71–74; payments in, 69–71. *See also* Patron-client relationship
Jamuna River, 29
Janeu, 66
Jan Sangh Party, 124–125, 202–203, 205–215
Jati, 63, 66, 86n, 164, 228
Jatpat, 89, 202, 204, 207
Jats, 203, 218n
Jaunpur District, 55
Joint family, 80–82, 84
Justice *panchayat.* See *Panchayati Raj, nyaya panchayat*

Kahars, 41, 69, 141, 150, 207, 210
Kalwars, 41, 78, 81, 210
Kamin. See *Praja*
Khandan, 79, 84–85
Khatris, 90
Kinship, 6, 21, 79, 86

Kisan, 11
Kohars, 46, 64, 71, 74, 75 (Fig. 9), 78, 150
Kshatriya, 9, 63–64, 67–68
Kurmis, 5, 46, 66, 86, 111, 159n; economic and social mobility of, 8, 44, 220; income and wealth of, 41, 81, 117, 169; *jajmani* relationships of, 63, 68, 76; land ownership, 33, 136–138, 186; other conflicts involving, 148–151, 160, 174, 207, 214, 216–217; and political involvement, 142, 144, 202, 205, 207, 214, 216–217; water disputes involving, 190–191, 193, 196, 198 (Chart 3)

Labor, 28, 37, 41, 82, 160, 162, 165–167, 169–170
Laborer. See *Mazdur*
Land, 33, 35, 37. *See also* Disputes, land
Landlord. See *Malik;* Zamindar
Landowner. See *Bhumidar*
Land ownership, 33, 35 (Table 3), 40–41, 42–44 (Tables 5, 6, 7), 46
Land tenure reform, 119–120, 133n. See *also* Zamindari, abolition of
Language, 202, 213
Lawsuits, 186, 189. *See also* Conflict, resolution of; Court
Leader, 113. See also *Agua; Bare admi; Neta; Rais;* Faction leaders
Leader-follower tie, 151–153
Leadership, 109–132, 132n, 157, 185, 223, 234n
Lekhpal, 33, 58
Lifestyle. *See* "Caste culture"
Lineage. See *Pattidar*
Literacy, 41. *See also* Education
Little Pura, 24–25, 139, 146; politics in, 207–208, 210; water allocation in, 186–188, 190, 193, 195–198
Little Pura Bhumihars, 25, 114; conflicts involving, 135–137, 141, 175–177, 186–188, 193–196; political involvement of, 150–151
Local Self-Government. See *Panchayati raj*
Lohars, 69, 86n, 150, 169, 207; occupations of, 70 (Fig. 7), 71, 74; personal relationships of, 76, 78
Lohia, Ram Manohar, 208, 213, 217–218n
Loo, 29
Lord. *See* Thakur
Love, forbidden, 96–97. *See also* Marriage

Mafi, 37, 161, 167–168, 184n
Maharajas, 20, 25, 64
Main Pura, 24, 126–127, 186–187, 190, 193–199

INDEX

Main Pura Bhumihars, 127, 135, 137, 141, 150–151, 186, 193–194
Malik, 11, 73, 162, 165, 168–169, 171–174; definition of, 167; political involvement of, 210, 212
Marriage, 64, 84, 91, 95, 98–101, 107n, 164–165. See also *Gauna*
MARX, KARL, 11, 18n, 205
MASON, PHILIP, 230–231
Master. See *Malik*
MAYER, ADRIAN, 132–133n, 234n
Mazburi, 162, 166–167, 172, 184n
Mazdur, 11, 15, 35, 67, 73–74, 87n, 167, 168 (Fig. 23); beatings of, 166, 170–173, 189; dependence on big men, 210, 232; as ploughman, 161, 166–173; threats of beatings, 191–192
Mazduri, 161, 163, 165–170, 181–182, 184n
Mediators. See Brokers
MEILLASSOUX, CLAUDE, 87n
MENCHER, JOAN P., 17–18n
Middlemen. See Brokers
MILLER, D. B., 86–87n
Misra, Vijay, 175, 188, 192–194, 196–197, 200n
Mobility, 19, 21, 62; occupational, 74
Mohan, 96–97
Molested boy, 145
Monetized economy, 74, 222, 226
Monsoons, 29
Moral duty. See *Dharma*
MORRIS-JONES, W. H., 3–4
Motorcycle, 48n
Mukhiya, 25, 59, 110, 114, 117, 119, 129, 132–133n, 155, 201, 223, 226. See also Singh, Chand; Singh, Cheddinath
Musahars, 40, 79, 189, 210, 212, 221; occupations of, 41, 71, 72 (Fig. 8), 73, 75, 168
Muslims: feelings against, 205; religion, 20

Nahiyan, 37
Nais, 41, 46, 61–62, 68–69, 90–91, 106, 152, 158, 194
Narain, Raj, 206 (Fig. 25), 208
Neta, 109–110, 182
Nichjat (low caste), 6n
NICHOLAS, RALPH W., 228
Non-Cooperation Movement, 28, 128, 201
Noniya Pura, 151
Noniyas, 46, 71, 74, 151
Nyaya panchayat. See *Panchayati raj*

Occupational mobility, 74
Occupations, 41, 45 (Table 7), 46, 163, 165–166, 226
OPLER, MORRIS, 68

Outcaste, 38, 40, 64–66, 87n, 150

Pancha, 37–38, 52. See also *Panchayat*
Panchayat, 20, 51–52, 105, 107, 170; *amin,* 28, 49, 114; *bare admi,* 21, 38–40, 53, 92–93, 102–105, 126; *bhavan,* 52, 56, 141, 157; *biradari,* 38–40, 91–93, 102–103; conduct of, 39–40; definition of, 37–38; elections, 53, 55, 66, 141–144 226, 228; informal, 39, 100, 146; lessening of influence of, 53–54, 59, 138, 185, 219–220, 225; and *mukhiya,* 25; village, 114, 116–117; and water, 197
Panchayati raj, 14, 17n, 115, 118, 135, 223; and community development, 50–51; and *gram panchayat,* 49–50, 53; and *gram sabha,* 49, 141; and *nyaya panchayat,* 50, 53–55, 59, 138; and *panchayat samiti,* 50–51; as patronage resource, 157, 221; as statutory *panchayat,* 49–51, 59; and *zila parishad,* 51
Panchayat leader. See *Sarpanch*
Panchayat member. See *Pancha*
Panchayat Samiti. See *Panchayati raj*
Parivar, 81
Parti, 110, 117, 119–120, 127, 129, 159n; village, 120, 188–190, 193–194, 196, 199. See also *Partibandi*
Partibandi, 3, 8, 10, 15, 133n, 221–222, 233, 235n; conflicts in, 6, 8, 12, 141–148, 179, 220, 227; definition of, 134, 156–157, 227; effects on class conflict, 8, 160, 179; effects on social relations, 57, 154–156; elections and, 142, 201, 207–210, 214–217; neutrality in, 150–151, 190–191; origins and history of, 24–28, 103–105, 135–141; recruitment of personnel, 106, 148–155, 158–159n; resources of, 144, 226
Pasis, 40, 73
Paternalism, 71
Patna, 123
Patron. See *Jajmani*
Patron-client relationship, 71–74, 86n, 230–233, 234–235n. See also *Jajmani*
Patti, 78, 85–86
*Pattidar*s, 24, 54, 85–86, 119–120, 123, 125, 127, 135, 147, 150, 152, 168, 179–180
Peasants, 18n, 28, 234n
"Peri-urban" community, 21, 24
Ploughman. See *Mazdur*
POCOCK, DAVID, 11, 71–73
Police, 25
Police Sub-Inspector, 171, 175, 177–178
Political activity, 3–5, 8–9, 11–12
Political affiliations, 28

INDEX

Political conflict, 12, 28, 156, 197, 200n, 220
Political idioms, 3-4, 233
Politics, xv, 3-6, 10-11, 62, 217, 222; clientelist, 233; village, 24, 201-217. *See also* Arena; Elections; *Partibandi*
Poverty, 5, 64, 67, 231
Power, 59, 67, 161, 194, 198-199
Power struggle, 25, 223, 226
Pradhan, 50, 52, 157; defined, 3; election of, 113, 118, 127, 141-144
Pradhan (Prasad Singh), 13, 53, 58, 118, 120, 121 (Fig. 16), 123, 126-127, 150, 152; as *agua,* 110; in dispute settlement, 96-97; in dispute with Chamars, 176-179, in land dispute, 136-137; kinsmen of, 99 (Fig. 14), 120, 124, 128, 130-131, 135, 153, 180, 199n; kinsmen of, as voters, 205, 215; life of, 120-122; in national elections, 207-208; opinions of, 3, 216; and *partibandi,* 3, 124-125, 135-137, 142-144, 146, 153-158; in water disputes, 186, 188, 190-199
Praja. See *Jajmani*
Pramukh, 50, 52, 130, 208, 213
President's Rule, 203
Prestige, 93, 95, 99, 112, 117-188, 128, 150, 171
Priest. See *Brahmans*
Primary schools, 48; for boys, 21; for girls, 21, 155
Prostitutes, 13, 114
Pumping set, 30-31, 46
Punishment, 40
Puras, 8, 24, 57, 76, 120, 164, 177, 209, 211
Purdah, 66, 83-84, 91, 95-96, 101, 127, 164-165, 178-179

Raidas, 162, 212
Railroad station, 21
Rais, 110-111, 113, 130, 132n, 162, 209, 220
Raisat, 111, 123, 129
Rajput. See *Thakur*
Ram, Bhaggu, 148-149, 203, 205-206, 208
Ram, Jagjivan, 79, 162, 181-182
Ram, Maggu, 175, 179-180
Ram, Mohan, 56, 138, 148, 178-180, 191-193
Ram, Raju, 177-179
Ram, Sita, 116, 118
Ram, Viren, 175, 178-180, 211
Ramapur, 53, 58, 71, 118, 120, 123, 135, 138, 187, 189-190
RATH, N., 231
Religion, 20, 182

Resources, 28, 40-46, 156, 226-227; competition for, 144, 186, 190, 194, 197-199; government, 55-59, 221-222, 225; patronage, 157
Rishi, 86
Ritual purity, 63, 67
Rivas, 162
Rulers. See *Kshatriya;* Maharajas; British Raj
Rules, 4-5, 9, 59, 61-63, 68-69, 78-79, 225-226

Sacred thread. See *Janeu*
Sahib, Babu, 21, 28, 33, 48n, 54, 68, 104-105, 115, 135, 148
Samyukta Vidhayak Dal (SVD), 203
Samyukta Socialist Party, 202-203, 205-208, 212-214
Saranpur, 124, 187-188
Sarpanch, 39, 130
Scandal, examples of, 64
SCHWARTZ, NORMAN, 228
Seed Store, 57, 129
Seed Store Inspector, 14, 56, 58, 60n
Senapur, 55, 68
Servant. See *Shudra; Mazdur*
Settlements. See *Puras*
Sex, 76, 78
Sharecropping. See *Mafi*
Shudra, 63, 66
SIEGEL, BERNARD J., 229, 235n
Singh, Ajay, 28, 116, 128-129, 135, 139-140, 148, 153
Singh, Amar, 30, 52, 116 (Fig. 15), 140, 142; aging, 116, 120; allies of, 129, 139, 153, 195; in disputes, 139-140, 142, 148-149, 195-196; as supporter of Jan Sangh, 207-208; kinsmen of, 28, 141-142; and Krishna Singh, 129, 148; and *partibandi,* 129, 142, 151, 153
Singh, Arun, 24-25, 28, 116, 135
Singh, Baljit, 141-142
Singh, Chait, 24-25, 28
Singh, Chand, 25, 115
Singh, Chandra *(bara admi),* 123, 124, (Fig. 18), 127, 133n, 142, 188; as *bara admi,* 131; and Chamars, 178, 179 (Case 28), 182-183; in competition with Jai Singh, 154-155; in disputes with *pattidars,* 103-105, 180; kinsmen of, 187; and midterm election, 207-209, 214-216, 225; in *panchayat* elections, 144; in *partibandi,* 124-125, 130, 136-139, 145-151, 153, 157; and water disputes, 189-190, 192-197

INDEX

Singh, Chandra (of Pradhan's family), 93–95, 208
Singh, Charan, 202–203
Singh, Cheddinath, 25, 28, 33, 104, 114–115, 118, 135
Singh, Jai, 125 (Fig. 19), 155, 178; as *bara admi*, 152, 154, 157, 170; and Chamars, 148–149, 180, 182, 191, 225; in the midterm election, 207–210, 214, 216; and *panchayat* elections, 142, 144, 151; and *partibandi*, 139, 146, 150, 156; and *pattidar*s, 103–105; as dispute settler, 102–103; and water distribution, 186–190
Singh, Kallu, 188, 194, 196–197, 199n
Singh, Kesar, 103–104
Singh, Krishna, 53, 58, 60n, 118, 128 (Fig. 20), 152, 157, 208; and dispute with kinsmen, 99–102; and legitimizing power, 224; life of, 128–130; and *partibandi* rivals, 123, 125–126, 136–139, 148–149, 190; and relationship with Pradhan's family, 120, 122, 135, 153–154; and state politics, 202, 213; and water dispute, 187, 189. See also Intercollege, Secretary of
Singh, Kumar, 189–190
Singh, Lalji, 124, 208–209
Singh, Moti, 189–190
Singh, Nagesh, 98–99
Singh, Nandalal, 188–190
Singh, Narain, 127, 155, 178, 207; as ally of Chandra Singh, 124, 130–131, 192, 208; kinsmen of, 83 (Fig. 12), 145, 147, 196, 200n; land transactions, 139–141; and *partibandi*, 134, 150, 156, 198–199, 208; and water disputes, 192, 196, 199, 200n
Singh, Prasad. See Pradhan
Singh, Raj Bihari, 203, 209, 213
Singh, Raj Kumar, 122 (Fig. 17), 123, 127, 130–131, 152, 179 (Case 28); in disputes, 136–137, 145–147, 149–152, 180, 187–190, 195; and *partibandi*, 105, 139, 154–155; political involvement of, 207–208, 210
Singh, Rampat, 104, 139–140, 144, 148, 151, 155, 188
Singh, Rudra Dutt, 68
Singh, Satya, 93–95
Singh, Vishwanath, 203, 205–209, 211
Sirdar, 31, 33
"Social drama," 146–148
Social ostracism, 40
Social relationships, 24, 63, 81
Socialist Party, 28, 217n
SOMJEE, A. H., 21, 24
Sons, 90–91, 93–96. See also *Bans*

SRINIVAS, M. N., 9, 17n, 63
SSP. See Samyukta Socialist Party
Status, 117, 161
Statutory *Panchayat*. See *Panchayati raj*
Subcaste. See *Biradari*

Taxes, 49, 51, 56
Teachers, 24
Telis, 69, 71, 74, 102–103, 150
Thakur, 210; Rajput, 20, 55; as referent for Bhumihar, 64
Thokdar, 126–127, 186–189, 192–194, 196–197
THORNER, DANIEL, 11
Tilak, 98–99, 108n
Transistor radios, 19, 48n
Tripati, Kamalapati, 209
Tubewell, 30, 126–127, 132, 175–176, 185–189, 191–192, 196, 198
Tubewell Operator, 56, 186–189, 192, 195
TURNER, VICTOR, 221

Unchjat (high caste), 6n. See also Caste, hierarchy
Untouchables. See *Harijan*s; individual names of Untouchable castes
Uttar Pradesh High Court. See Court, high
Uttar Pradesh *Panchayati Raj* Act (1947), 49
Uttar Pradesh (U.P.), 19, 24, 29, 109, 130, 202–203, 213, 222

Varna, 63, 86–87n
Vasectomies. See Family planning
Vertical cleavage. See Factional conflict; *Partibandi*
Village assemblies. See *Panchayati raj, gram sabha*
Village Council. See *Panchayat*
Village council house. See *Panchayat bhavan*
Village headman. See *Mukhiya*
Village leadership. See Leadership
Village Level Worker (VLW), 14, 50, 55–58, 120, 178, 228
Village officials, elected, 115
Village *Panchayat*. See *Panchayat*
Village politics. See Politics, village
Village record-keeper. See *Lekhpal*
Village unity, 24, 156
VLW. See Village Level Worker
VON VORYS, KARL, 230, 235n
Voting, 203–207

Wages. See *Mazburi*
Warriors. See *Kshatriya*

Water, 8, 28, 31, 185, 199; distribution of, 37, 86, 127, 149, 186–199. *See also* Disputes, water; *Thokdar;* Tubewell
Wealth, 80–81, 161, of *bare admi,* 110, 113–114, 131–132; distribution of, 40–48, 67; of dominant caste, 9; importance of, 64; of *rais,* 110–111. *See also* Land
Wells, 46, 121, 155, 175
Wives: buying of, 66, 90–91; jealous, 91–93
Women, 21, 62, 83–84, 164–165, 169

Wrestling match, 77 (Fig. 10)

Youth club, 205

Zamindar, 33, 49, 114–115, 117, 133n, 135, 220, 223
Zamindari, 33, 161; abolition of, 28, 33, 74, 104, 119, 222–223; Uttar Pradesh Abolition of Zamindari Act, 31, 135
Zila parishad. See Panchayati Raj

Miriam Sharma received an M.A. in history from the University of Virginia and a Ph.D. in anthropology from the University of Hawaii. She has been the recipient of a Fulbright Predoctoral Dissertation Research Grant and has held a National Endowment for the Humanities Postdoctoral Fellowship. She is presently Interim Director of the Ethnic Studies Program at the University of Hawaii.

Asian Studies at Hawaii

No. 1 *Bibliography of English Language Sources on Human Ecology, Eastern Malaysia and Brunei.* Compiled by Conrad P. Cotter with the assistance of Shiro Saito. September 1965. Two parts. (Available only from Paragon Book Gallery, New York.)

No. 2 *Economic Factors in Southeast Asian Social Change.* Edited by Robert Van Niel. May 1968. Out of print.

No. 3 *East Asian Occasional Papers (1).* Edited by Harry J. Lamley. May 1969.

No. 4 *East Asian Occasional Papers (2).* Edited by Harry J. Lamley. July 1970.

No. 5 *A Survey of Historical Source Materials in Java and Manila.* Robert Van Niel. February 1971.

No. 6 *Educational Theory in the People's Republic of China: The Report of Ch'ien Chung-Jui.* Translated by John N. Hawkins. May 1971. Out of print.

No. 7 *Hai Jui Dismissed from Office.* Wu Han. Translated by C. C. Huang. June 1972.

No. 8 *Aspects of Vietnamese History.* Edited by Walter F. Vella. March 1973.

No. 9 *Southeast Asian Literatures in Translation: A Preliminary Bibliography.* Philip N. Jenner. March 1973.

No.10 *Textiles of the Indonesian Archipelago.* Garrett and Bronwen Solyom. October 1973. Out of print.

No.11 *British Policy and the Nationalist Movement in Burma, 1917-1937.* Albert D. Moscotti. February 1974.

No.12 *Aspects of Bengali History and Society.* Edited by Rachel Van M. Baumer. December 1975.

No.13 *Nanyang Perspective: Chinese Students in Multiracial Singapore.* Andrew W. Lind. June 1974.

No.14 *Political Change in the Philippines: Studies of Local Politics preceding Martial Law.* Edited by Benedict J. Kerkvliet. November 1974.

No.15 *Essays on South India.* Edited by Burton Stein. February 1976.

No.16 *The* Caurāsī Pad *of Śrī Hit Harivaṁś.* Charles S. J. White. 1977.

No.17 *An American Teacher in Early Meiji Japan.* Edward R. Beauchamp. June 1976.

No.18 *Buddhist and Taoist Studies I.* Edited by Michael Saso and David W. Chappell. 1977.

No.19 *Sumatran Contributions to the Development of Indonesian Literature, 1920–1942.* Alberta Joy Freidus. 1977.

No. 20 *Insulinde: Selected Translations from Dutch Writers of Three Centuries on the Indonesian Archipelago.* Edited by Cornelia N. Moore. 1978.

No. 21 *Regents, Reformers, and Revolutionaries: Indonesian Voices of Colonial Days, Selected Historical Readings, 1899–1949.* Translated, edited, and annotated by Greta O. Wilson. 1978.

Orders for Asian Studies at Hawaii publications should be directed to The University Press of Hawaii, 2840 Kolowalu Street, Honolulu, Hawaii 96822. Present standing orders will continue to be filled without special notification.